# Leading Issues in Cyber Warfare & Security Research
## Volume 2

Edited by Julie Ryan

Leading Issues in Cyber Warfare & Security Research
Volume Two

Disclaimer: While every effort has been made by the editor, authors and
the publishers to ensure that all the material in this book is accurate and
correct at the time of going to press, any error made by readers as a result
of any of the material, formulae or other information in this book is the
sole responsibility of the reader. Readers should be aware that the URLs
quoted in the book may change or be damaged by malware between the
time of publishing and accessing by readers.

Note to readers: Some papers have been written by authors who use the
American form of spelling and some use the British. These two different
approaches have been left unchanged.

ISBN:    978-1-910810-64-4 (print)

Printed by Lightning Source POD

Published by: Academic Conferences and Publishing International Limited,
Reading, RG4 9AY, United Kingdom, info@academic-publishing.org
Available from www.academic-bookshop.com

# Contents

# About the Editor

Dr. Julie Ryan has been working in the field of information security for over 30 years. Starting out as an intelligence officer in the US Air Force, she has tackled problems in the military, in government, in industry, and in academia. Currently, she is Associate Professor of Engineering Management and Systems Engineering at the George Washington University, located in downtown Washington, D.C., where she teaches and directs research in information security, cyber warfare, systems dynamics, and analytics. Her books include "Defending Your Digital Assets Against Hackers, Crackers, Spies and Thieves" (McGraw-Hill 2000), "Leading Issues in Information Warfare and Security" (API 2011), and "Detecting and Combatting Malicious Email" (Elsevier 2014). Her degrees include B.S. from the U.S. Air Force Academy, MLS from Eastern Michigan University, and D.Sc. from George Washington University.

# List of Contributing Authors

**Andre' Ara Karamanian**, Carnegie Mellon University, CERT, Cisco Systems, USA

**Chad Arnold,** Department of Computer Science and Engineering, Wright State University, Dayton, Ohio, USA

**Kris Barcomb,** Air Force Institute of Technology, Wright-Patterson AFB, USA

**Larisa Breton,** The University of the District of Columbia, Washington, D.C., USA

**Ivan Burke,** Defence Peace Safety and Security department, Council for Scientific and Industrial Research **Jonathan Butts,** Department of Electrical and Computer Engineering, Air Force Institute of Technology, Wright Patterson AFB, Dayton, Ohio, USA

**Mainak Chatterjee,** University of Central Florida, Electrical Engineering and Computer Science Dept, Orlando, Florida, USA

**G Commin,** *ESIEA, (C+V)° Laboratory*

**Matthew Crosston,** Bellevue University, USA

**José Fernandez,** Département de génie informatique et génie logiciel, École Polytechnique de Montréal, Montréal, Canada

**E Filiol,** *ESIEA, (C+V)° Laboratory*

**Tim Grant,** Faculty of Military Sciences, Netherlands Defence Academy (NLDA), Breda, The Netherlands and R-BAR, Benschop, The Netherlands

**Håkan Gunneriusson,** Swedish National Defence College, Stockholm, Sweden

**Patrick Hurley,** Air Force Research Laboratory, Information Directorate, Cyber Assurance Branch, Rome, New York, USA

**Charles Kamhoua,** Air Force Research Laboratory, Information Directorate, Cyber Assurance Branch, Rome, New York, USA

**Scott Knight,** Department of Electrical and Computer Engineering, Royal Military College of Canada, Kingston, Canada

**Dennis Krill,** Air Force Institute of Technology, Wright-Patterson AFB, USA

**Marina Krotofil,** Institute for Security in Distributed Applications, Hamburg University of Technology, Germany

**Kevin Kwiat,** Air Force Research Laboratory, Information Directorate, Cyber Assurance Branch, Rome, New York, USA

**Antoine Lemay,** Département de génie informatique et génie logiciel, École Polytechnique de Montréal, Montréal, Canada

**Andrew Liaropoulos,** University of Piraeus, Department of International and European Studies, Piraeus, Greece

**Robert Mills,** Air Force Institute of Technology, Wright-Patterson AFB, USA
**Rain Ottis,** University of Jyväskylä, Jyväskylä, Finland
(CSIR), Pretoria, South Africa
**Joon Park,** Syracuse University, School of Information Studies (iSchool), Syracuse, New York, USA
**Char Sample,** Carnegie Mellon University, CERT, Cisco Systems, USA
**Michael Saville,** Air Force Institute of Technology, Wright-Patterson AFB, USA
**Krishnaprasad Thirunarayan,** Department of Computer Science and Engineering, Wright State University, Dayton, Ohio, USA
**Renier van Heerden,** Defence Peace Safety and Security department, Council for Scientific and Industrial Research (CSIR), Pretoria, South Africa

# Introduction to Leading Issues in Cyber Warfare and Security Volume 2

## 1   Introduction

The past several decades have seen an explosion of thought and capabilities associated with cyber warfare. It is useful to sit back and put the changes into perspective so that one may develop an understanding of where the concepts are heading. There are three main axis along which the changes have advanced: organizational, technological, and environmental. The interactions of the changes within the three dimensional conceptual space have created a need for new thoughts and approaches. The papers in this book contain some of the more original thoughts in this area, each contributing gems of ideas that can help drive the thinking forward. It is not necessary to read the papers in any particular order to gain the most from this book. Each paper is introduced with commentary that ties the paper to the overarching theme of advancement in cyber warfare. For those who would like to take a structured approach to using this material, a syllabus is provided as an appendix that includes ancillary sources to complement the reading and questions that stimulate ideas. These introductory comments are meant to lay the scene for the contemplation of these ideas.

## 2   A Generational View of Information Warfare

We are now in what might be considered the third generation of information warfare. In order to characterize these generations, we can refer to them as the Information In Warfare Generation, the Information as Warfare Generation, and the Information Warfighting Domain Generation. The Information In Warfare Generation, IW 1.0, lasted from the dawn of sentience to roughly the 1940s. The Information as Warfare Generation, IW 2.0, emerged from the amazing technological advances and the strategic information battles of WWII and lasted until roughly the 1980s. The Information Warfighting Domain Generation, IW 3.0, is the one in which we are now. Each of the generations are sufficiently different that they evince different artifacts and effects, but each is important to understand because as a new generation emerges, the older one has not disappeared but has been wholly subsumed into the new generation.

## 2.1    The First Generation: Information in Warfare

The Information in Warfare Generation (IW 1.0) strategies focused on the use of information as a leveraging function.  Thinkers ranging from Sun Tzu[1] to Napoleon Bonaparte[2] focused on the use of information as a way of optimizing the use of forces while reducing the actual necessity of engaging in combat, which is fundamentally resource intensive.  Carl von Clausewitz wrote about the fog of war and the warfare as engaging in politics by other means, identifying the critical role of information in geopolitical activities.  Information was used as a force multiplier, but also as a weapon of sorts, generally to undermine the will of the opponent or as a way of get the enemy to commit to a course of action that benefited the other side.  The protection and use of information to support and advance conventional warfare is the defining characteristic of this generation of information warfare, which is why it is characterized more as information <u>in</u> warfare than actually information warfare.

## 2.2    The Second Generation: Information As Warfare

The transition from the first to the second generation was a gradual thing, as these things tend to be.  The contributions of science and the development of operations research[3] as a way to leverage information in systems and engineering led the way in the developing appreciation for the role of information.  Tactical information victories, such as the information skirmishes that preceded the Battle of Midway, highlighted the increasing interaction of advanced communications technologies with strategic deception tactics for operational advantage.  This distinction really underscores the differences that mark the birth of the second generation: the increasing sophistication of the information carrying and processing technologies provided a substrate for the development of new ways of executing strategic operations.

---

[1] Much has been written about the application of Sun Tzu's writings have to information warfare.  A translation of the text of "The Art of War" can be found at
http://www.au.af.mil/au/awc/awcgate/artofwar.htm.
[2] An accessible overview of the various thinkers and effects on geopolitical contests can be found in "Military Theory and Information Warfare" by Ryan Henry and C. Edward Peartree.  Originally published in Parameters, Autumn 1998, pp. 121-35, it is available online at http://strategicstudiesinstitute.army.mil/pubs/parameters/Articles/98autumn/henry.htm
[3] Several excellent books have been written on these developments.  One of my favorites is "Engineers of Victory: The Problem Solvers Who Turned the Tide in the Second World War" by Paul Kennedy (Random House, 2013).

It is worth spending some time thinking about the role that information operations played in the Battle of Midway from an information contest perspective, since it is an example (by no means unique) of the transition from information as a relatively passive aspect of geopolitical competition to a more active form of competition in the information dimension. The context of the situation was that Japan, after having attacked Pearl Harbor six months prior, intended to launch a full out offensive to destroy the US naval capability in the Pacific. As part of the US battle preparations, what might be called an information feint was performed. This feint had the same structural components as a physical force structure feint designed to draw an opposing force out: it was designed to look legitimate but it's real goal was to cause the opposition to act in a way that was advantageous to the mission strategy.

A feint is a deceptive movement, designed to draw out an opponent. In sports, such as boxing, a feint might be a pretended jab by one hand in order to cover the real punch by the other. In warfare, a feint can be used to draw an opponent into an unsustainable position or to cause them to misunderstand force structure.[4] The information feint preceding the Battle of Midway[5] consisted of two parts: the first part was an information trojan horse and the second part was classic disinformation. The two parts came together to both reveal the location of the intended attack and to cause Japan to misunderstand the deployment of US naval force elements. The US did not know where the Japanese were going to attack, but thought it might be Midway Island. The Japanese cipher had been broken, but the Japanese had also encoded the target as "AF" rather than using the common name of the intended destination. The US Navy used the first part of the information feint to cause Japan to reveal the actual identity: messages were sent over a relatively insecure communications channel to other US forces reporting that Midway Island was running low on water. This information trojan horse hid the true intent of the message behind a compelling story: the Japanese almost immediately relayed the information that "AF" was running low on water, thereby providing the US forces with con-

---

[4] A discussion of military feints in recent history can be found at http://www.axis-and-allies.com/military-tactics-feint.html

[5] A very nice description of the activities associated with this effort was written by Brayton Harris, entitled "Code Breakers Crack Japan's Plan for Battle of Midway" (June 2013). It can be accessed at http://www.commandposts.com/2013/06/code-breakers-crack-japans-plans-for-battle-of-midway/

firmation of the identity of the intended target. The second part of the information feint was false radio chatter in the vicinity of the Coral Sea, leading the Japanese to believe that the carrier task force associated with the USS Yorktown was far away from Midway Island. These two information operations constituted an important feint in the Battle of Midway and can be viewed as a generational advancement in the use of information for aggressive purposes.

This was an example of information as a tool of aggression, complementing and supporting the overall battle strategy. The use of information technologies as weapons was also seen during this time period. One example, again not unique, was that of the Battle of the Beams, the name given to the British use of electronic countermeasures against the radio frequency techniques used for navigation by the German Luftwaffe. The Luftwaffe capitalized on the pre-war scientific advances in radio based navigation techniques to improve the accuracy of bombing campaigns against the United Kingdom. In reaction, the British developed a way of interfering with those signals in such a way as to cause the bombers to drop the bombs in relatively isolated areas rather than on the intended targets. This was a direct attack on the information veracity of the supporting technologies for warfare.

These two examples illustrate the increasing incorporation of both information and information technologies into active warfare operations, a process that continued as observers mimicked and improved upon the successes of others. However, the state of technology held back the potential. When the confluence of transistors[6], electronic databases[7], and packet based information networks[8] revolutionized the information technology landscape, the stage was set for another generational leap. These technologies really took off during the 1970s, became integrated into con-

---

[6] Transistors have been called the most important invention of the 20th century, with mass production for incorporation in a wide range of technologies ramping up in the 1950s and 1960s. An accounting of their invention can be found at
http://www.pbs.org/transistor/album1/
[7] A discussion of the development and advancement of electronic database management systems, beginning with the 1960s, can be found at
http://quickbase.intuit.com/articles/timeline-of-database-history
[8] A "Brief History of the Internet", including Licklider's 1962 concept for a "Galactic Network", can be found at http://www.internetsociety.org/internet/what-internet/history-internet/brief-history-internet

sumer electronics, and exploded during the 1980s. With the commercialization of the internet in the early 1990s, the stage was set for something completely new.

## 2.3    The Third Generation: Information as a Warfighting Domain

The third generation of information warfare, in which information is seen as a separable domain of warfare, similar to the other domains of land, sea, air, and space, is one which is still being analyzed and considered for implications.    The development of the idea of information warfare as something new and different from what had gone on previously emerged during the 1980s. Various names were given for the observed phenomenon, such as Revolution in Military Affairs, and discussions were held about what would constitute offensive and defensive actions in the information dimension[9].   The perception of the promise of the nascent conceptualization of information warfare as a distinct aspect of war ranged from those who considered the potential for bullet-free wars to those who warned ominously about "an information Pearl Harbor"[10].  It was apparent to all that a new class of weapons had come into existence: software viruses, trojan horses, worms, and logic bombs took their places in the lexicon of warfare.  And if weapons existed, then targets must also exist.  If targets exist, then it should be possible to create a targeting plan in support of mission objectives.  These thought processes led to an increasingly focused examination of the role of the new capabilities in warfare[11].

A distraction to the information network focused analyses came from the electronic warfare and psychological operations communities, who argued loudly that the concepts of information warfare must include what had emerged from the post-World War II technology base as conventional aspects of military operations: electronic countermeasures (ECM), electronic counter-countermeasures (ECCM), and influence operations, amongst oth-

---

[9] An example of the thought of the time can be reviewed in Martin Libicki's classic, "The Mesh and The Net", from 1994.  A copy can be found at various sources on the internet in pdf format.

[10] See "Protecting the National Information Infrastructure Against InfoWar", published in Colloquy, Vol. 17, No. 1, July, 1996.  A copy is available at http://members.tripod.com/dan_ryan/SASA.htm

[11] An example of the scholarship on this is Greg Rattray's 2001 book, "Strategic Warfare in Cyberspace," available from MIT press: https://mitpress.edu/books/strategic-warfare-cyberspace

ers. From this debate emerged the terminologies of information operations (IO), computer network attack (CNA), computer network exploitation (CNE), and computer network defense (CND)[12].

# 3    Apples Plus Carts = Something Entirely Different

The term "cyberspace" came into prominence as well, figuratively describing the area in which these actions could take place. The recognition that something new was emerging prompted various analogies, including the one offered by Porche et al in their book, "Redefining Information Warfare Boundaries for an Army in a Wireless World" (RAND 2013)[13]. In this book, the analogy is given of apples and apple carts (p 23). Both apples and carts are physical elements, subject to the laws of physics and static analytical methods. But when you place apples into a cart and join that combination with an entrepreneur, you get something entirely and completely different: mobile commerce. The new entity can still benefit from the underlying component understanding, but that is not sufficient for understanding the potential of the new aspect. New ways of analyzing, organizing, and operating the mobile commerce version of apples and carts must be developed. This is, admittedly, a simplistic example but it serves to underscore the need to consider the domain of information from a perspective that includes more than simply the component aspects.

Along with the challenges of understanding what the Information Warfighting Domain might be, what an information operation consists of, and how to integrate information operations into operational missions, there arose the questions of who should be able to conduct military information operations and what would constitute an act of war in cyberspace.

The question of "who" would seem to have been addressed by international treaties on the conduct of war, such as the Geneva Conventions. Does this mean that only members of an armed force associated with a geopolitical state can legally conduct information operations? This is up

---

[12] An example of the type of direction provided by western military leadership regarding these terms can be observed in "Joint Terminology for Cyberspace Operations", http://www.nsci-va.org/CyberReferenceLib/2010-11-joint%20Terminology%20for%20Cyberspace%20Operations.pdf

[13] A copy of this book can be obtained at http://www.rand.org/content/dam/rand/pubs/monographs/MG1100/MG1113/RAND_MG1113.pdf

for some debate, particularly if computer network defense is considered to be part of warfare in the information domain. Countries like Estonia have taken the lead in developing citizen defense leagues to support their nation's information infrastructure against attack. Other developments have been the rise of what has been called "the patriotic hacker", someone who acts without military or governmental authority against perceived wrongs.

The already complicated situation is further confused by what is being called "hybrid warfare[14]." This hybrid warfare is the combination of information operations of all types combined with a low level conventional arms contest. As this is being written, the hybrid war attracting the most attention is that being waged by Russia against various targets[15]. While the activities included in this hybrid style of war include propaganda and information systems attacks, the most notable aspect of it has been the use of "trolls", both automated and human, to achieve several information goals: first, the trolls overwhelm comment threads to make it seem as though public opinion is vastly different than it actually is; second, the trolls populate the social media space with both direct and indirect messaging; and finally, the trolls attack individuals who dare to post commentary contrary to the desired messaging[16]. The sheer volume of activity created by the trolls makes it increasingly difficult to use social media for informed conversations. It also serves to sway the opinion of those who may have been more neutral in outlook. These same tactics have been adopted by insurgent operator, such as the self-titled "Islamic State," which uses troll armies for direct messaging, recruitment, and harassment of adversar-

---

[14] Mark Galeotti wrote an interesting piece exploring this concept, titled "Hybrid War and Little Green Men: How It Works, and How it Doesn't", republished on 1 May 2015 in the International Relations and Security Network, available at http://isnblog.ethz.ch/government/hybrid-war-and-little-green-men-how-it-works-and-how-it-doesnt. A more in-depth analysis was published in April 2015 by Michael Korman and Matthew Rojansky, titled "A Closer Look at Russia's Hybrid War", which is available online at http://www.wilsoncenter.org/sites/default/files/7-KENNAN%20CABLE-ROJANSKY%20KOFMAN.pdf

[15] Two sources of interest include Vitaly Shevchenko's article from March 11, 2014 published in the BBC entitled, "Little Green Men or Russian Invaders?" (available at http://www.bbc.com/news/world-europe-26532154) and Sam Jones' article in the Financial Times from May 13, 2015 (available at http://www.ft.com/cms/s/0/03c5ebde-f95a-11e4-ae65-00144feab7de.html#axzz3dLZGFuaz).

16 The New York Times published an excellent analysis of the activities of the Russian Troll Army in June 2015. The citation is Chen, Adrian, "The Agency", New York Times, June 2, 2015. Available online at http://www.nytimes.com/2015/06/07/magazine/the-agency.html

ies. In this manner, cyberspace has itself been militarized, complete with virtual mine fields. Interestingly, it has also been used to confuse both sides of a conflict through the creation of fake reports[17] on activities, a twist on the classic disinformation types of campaigns.

# 4 Trench Warfare in Cyberspace

The world we find ourselves in can be thought of as equivalent to the stalemates of World War I. Dueling denial of service attacks, malicious software intrusions, and website defacements are wearing and difficult, but in the end manageable. The trench warfare of WWI did nothing to advance either side's cause, and created enormous damage to the force structure, the landscape, and to society. While few would claim that the information skirmishes of today are killing people or ruining environments, thinking about the unceasing level of conflict in cyberspace between all of the players — geopolitical entities, criminals, and others — as trench warfare puts a perspective on the situation that is useful. Development of new defenses, new weapons, and new strategies will obviate the state that we find ourselves in now eventually. Recognizing the state we are in helps lay the foundation for considering the future.

# 5 Next Generation Cyber Warfare

The campaigns of today feature denial of service attacks[18], information gathering malicious software[19], a very few sophisticated targeted cyber-weapons such as Stuxnet[20], and a great many infiltrations of systems for

---

[17] An entire battle between Iraqi and Islamic State forces was created by a twitter user, whose efforts were noticed, supported, and spread by other twitter users. The results were a crowd-sourced disinformation campaign that fooled many expert observers. Two sources for the story include coverage on Gizmodo by Chris Mills, available at http://gizmodo.com/how-one-twitter-troll-created-a-fake-islamic-state-batt-1711579420, and coverage at the BBC Trending Blog, titled "The fake battle that fooled IS supporters — and their opponents", available at http://www.bbc.com/news/blogs-trending-33111934.

[18] For example, see the review on the Estonia attacks of 2007 published in International Affairs Reviews: "Denial-of-Service: The Estonian Cyberwar and Its Implications for U.S. National Security", http://www.iar-gwu.org/node/65

[19] For example, see the discussion on the Kaspersky website, written by Ryan Naraine, on the Duqu collection of malicious software which has been described as being purposed for stealing information: https://securelist.com/blog/incidents/32463/duqu-faq-33/

[20] There are many well written reports Stuxnet. A very nice summary was written by David Kushner for IEEE Spectrum, "The Real Story of Student", 26 Feb 2013. It is available online at http://spectrum.ieee.org/telecom/security/the-real-story-of-stuxnet

the purposes of espionage and data exfiltration[21]. The use of malicious software to encrypt large blocks of data for denial is possible and could have devastating consequences, removing en masse capabilities for control and coordination as relevant information is rendered inaccessible[22]. The recent revelations of the compromisability of aircraft control systems inspires scenarios of hostile actors compromising the air transportation system, perhaps even commandeering aircraft to serve as weapons[23]. As such a compromise became known, the attacked air system(s) would come to a halt, giving the aggressor almost exclusive air supremacy. Such an advantage could tip the balance of power significantly.

The papers selected for this volume were chosen for their contribution to the consideration of what comes next. This book does not stand alone: it is intended to be a companion volume to the first book, Leading Issues in Information Warfare and Security (Volume 1).

The papers in this Volume can be considered to fall into two broad categories: considering the future of cyber warfare and structural issues that should be considered. The papers are ordered in such a way as to develop a complicated appreciation for the challenges facing all of us, from gov-

---

[21] These infiltrations have been done primarily by human actors with direct access to systems but also through whole sale compromises of systems, such as the US Government's Office of Personnel Management (OPM) network. A review of the implications of this compromise was written by Ryan Evans for the Washington Post on June 17, 2015. Entitled "Why the lastest government hack is worse than the Snowden affair", it can be found online at http://www.washingtonpost.com/opinions/hitting-an-agency-where-it-hurts/2015/06/17/ffca6c6a-1512-11e5-9ddc-e3353542100c_story.html

[22] There have been periodic reports of towns and police departments being victimized by CryptoLocker or CryptoWall, both of which encrypt the contents of systems in order to extort ransom payments. One story that describes the effects of such an attack on a police department in Tennessee, USA, explains the problem: {quote} "My first response is we are not going to be held hostage. We are not going to pay a fee to get our records back," Bledsoe said. "But once it was determined which records were involved and that they were crucial to victims of crimes in this county, and to the operations of the sheriff's office and the citizens of this county...I had no choice but to authorize to pay this." {end quote} "Dickson Sheriff's Office pays ransom to cyber criminals" by Chris Gadd, Nov 11, 2014, The Tennessean. Available online at http://www.tennessean.com/story/news/local/dickson/2014/11/11/dickson-sheriffs-office-pays-ransom-cyber-criminals/18868325/

[23] A researcher claims to have been able to make a plane fly sideways through compromise of the software systems: "Feds say that banned research commandeered a plane," by Kim Zetter, May 15, 2015, Wired Magazine, available online at http://www.wired.com/2015/05/feds-say-banned-researcher-commandeered-plane/

ernmental policy makers to social activist to teachers and economists. Beginning with a discussion of possible actions and uses of cyberspace for offensive purposes, the topics of the papers build upon each other through structural components needed for cyber warfare and control of cyber-space, culminating in discussions of controls and sovereignty in cyber-space.

While papers can be read in any order, some of them are logically connected in order to provide a nuanced examination of some elements. Where this has occurred, it is noted in the introduction to the papers.

The papers begin with one that explores the potential for harm through cyber operations. In her paper, "Cyber Can Kill and Destroy Too: Blurring Borders Between Conventional and Cyber Warfare", Marina Krotofil reviews and explores the cyber equivalent of combined arms campaigns: the intersection of cyber and physical attacks. The paper focuses on the current state of integration between information technology and physical systems, with a focus on the control of the physical systems by the information technology, with an eye towards understanding how subversion of the information technology can result in the subversion of, damage to, or destruction of the physical system.

Following that is a discussion of formalization of this integration through the concept of hybrid warfare models. An important problem facing the strategists trying to understand how competition in cyberspace can, will, and has integrated with other elements of life is developing a framework for discussing combined arms activities using information warfare elements. An emerging concept, dubbed "hybrid" warfare, is being used as a structural way to describe the integration of information activities on the broadest spectrum into aggressive actions. Gunneriusson and Ottis provide a great service to this discussion by exploring many different concepts of what "hybrid" threats might be.

Based on the idea that offensive cyber operations should be studied and emerge from the darkness in which they typically hide, Grant and his colleagues embarked on a research program to explore the potential answers to the question, "What resources would be needed by a Cyber Security Operations Centre in order to perform offensive cyber operations?" in their paper "Comparing Models of Offensive Cyber Operations".

Building upon those three papers, the next one, "Duqu's Dilemma: The Ambiguity Assertion and the Futility of Sanitized Cyber War," starts the discussion of structural considerations. The dilemma, which is a difficult choice between two (or more) alternatives, is fundamentally expressed as a control problem: "the reality of cyber-attacks and initiatives can be for information gathering or physical attack potentiality; they can be originated from a government effort but executed through major commercial assets; they can be aimed for political/military objectives yet facilitated by piggy-backing on civilian systems." The implication is that since the controls associated with the conventional laws of armed conflict only apply to about half of that list, adopting and enforcing that control would be less than effective in meeting the goals of such a control structure. The alternative, however, is equally bleak: accepting the ambiguity associated with the nature of cyberspace in both structure and usage, where ambiguity as a concept is rather foreign to international norms, blame-finding, and legal structures.

This discussion is followed by a consideration of unrestricted warfare potential in the paper "Unrestricted Warfare Versus Western Traditional Warfare: A Comparative Study". This paper builds upon the themes touched upon in the previous papers. The inherent changes in how humans interact and how the boundaries of state interests have diffused and broadened require some reaction, some accommodation. The proposal that warfare would necessarily evolve to embrace all aspects of life, both traditionally military and non-military, is a notion that must be considered carefully, particularly because of the problems associated with integrating traditional military approaches with what can be called the "new warfare". The point is made that these efforts should "pass not only the physical borders, but also domains such as the economy, finance, religion and culture to attain the enemy."

The informing influences of national culture are touched upon in the next paper, "Hofstede's Cultural Markers in Computer Network Attack Behaviors." The research reported in this paper could provide interesting insights into issues associated with structural aspects of organizing, training, and equipping for cyber operations, as well as with the development of cyber warfare engagement strategies.

Building upon the previous paper's exploration of the cultural aspects of patriotic website defacements, Larisa Breton considers the problem of understanding the groups that are likely actors in those attacks. Intriguingly, the exploration is not just in and of themselves as entities, but through the lens of the Clausewitzian concept of centers of gravity (CoG). Nonstate actors have increasingly used information technologies to create the connectivity, and thus the unifying motivation, for their community of influence. Virtual non-state actors, such as Anonymous, have emerged that exist in online venues and operate primarily in the information domain. In this analysis, Breton uses a geologic metaphor, that of islands, to explore how these emergent actors affect the rest of the environment. Her conclusions are that virtual non-state actors have the potential to affect both warfare and governance.

Moving into a more specific set of analyses on the structural requirements for cyber warfare, the next paper explores the notion of geography in cyberspace from a military perspective. This is an important consideration with implications well beyond that of warfare operations. When cyberspace can be mapped as a geography, what does that mean in terms of governance and control of parts of that geography? We are used to thinking about governance issues in terms of real space: land, negotiated borders, population centers, etc. These are intuitively represented in physical models of terrain. A radically different approach to modeling cyberspace from the perspective of a cyber-geography might provide a very different perspective on collective groupings, governance, and control.

Just as understanding the geography of cyberspace is critical to being able to formulate military plans in cyberspace, developing a comprehensive approach to the underlying intelligence data needs, analytical structures, and applications is important. Structural approaches to intelligence preparation of the potential cyber battlespace could be used to develop tactics resulting in the reshaping of the battlespace, changing the dynamics of the conflict. Combined with the previous paper on the "Military Geography in Cyberspace", the notion of being able to treat cyberspace as a real domain, rather than something that is hard to comprehend, is progressing apace.

Having touched on the geography of cyberspace and preparing intelligence analyses for the cyberspace environment, this next paper looks at how sophisticated attacks might be dealt with. The focus of this analysis is industrial control systems (ICS), which are used to control various utility functions, such as mining operations, electrical grids, and multimodal transportation systems. In "Strategies for Combating Sophisticated Attacks", the authors describe the components of a generic ICS and then explore the current defense strategies. After exploring the limitations of those strategies, using real world examples, they propose that an inside-out analysis of the system from a security perspective is just as critical as having effective defense-in-depth strategies. This is very complementary to the conclusions derived in the IPCE paper but from a civilian operator perspective. It also is complementary to the next paper, "Replication and Diversity for Survivability in Cyberspace: A Game Theoretic Approach", which analyzes defense in depth effectiveness. The three papers taken together combine synergistically to describe the knowledge needed for both civilian and military organizations to effectively confront cyber challenges.

In "Replication and Diversity for Survivability in Cyberspace: A Game Theoretic Approach", a game theory approach is used to considering potential strategies from both the attacker and defender perspective. There are two key findings: first, that the relative skills of the adversaries are important to the outcome; and second, that when both are competent, then the design of the system becomes important. From the perspective of the military commander focused on developing attack and defense strategies, this analysis provides insights into how target selection might be considered and how defenders might be deployed.

The final two papers deal with the question of sovereignty and, by extension, the viability of the current Westphalian construct of nation-states. First, Liaropoulos presents a cogent discussion of what constitutes "sovereignty" and the challenges associated with expressing control of associated elements in the domain of cyberspace. He argues, citing a broad range of sources and authorities, that the expression of sovereignty in cyberspace is a needed and appropriate course of action for states, and that it is a necessary condition for the development of an international cyber order. Following that paper, Barcomb et al lay out an analysis framework based on a five layer internet protocol stack in order to differentiate where control lies and where sovereignty might appropriately be established. The context of the analysis is the experience of the United States, with references to control and use of exoatmospheric space and the development of international norms for such control. The point is made that "international norms governing appropriate conduct in cyberspace are immature. As nations become more cyberspace-dependent, they are struggling to clearly define their claims within it and to determine appropriate responses when those claims are jeopardized." This is, of course, true and serves as a fitting conclusion to the thoughts developed through the presentations of all the papers in this volume.

*Julie Ryan*

# Cyber can Kill and Destroy too: Blurring Borders Between Conventional and Cyber Warfare

**Marina Krotofil**

Institute for Security in Distributed Applications, Hamburg University of Technology, Germany

marina.krotofil@tuhh.de

*Originally Published in the Proceedings of ICCWS, 2014*

**Editorial Commentary**

Much of the discussion of what would constitute an act of armed aggression in the information domain has centered on attacks on information systems. In her paper, "Cyber Can Kill and Destroy Too: Blurring Borders Between Conventional and Cyber Warfare", Marina Krotofil reviews and explores the cyber equivalent of combined arms campaigns: the intersection of cyber and physical attacks. The paper focuses on the current state of integration between information technology and physical systems, with a focus on the control of the physical systems by the information technology, with an eye towards understanding how subversion of the information technology can result in the subversion of, damage to, or destruction of the physical system.

The paper is thought provoking, particularly given the emergence of the internet-of-things (IoT) and increasingly sophisticated bio-mechanical engineering solutions. The IoT is increasingly linking the most mundane pieces of daily lives, such as televisions, refrigerators, home electricity systems, in ways that enable information sharing and control across widely diverse systems. Emerging bio-mechanical solutions include varying contraptions for integrating human bodies with information technologies for varying purposes, including control of office lighting and coffee pots. The same considerations for defense, intelligence, forensics, and management considered by Marina Krotofil need to be expanded to the IoT and cyber-physical systems of all scale. This supports the argument that the emerging realities of cyberspace are sufficiently different and concerning that cyber deserves to be treated as a domain separate from the conventional war fighting domains of air, land, sea, and space. The integration, the potential operational tempo of operations using these systems as conduits, proxy actors, or targets create a potential that is sufficiently different than military operations in conventional space that it is possible that a new branch of military science may need to be created.

**Abstract:** Cyberwarfare has become a fashionable topic in the last decade, partly because of the ever increasing sophistication of computer attacks, partly because of malicious actors setting their sight on industrial systems such as plants. Modern production systems are characterized by an IT-infrastructure controlling effects in the physical world. Such systems are called cyber-physical systems. In this paper we draw a distinction between information cyberattacks and cyber-physical attacks. Thereafter we provide insights into the specifics of cyber-physical attacks and examine to which extent they are similar to conventional warfare.

**Keywords**: critical infrastructure, security, safety

# 1   Introduction

The invention of computing machines and the subsequent creation of the Internet induced the emergence of a new space – digital space or cyberspace. Information technologies have quickly found their applications in all areas of life. They have also quickly become regular means of fraud and abuse. In the modern world there is a broad range of malicious actions in cyber space, ranging from abuses by script-kiddies to crime, espionage, attacks and political actions (hacktivism). Particularly damaging activities such as espionage and targeted attacks are often referred to as cyber warfare. Questions persist whether offensive cyber capabilities can be utilized for strategic and tactical war operations.

Technological change as a product of industrialization has transformed warfare from gunpowder to precision-guided munitions and stealth fight machines. The ability to create new technologies and transform them for martial benefits had been an essential part of military evolution. It is therefore not surprising that cyber means has also found their way into military affairs. Nevertheless the hostility, self-sufficiency of cyber weaponry and its particular role in conventional conflicts remains a topic of heated dispute (Leed, 2013; Libicki, 2013; Rid, 2013).

Discussions on cyber war mainly revolve around information and communications matters such as mass-harvesting of online communications, immense exfiltration of documentation, computer crime as well as disruption of the information and communications systems, including military and civilian command and control channels. It is therefore often contended that cyber activities cannot cause destructive causalities similar to conventional war. This assertion holds for data-targeting cyber attacks in the context of information cyber warfare.

Miniaturization of processors has enabled them to replace analog components in many electronic products. Further integration of microprocessors with input and output system components has evolved into microcontrollers. They became ubiquitous with applications ranging from consumer electronics to complex industrial systems. Many microcontrollers are part of purpose built computational systems embedded in applications in the physical world. Such collaborating environments consisting of computational and communication elements controlling physical entities with the help of sensors and actuators are called cyber-physical systems (CPS). On one hand embedded computers enable governing of physical applications to achieve desired outcomes. On the other hand, in the same way physical systems can be instructed to perform what is not intended. Thereby, software code which does not inherently possess tangible force acquires destructive capacity through the ability to instruct physical systems to malfunction. Cyberattacks on physical systems are correspondingly called cyber-physical attacks. The implications of this class of cyberattacks (the ability to inflict physical damage) can be compared to the kinetic impact of conventional weaponry. At that, malicious software can be seen as a warhead or as a detonator – one can choose.

At the current time the discussion about potential combativeness and actual feasibility of cyber-physical attacks is nevertheless largely premature as the world has not seen many full-fledged cyber-physical attacks yet. Advancing the state of knowledge about these questions, however, could and should be persevered. In the absence of a physical experimental infrastructure it can be pursued through ways that are relatively inexpensive, e.g. through modelling and simulations. For that purposes we adapted the public plant-wide process control model of the Tennessee Eastman (TE) chemical process (Ricker, 2002) to study physical processes exploitation and defence techniques. Some results of our research are included in this work.

The aim of this paper is twofold. Firstly, after drawing a distinction between information cyber attacks and cyber-physical attacks we give evidences that due to the ability of cyber-physical attacks to cause impacts beyond digital space the line between conventional and cyber ammunition is becoming very thin. Secondly, we provide insights into the specifics of cyber-physical attacks. In particular we dwell on a case of targeted cyber-physical attacks on process control systems such as a chemical plant or a refinery. We will show that general rules and attributes of conventional war are equally applicable to the cyber-physical assaults.

## 2    Terminators in cyberspace

While there has been no publicly known murder committed by means of a computer-enabled attack yet, there have been public demonstrations that cyber-physical attacks can be launched to cause fatalities. At the same time, history has already witnessed examples of remote attacks causing physical damage.

Medical devices are meant to save lives. E.g., a pacemaker implanted in the chest sends regular electrical pulses to help maintaining a regular heart beat. Howbeit, these devices have little protection against unauthorized access via the wireless protocols used to access the widget. In a public video a researcher showed how he could remotely cause a pacemaker to suddenly deliver a lethal 830-volt shock from 50 feet (15.4 m) away (Kirk, 2012). In another presentation it was shown how insulin pumps from a particular vendor could be exploited wirelessly and made to deliver fatal doses of insulin to someone wearing the device (Radcliffe, 2011). Being aware of the medical devices remote exploitation danger Dick Cheney the former US Vice President had the wireless access to his pacemaker disabled (Gupta, 2013).

The most violent cyber attack to date is likely to have been Siberian pipeline explosion in 1982 in Russia. It was supposedly caused by CIA-initiated and covertly transferred hidden malfunctions in the Canadian automated control software. The malicious pipeline software was programmed to reset pump speeds and valve settings to produce pressures far beyond those acceptable to the pipeline joints and welds" yielding most monumental non-nuclear explosion and fire ever seen from space" (Hoffman, 2004). However, according to Thomas Rid the available evidence on the event is so thin and questionable that it cannot be counted as a proven case (Rid, 2013). The laboratory attack on an electric generator is a proven case though; the machinery was caused to self-destruct by virtue of a remotely executed attack (Meserve, 2007). Stuxnet a tailored subversive malware which caused a number of centrifuges to fail physically (Langner, 2013) has certainly convinced many that sophisticated abuses in cyber space are possible. While one may argue that the list of examples is too scant, the feasibility of the attacks should not be underestimated. Accident databases contain enough examples of both cyber-related and operations-related industrial incidents and disasters with human, machinery and environmental losses. Those scenarios might also be provoked intentionally. It would not be wrong to assume that national agencies are silently exploring the offensive potential of cyber-physical capabilities. It is also clear why the development of such arms is kept clandestine. Cyber attacks are single-use weapons. Every vulnerability disclosure and attack demonstration leads to fixes that make the next exploitation much harder.

Meanwhile the "Tallinn Manual on the International Law Applicable to Cyber Warfare" (Schmitt, 2013) which was written by 20 legal scholars and practitioners has captured the current reasoning on how current international law may apply to cyber war. In particular according to the authors, it is acceptable to retaliate against cyber attacks with traditional weapons if a state can prove that the attack lead to fatalities or to severe property damage. It is also stated that hackers who perpetrate attacks are legitimate targets for a kinetic counter strike. In this regard the delimitation between cyber and conventional wars seems to loose its definition even further.

## 3    Process control systems as theater of war

Process control system (PCS) is an aggregated term for architectures, mechanisms and algorithms which enable processing of physical substances or manufacturing end products. Process industries include assembly lines, water treatment, pharmaceutical, food and other industries. Plants are strategic objects, especially those which are involved in military manufacturing, (petro)chemical production and utilities. The adversary might want to take control of them in order to disrupt production, break machinery or induce hazardous situations. Plants dealing with explosives, toxic and flammable chemicals and the like are thus subjected to risks of catastrophic accidents with lethal consequences for both plant personnel and members of the public. The Bhopal disaster in India in 1984 (Jung and Bloch, 2012) is one of the largest industrial accidents on record. A runaway reaction in a tank containing poisonous methyl isocyanate caused the pressure relief system to vent large amounts of chemicals into the atmosphere. The estimate of the death toll ranges from 4000 to 20000, with severe health problems persisting to the present.

In the past few decades plants have undergone tremendous modernization. Technology became an enabler of efficiency but also a source of problems. What used to be a panel of relays is now an embedded computer. What used to be a simple analog sensor is now an IP-enabled smart transmitter (McIntyre, 2011) with multiple wired and wireless communication modes, numerous configuration possibilities, and even a web-server, so that maintenance staff can calibrate and setup the device without even approaching it. Thereby the possibility of remote exploitation of the physical processes and equipment became a reality. What is not always understood yet is that breaking into a system and taking over a device is not enough to carry out an attack. To actually break the system requires a different set of knowledge such as good understanding of mechanics, physics, chemistry and control principles.

Due to the multidisciplinary nature of plants it would require a team of technologists with highly specialised skills to design and conduct targeted large-scale attacks. Even if the cyber-warriors manage to break through all the IT-defences achieving the desired effects will be hampered by the plant operators' protective defences thus converting the plant floor into a battlefield. In the next sections we will show that strategies and tactics used in conventional military conflicts are the same as used for offence and defence in the industrial cyber-physical war game.

## 3.1 Espionage, reconnaissance, deception

As each facility is uniquely customized even operational sites within the same company can be very dissimilar. The same applies to systems failure modes. Therefore offensive capabilities in the cyber-physical domain exist only in relation to a specific target, which must be scoped to be understood.

The last few years were marked by the discovery of a large number of espionage campaigns and sophisticated spying malware directed at industry-related companies, e.g. (Chien and O'Gorman, 2011). The attackers were especially interested in user credentials and in intellectual property such as design documents, formulas, manufacturing processes, etc. While information on supporting IT and communication infrastructure is necessary for obtaining persistent access and gaining control, the data on processes, configurations and equipment is required to design actual cyber-physical attacks. Different equipment is susceptible to different classes of physical damage (Larsen, 2007). In addition carrying out an attack requires identification of process control system weaknesses and flaws which can be exploited.

Let us assume that the analysis of stolen information suggests that a chemical reactor relieve system is only designed to cope with the first exothermic reaction during normal operating conditions. This design weakness can be exploited by inducing a second exothermic reaction causing overpressure the relieve system would not be able to control. There are few approaches which may be applied for achieving the latter. One can manipulate the inflow or reactants, disable the cooling system or stop the mixer in the reactor. The decision on the strategy will depend on further weaknesses identified from the exfiltrated documentation, strategic considerations and/or personal preferences of the attackers (probably based on the expertise they possess). E.g., the root cause of the explosion at T2 Laboratories (4 killed, 28 insured) was a failed cooling system (CSB, 2009). The lack of cooling redundancy resulted in a runaway reaction. Because of insufficient relieve capabilities the pressure burst the reactor, the reactor content ignited and exploded. If the attacker is aware of both weaknesses, she only needs to disable the cooling system, which is subjected to a single point of failure, in order to achieve her goal.

As with many things in cyberspace a lot is simpler on paper than in reality. Hitting at outright success is difficult. The exact dynamic behavior of a process, precise mapping of I/O points, subtle correlation and interdependencies between components and physical phenomena are often not known even to the operators. The attacker can do her home work well and design most of the attack in advance; however she will have to tune the attack locally through reconnaissance activities such as changing configuration parameters or turning components on and off while observing the system's reaction. Getting the desired results also requires evading intrusion and anomaly detection guards so that those who administer the system cannot detect and eradicate the attack, and repair the damage quickly. Persisting within the target would therefore require reconnoitring the cyber assets, network design, security defences and safety countermeasures.

Military deception techniques aim to deliberately mislead adversary decision makers by luring them into taking specific actions or inactions. Deception can take different forms such as placing dummy and decoy equipment and devices or spreading false information on tactical actions or movement of forces. Similarly plant administrators may strategically place misleading or false technical documentation and use a simulated infrastructure to influence the attacker's target selection process and pilot her towards decoy physical processes as demonstrated in (Rrushi, 2011) for the example of a boiling water reactor. A particular case of deception in cyber space is the usage of honeypots – decoying vulnerable-looking cyber assets for studying attackers and their techniques. A recent report about a honeypot specifically developed to catch attacks against industrial control systems (Wilhoit, 2013) has demonstrated that the attackers not only have the skills to gain access to industrial systems but also posses knowledge on how to manipulate the equipment under control. The attacker may in turn use deception offensively. Among frequent causes of industrial accidents are missing alarms or wrong responses to abnormal events by the operators (ASM, 2013). The attacker may intentionally trigger certain alarms or cause alarm flooding to divert operator attention from the real problem or forcing her taking wrong actions.

## 3.2    Attack strategies and success factors

Conventional warfare is known as a strategic and tactic undertaking. Thorough planning and tailoring of activities to the situation at hand are necessary prerequisites for achieving success. Cyber-physical strikes are not different. The attacker might want to upset production, maximize physical damage, leave no traces, achieve results quickly, etc. Inducing specific unwanted effects requires playing radically different strategies specific to the process being attacked, but there are some general concepts that can be discussed. Foremost among those is time.

Misuse in IT the domain does not usually deal with time. One flips a bit and software changes happen faster than a human can observe. In cyber-physical systems it may take hours to heat a water tank or burn a motor. In our previous work (Krotofil and Cardenas, 2013) we have shown that the time it takes to bring a process to an undesired state depends greatly on a large number of parameters, among those the kind of relationships between the interdependent physical parameters and the way a physical phenomenon is being controlled, in particular, the configuration of the control loop which includes the choice of the manipulated variable (valve), type of the control algorithm and tuning parameters of a controller. Figure 1 depicts TE process failure due to high reactor pressure brought on by attacks on different sensors. As can be seen the time to shutdown greatly differs. To obtain knowledge on such timing parameters the attacker would need to derive a behavioural process model of sufficient precision. This is a non-trivial task which is an active research area in process control engineering (Vodencarevic, et al., 2011).

Due to noise, disturbances, non-linearity and instability of process behaviour the timing of the attack is another important strategic factor. Peak values (low and high) are usually of interest, in particular for launching resonance attacks, such as water hammers (Leishear, 2013). Water hammers are formed due to waveform additions in fluids leading to a physical failure of the pipe. In our experimental work we conducted an empirical study of the influence of attack time on the success of DoS attacks on sensors. Figure 2 demonstrates the outcome of a 10 hours long DoS attack on a reactor pressure sensor initiated at a random time. Depending on the time of attack the impact varies from negligible to a shutdown (experiment stopped before simulation time elapsed). If the attacker's goal is to induce an unsafe situation as soon as possible she would prefer to strike at one of the measurement's peak values. The next question to answer is how to decide on the best peak value to launch an attack as the sensor signal is relatively variable. This class of decision problems is known as stopping problem (William, Darryl and Rapoport, 2003). We currently evaluate different stopping algorithms to maximize the impact of DoS attacks (work in progress).

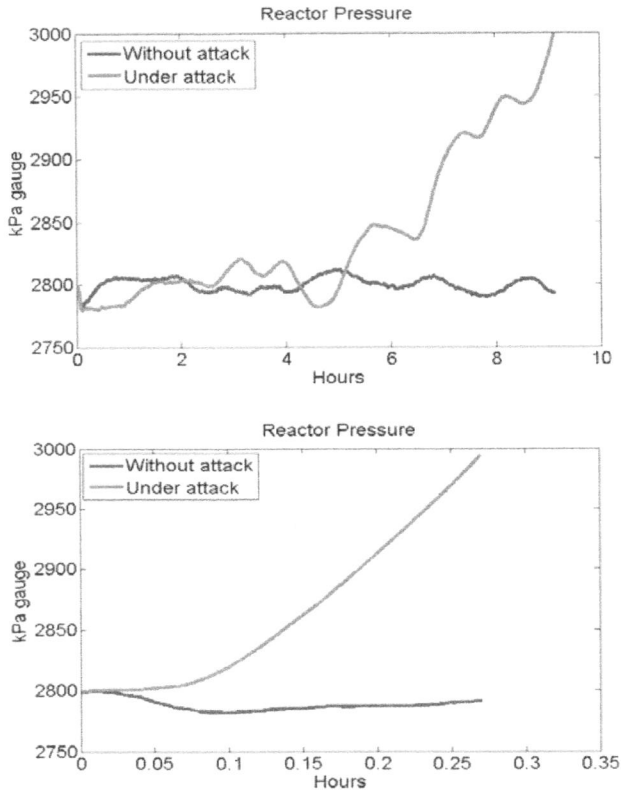

**Figure 1:** Integrity attack on separator recycle flow sensor (left) and reactor temperature sensor (right)

If the desired process upset is not instantaneous, plant operators may take corrective measures to bring the process back into its steady state. Moreover, if the operator attributes the process behaviour to unnatural causes, she can initiate an immediate incident investigation. Out of these considerations the attacker might prefer to hide the real process measurements from the operator. As a result, the operator loses situational awareness. This is one of the most dangerous attacks on process control. Besides changing the content of the operator's display, the adversary can spoof process data or play back pre-recorded normal operations measurements as implemented in the Stuxnet attack (Falliere, Murchu and Chien, 2010). A radically different approach would be to influence the process of taking measurement itself. This could be achieved through the manipulation of the surrounding environment or through miscalibration of the transmitters (sensors). Such an attack violates one crucial and predominantly over-looked security property of information called trustworthiness or veracity (Gollmann, 2012). E.g., in 2005 BP Texas City Refinery (CSB, 2007) suffered one of the worst industrial disasters in recent

USA history: Explosions and fires killed 15 people and injured another 180. The root cause of the tragedy were critical alarms and control instrumentation providing false indications. Due to wrong calibration the splitter tower level indicator showed that the tower level was declining when it was actually overfilling with flammable liquid hydrocarbons. As a result the operator kept filling the tower. The further chain of events eventually led to an explosion.

## 3.3   Response

Despite of the full automation of most plants, human operators und maintenance personnel play a key role in process management and control, and are the main troops on the plant battlefield. During normal operating conditions operators are mostly responsible for the fine-tuning of control parameters to minimize the usage of raw materials, energy and efforts to produce best quality products. If process conditions are abnormal, the operator has the critical function of fault administration. Upon fault detection the problem has to be diagnosed and a decision has to be made on corrective measures. Sounds simple, but it is not.

Processes are generally highly complex and involve a high number of interacting variables and many degrees of freedom (valves). Variables can be cross-coupled, so that changes in one variable affect several other variables simultaneously. Modern control rooms comprise multiple displays with large number of controls and alarms to display these processes. In critical situations such complexity can severely overburden the operator and make it extremely difficult for her to identify the state of the plant. Furthermore, the decision-making process is predominantly based on experiences and training. Every previously unseen disturbance poses a significant mental challenge for the personnel. E.g., if the operator had never had to deal with water hammers before, she would likely not to be able to figure out easily how to resolve it (e.g. slowing down the valve). Withal, the process variables and system responses can be slow and a control action may not produce a visible system response for seconds or minutes.  As a result, stress and fatigue are intrinsic attributes of this job.

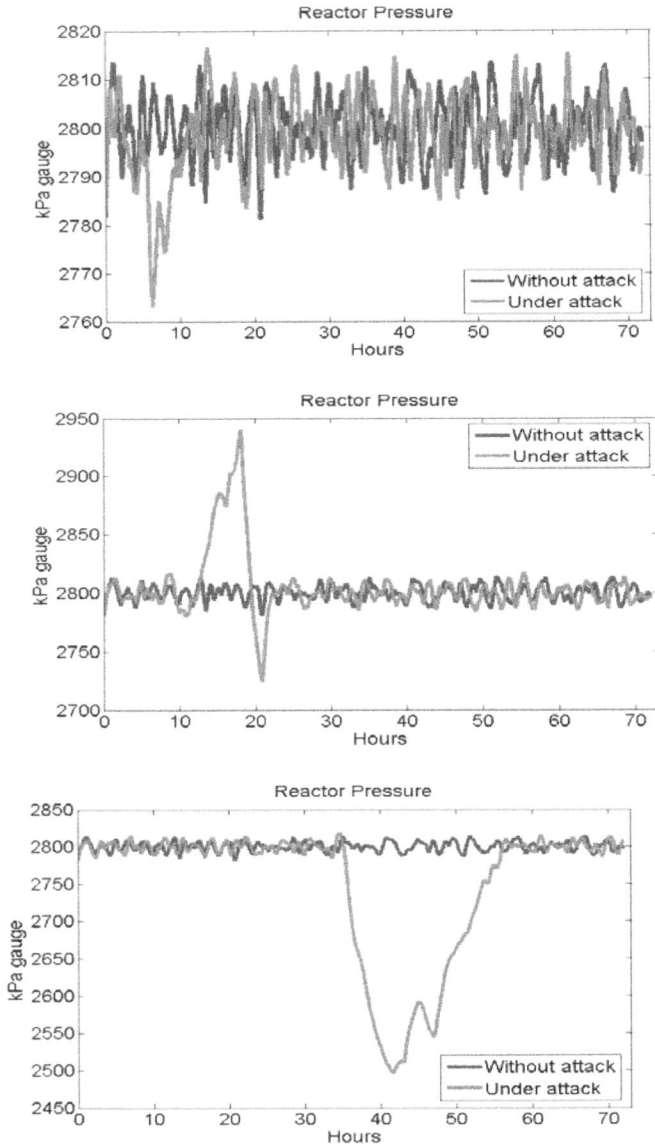

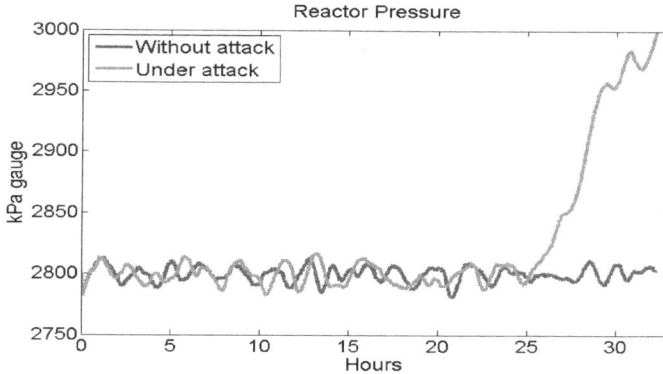

**Figure 2:** Impact of 8h long DoS attacks on reactor pressure sensor at random time

Despite of the challenges outlined operators are largely capable of dealing with accidental process perturbations without initiating unit shutdown. However, during a coordinated attack events are not happening on the basis of statistical independencies and normal process flows. Hence there is a significant danger of operators taking wrong actions. Moreover the intruder might have endeavoured to estimate the operators' responses and develop strategies to withstand the defender's corrective actions. Hence gaining the upper hand can be difficult. Therefore it is crucial to be able to locate and isolate the source of an attack. This would first and foremost require collaborative activities with IT and security personnel as cyberattacks may leave traces in system logs and traffic dumps. Modern plants may also take advantage of Asset Management Systems which keep detailed diagnostic and maintenance-related information about field instrumentation to detect unauthorized manipulations.

Detection of compromised nodes requires conducting forensic activities. Uncovering controllers compromised by the authorized engineering station might be challenging due to the absence of anomalous activity logs. Since in cyber-physical systems the major evidences of misuse are in the physical world, it might be possible to trace perturbations back to the compromised end points. It is therefore desired to keep a process running to facilitate the attribution of the sources of the problems. In the TE process loss of certain reactant feeds inevitably leads to plant shutdown due to exceeding safety limits. However by adjusting the feed flows of other reactants it is possible to prolong plant survivability (at a cost of suboptimal product

13

quality). In our experimental work we were able to keep the plant running up to 4 hours longer.

## 3.4 Defenses

To mitigate the threats one has to develop defenses. Any pilot knows when flying blind one has to trust the instruments. Fault diagnosis fully depends on the instrument readings. Hence it is important for the operator to have confidence that the measurements are correct. Preserving situational awareness is thereupon the cornerstone in PCS defence. This could be achieved through taking orthogonal measurements, performing plausibility and data consistency checks, calculating estimates, etc. What is important, implementation of such defences does not require physical changes in plant configuration and thus can be brought into practical service.

One of the most eminent similarities between military operations and cyber-physical systems is exposure to hazards and – consequently – requirement for safety measures. Process control history has accumulated substantial experience in identifying and addressing potential hazards and operational problems in terms of plant design and human error to minimise the effects of atypical situations and achieve a safe outcome from a situation that could have resulted in a major accident. However such analysis only considers natural causes of events and unintentional human mistakes within the organization. Communication technologies have in contrast introduced security issues such as external threats. The distinctive feature of intended abuses is the impossibility of predicting them (where, when and how). As a result it is difficult to asses whether system design will remain flaw-less and safety measures suffice if confronted with cyber-physical assaults. Conducting process-aware security risk assessment will help to identify PCS weaknesses in the presence of cyberattacks. While prioritizing equipment and systems which require most protection would require a list of hypothesized attack and evaluation of their probabilities, some steps of an security assessment such as the discovery of the latent abilities of the components can be conducted without having a particular misuse case in mind. Thus most of the equipment is manufactured for more than one purpose. E.g., a motor that can be run in reverse but never used that way should have that option disabled.

Military exercises serve the purpose of studying warfare and training available skills and techniques in simulated scenarios. Similarly cyber-security drills strengthen readiness to accidental and targeted attacks and bolster defences. Such an exercise simulates what would happen if the assailant penetrates certain systems and carries out a specific attack. Since in CPS the attacker ferrets her way to the physical world through the cyber layer it is crucial to conduct collaborative trainings including both IT and process control divisions. Such joint exercises will enable these usually disjoint groups to practice sharing information with each other, learn making real-time critical decisions for mitigating threats and conduct coordinated forensic activities. Also, the process control group should include multidisciplinary participants to train diverse attack detection (e.g., plausibility checks) and response techniques (e.g., dynamic controllability).

# 4 Discussion

In the modern Information Age information has become a valuable asset. This being the case, information warfare has become an attractive domain for most small countries and developing nations because the amount of resources and effort that a country must invest to launch a cyber attack is significantly lower than fielding tanks, launching satellites, developing a secret agency or refining uranium (as is the visibility of such preparations). Besides, cyber attacks can be launched across borders. The advanced nation-states have therefore no longer a monopoly on war. Moreover, minor actors such as organized crime groups, insurgents and terrorist can also engage independently or at the behest of nation-states.

While acquisition of cyber capabilities is easy and tools are cheap, the cost of large-scale cyber attacks should not be underestimated. Even more resources are required to prepare a targeted attack on a complex cyber-physical target such as a plant. It would require lengthy coordinated preparatory work and a multi-skilled team with advanced competences. Thus, feasibility testing and tuning of the devised physical attack requires experimental labs with specialized industrial equipment similar to the one installed at the target site. Implementation and carrying out of an attack further (optionally but very likely) depends upon sophisticated and time-consuming firmware reverse engineering, root-kitting of embedded systems and discovery of 0-days vulnerabilities. Therefore the ability to design and conduct a full-fledged cyber-physical attack is likely to be beyond the capacities of individual groups and countries without sufficient resources. As follows, cyber-physical weaponry is likely to remain a privilege of developed countries or well-financed nations which can draw in mercenaries.

Concerning conventional war, certain countries have cut military expenditures out of economic considerations and accept the risk of being conquered. Similarly the defence capacity of plants might be consciously kept weak if addressing security concerns is not deemed justifiable. E.g., it was shown that the optimal operating condition for reactor pressure in the TE process is close to the upper shutdown limit of 3000kPa. In this case the attacker will be able to bring the system into an unsafe state quickly. To ensure secure operations it would be desirable to maintain a sufficient safety margin. However, maintaining a safety margin of at least 100 kPa is equivalent to a 5% increase in cost. Ease of maintenance and plant administration also clashes with security concerns. Usage of standard configurations and operating procedures, utilization of equipment and instrumentation of a single preferred vendor makes vulnerabilities predictable but is convenient for managing the plant. Particularly dangerous is the homogeneity of field instrumentation firmware. In this case the attacker would need to discover vulnerabilities just once to invade multiple devices. An advanced attacker may further co-opt compromised devices into a botnet.

As can be seen from this short review paper, cyber-physical attacks, despite of carrying cyber component in them, are much closer to the essence of conventional warfare than to information cyber attacks. However more practice-oriented research is required to determine further aspects of cyber-physical assaults.

# References

Abnormal Situation Management (ASM) Consortium. [online] Available at:https://www.asmconsortium.net [Accessed June, 2013].

Chien, E., O'Gorman, G. (2011) The *Nitro Attacks: Stealing Secrets from the Chemical Industry*. Symantec: Technical report.

Falliere, Nicolas, Murchu L. O., Chien, E. (2010) *W32.Stuxnet Dossier*. Symantec: Technical report.

Gollmann, D. (2012) Veracity Plausibility, and Reputation. In *Information Security Theory and Practice, LNCS 7322,* pages 20-28.

Gupta, S. (2013) Dick Cheney's heart. *CBSNews*, [online] Available at: http://www.cbsnews.com/news/dick-cheneys-heart/ [Accessed October, 2013]

Hoffman., E.D. (2004) CIA slipped bugs to Soviets. *The Washington Post*, [pdf] Available at: http://industrialdefender.com/general_downloads/incidents/1982.06_trans_siberian_gas_pipeline_explosion.pdf [Accessed October, 2013]

Jung, B., Bloch, K. (2012) The Bhopal disaster. *Hydrocarbon Processing*, [online] Available at: http://www.hydrocarbonprocessing.com/Article/3035763/The-Bhopal-disaster.html [Accessed October, 2013]

Kirk, J. (2012) Pacemaker hack can deliver deadly 830-volt jolt. *Computerworld*, [online] Available at:
http://www.computerworld.com/s/article/9232477/Pacemaker_hack_can_deliver_deadl
y_830_volt_jolt [Accessed October, 2013]

Krotofil, M., Cardenas, A. (2013) Resilience of Process Control Systems to Cyber-Physical Attacks. In *Secure IT Systems, LNCS 8208,* pages 166-182.

Langner,R. (2013) To kill a centrifuge, [pdf] Available at:http://www.langner.com/en/wp-content/uploads/2013/11/To-kill-a-centrifuge.pdf [Accessed October, 2013]

Larsen, J. (2007) *Breakage.* [pdf] Black Hat USA. Available at:
http://www.blackhat.com/presentations/bh-dc-08/Larsen/Presentation/bh-dc-08-larsen.pdf [Accessed October, 2013]

Leed, M. (2013) *Offensive Cyber Capabilities at the Operational Level* [pdf] CSIS. Available at:
http://csis.org/files/publication/130916_Leed_OffensiveCyberCapabilities_Web.pdf [Accessed September, 2013]

Leishear, R. A. C. (2013) *Fluid Mechanics, Water Hammer, Dynamic Stresses and Piping Design.* Asme Intl.

Libicki, M.C. (2013) *Brandishing Cyberattack Capabilities* [pdf] RAND Corporation. Available at:
http://www.rand.org/content/dam/rand/pubs/research_reports/RR100/RR175/RAND_R
R175.pdf [Accessed September, 2013]

McIntyre, C. (2011) Using Smart Instrumentation. *Plant Engineering*, [online] Available at:
http://www.plantengineering.com/home/single-article/using-smart-instrumentation/a0ec350155bb86c8f65377ba66e59df8.html [Accessed October, 2013]

Meserve, J. (2007) Staged cyberattack reveals vulnerability in power grid. *CNN*, [online] Available at:http://edition.cnn.com/2007/US/09/26/power.at.risk/ [Accessed October, 2013]

Radcliffe, J. (2011) *Hacking Medical Devices for Fun and Insulin.* [pdf] Black Hat USA. Available at: http://media.blackhat.com/bh-us-11/Radcliffe/BH_US_11_Radcliffe_Hacking_Medical_Devices_Slides.pdf [Accessed October, 2013]

Ricker, N. L. (2002) Tennessee Eastman Challenge Archive. Available at:
http://depts.washington.edu/control/LARRY/TE/download.html [Accessed June, 2013].

Rid, T. (2013) *Cyber War Will Not Take Place.* Hurst & Co.

Rrushi, J.(2011) An exploration of defensive deception in industrial communication networks. *International Journal of Critical Infrastructure Protection* 4(3):66-75.

Schmitt, M. N. (2013) *The Tallinn Manual on the International Law Applicable to Cyber Warfare.* Cambridge University Press.

U.S. Chemical Safety Board (CSB). (2007) *BP America Refinery Explosion: final investigation report.*

U.S. Chemical Safety Board (CSB). (2009) *T2 Laboratories Inc. Reactive Chemical Explosion: final investigation report.*

Vodencarevic, A., Kleine Buning, H., Niggemann, O. , Maier, O. (2011) Identifying behaviour models for process plants. In *Emerging Technologies Factory Automation*, pages 1-8.

Wilhoit, K. (2013) *Who is Really Attacking Your ICS Equipment*? Trend Micro Incorporated: Research Paper.

William E. S, Darryl A. S., Rapoport, A. (2003) Analysis of heuristic solutions to the best choice problem. *European Journal of Operational Research*, Volume 151, Issue 1, 151(1):140-152.

# Cyberspace from the Hybrid Threat Perspective

## Håkan Gunneriusson[1] and Rain Ottis[2, 3]

[1]Swedish National Defence College, Stockholm, Sweden
[2]University of Jyväskylä, Jyväskylä, Finland
[3]Tallinn University of Technology, Tallinn, Estonia
rain.ottis@jyu.fi

*Originally Published in the Proceedings of ECIW, 2013*

**Editorial Commentary**

An important problem facing the strategists trying to understand how competition in cyberspace can, will, and has integrated with other elements of life is developing a framework for discussing combined arms activities using information warfare elements. An emerging concept, dubbed "hybrid" warfare, is being used as a structural way to describe the integration of information activities on the broadest spectrum into aggressive actions. Gunneriusson and Ottis provide a great service to this discussion by exploring many different concepts of what "hybrid" threats might be. Rather than confining their conceptualization to arms and geopolitical competition, they expand the conversation to include non-state actors, such as Anonymous, and the implications of "cheap and easily accessible computing devices and global networking."

Their exploration of the increasing intimate nature of information technologies is sobering to consider after having read Krotofil's exploration of how physical damage can result from cyber attacks. Another interesting avenue of discussion is triggered by the exploration of how nation states may try to confine citizen behavior in cyberspace, as illustrated by the contextual aspects of use, oversight, monitoring, and control of cyberspace.

The potential for governments to create and enforce virtual enclaves in cyberspace is already a reality; considering the near term potential for geopolitical organizations to fully embrace the notion of cyberspace as a predominantly national security problem leads to default militarization on both the offense and the defense. This in turn has profound implications for the global economy, access to information, and fair competition in trade, education, and research.

**Abstract:** Hybrid threats use conventional and unconventional means to achieve their goals. In this paper we explore the cyber threats as one possible aspect of hybrid threats. We describe three ways of approaching cyberspace (operations) from the hybrid threats perspective: supporting conventional operations, exploiting non-military systems, and exploring the opportunities provided by this environment. In particular, we highlight the aspects that are or likely will be relevant to the military community.

**Keywords**: hybrid threat, cyberspace, cyber operation, Internet, military

# 1    Introduction

One of the problems with the concept of hybrid threats is that it is very difficult to define. Hybrid threats are not defined by the actors, since states, non-state actors and even individuals might be considered (part of) hybrid threats. They are not about some specific technology, since the list here keeps growing as new technologies become available. They are not about specific effects, as a hybrid campaign may result in casualties, changed decisions, altered public perception, etc. Perhaps the best way to put it, hybrid threat is a manifestation of total war. It is about making the other side submit to one's will, with any means available.

Threats from or using cyberspace are similarly difficult to define, and can in fact be viewed as a subset of hybrid threats. Cyber threats come in the form of state actors, criminal groups, terrorist organizations, hacktivists, professional hackers for hire (mercenaries), etc. The list of exploitable technologies also keeps growing – aside from servers, personal computers and laptops we also have to worry about smart phones, smart meters (electricity distribution to our homes), wireless-enabled pacemakers, industrial control systems, etc, and that is just the hardware side. Possible effects can range from tongue-in-cheek publicity campaigns to destruction of critical infrastructure components and potentially – deaths.

Cyber threats operate in a man-made environment. As such, they are constrained by the capabilities built into that environment. However, this is in fact an enabler for the cyber attacker. Non-trivial man-made systems (such as computers, airplanes, etc.) are rarely perfectly implemented and may be based on flawed design assumptions. These assumptions may be about type of input, length of input, number of simultaneous user sessions, etc. Cyber attacks work by exploiting design assumptions or implementation flaws. It is important to realize, however, that while cyberspace is the "home" environment for cyber threats, they can and do affect other environments as well. Consider, for example, the case of StuxNet, where a cyber-attack disrupted the uranium enrichment process and caused a number of physical devices to break in Iran. (See, for example, Falliere, Murchu and Chien 2011, Sanger 2012, The Economist 2010a) Or consider the case of cyber-attacks against Georgian government and news sites during the 2008 Russia-Georgia war, which hampered the Georgian government's ability to communicate with the citizenry. (Markoff 2008)

These risks from cyberspace have a serious effect on society. On one hand, we are concerned with various threats – hacktivists, criminals, spies, etc. In order to protect ourselves (our systems, our data, our way of life) we are constantly endeavoring to improve the security situation in cyberspace. On the other hand, however, we are concerned with the opportunities and liberties associated with cyberspace – freedom of speech, privacy, etc. Unfortunately, in many cases, an increase in security tends to undermine the open and liberal society. Therefore, it is important that (military) security professionals are aware of these concerns and will take steps to minimize the adverse effects of new security solutions.

In this paper we describe three ways of approaching cyberspace (operations) from the hybrid threats perspective. In an effort to better explain this new type of threat to commanders, planners and soldiers, we highlight the aspects that are or likely will be relevant to the military community.

## 2    Hybrid threats in relation to cyber threats

Hybrid threat as a concept has changed over time. This is not unusual when it comes to the combination of the military culture and theoretical concepts. The now dead acronym EBO (Effects Based Operations) had a similar story. (See, for example, Mattis 2008 or Ho 2005) The stake holders agreed that the term held some truth but they could not come to an agreement of the content or meaning of the concept. The terms used in EBO were so hollow yet so widely discussed that it was considered better to leave that debate open and to concentrate on developing our theoretical thinking on military operations instead.

The initial meaning of hybrid threat was described as a non-state actor wielding a conventional capability as if it were a state-actor. (Matthews 2008) The concept has evolved to a catch-all phrase for unconventional and unexpected threats which strike asymmetrically. Now, as with EBO, NATO has abandoned the development of the concept of hybrid threats. However, this does not mean that the underlying concept is not of any use.

In the early days of the Internet, many wondered about the possibilities that global networking would bring. In historical terms, this was similar to the time when electricity was harnessed for the benefit of society. Such advances in science and technology bring about all-encompassing effects to the entire society, not just specific markets, businesses or governments. Instead of talking about, for example, *the electricity threat* or *the cyber threat,* it might be better to use the hybrid threat concept as a way to describe the interplay between conventional and unconventional threats to our society. In this paper we have taken this route in order to explore the cyber threat from a new perspective, since the military is already somewhat familiar with hybrid threats.

Although this is not a firm rule, hybrid threats tend to target the civil society rather than the military. This is a double asymmetry as it both strikes in unconventional ways and targets parts of society that may not be prepared for the attack. Defending against cyber threats requires a comprehensive approach, involving all relevant stakeholders from responsible government agencies (including the military) to private companies to individuals.

## 3    Cyberspace and cyber operations

Cyberspace is the extension of some of the greatest technological developments of the 20th Century: the electronic computer, the Internet and the World Wide Web. In 1948 Norbert Wiener coined the word cybernetics, which refers to "communication and control in the animal and the machine" (Wiener 1948). The discipline of cybernetics plays an important role in understanding and developing the underlying infrastructure of cyberspace. In 1984 William Gibson, a science fiction writer, first used the term cyberspace to describe the "consensual hallucination" of a new domain formed by interconnected computers. (Gibson 1984) Over the last decade the term has been widely adopted, but there are numerous ways of defining, interpreting and using the underlying concept.

One of the most prominent concepts of cyberspace is the one that has emerged in the national defense and security sector. It refers to cyberspace as a new domain of (military) operations, on equal footing with land, air, sea, and sometimes – space. (The Economist 2010b) The western military doctrine generally divides the operations in cyberspace into two or three categories. Perhaps the best known is the US approach, which uses the term 'computer network' instead of 'cyberspace'. According to this doctrine, computer network operations (CNO) are a component of Information Operations and break down into computer network defense (CND), computer network exploitation (CNE) and computer network attack (CNA). (Joint Publication 3-13)

While the main purpose of CND and CNA is self-evident, CNE is somewhat more controversial. It primarily refers to covert intelligence gathering, but it is unclear where the 'exploitation' ends and the 'attack' starts. From the defender's perspective, it is very difficult to tell if an intrusion into their systems is an attempt to gather military intelligence (CNE), to prepare for a subsequent attack (CNA), to make money (criminals), or to make an ideological statement (hacktivist).

Of the three, CND is the most mature discipline. This does not mean that the art of defense is perfected - just that know-how is available and widespread. The offensive forms of operations (CNE, CNA) are comparatively rarely discussed in public and the actual capabilities of various actors are difficult to assess. It is this emergent quality that raises offensive cyber operations into the hybrid threat discussion.

The western doctrine is by no means finalized, nor is it the only one. For example, the Chinese military has spent nearly two decades of developing 'informationized warfare'. Inspired (shocked) by the US performance against the Soviet style forces of Iraq in the Gulf War, Chinese scholars and military leaders have blended the techno-centric approach of the US doctrine with the ancient 'Art of War' of China. (See, for example, Thomas 2007, 2009) The resulting mix offers a potentially more holistic approach than the often stove piped and limited Western IO doctrine.

The Russian military doctrine (or vision) of the future wars also combines conventional and unconventional approaches. For example, there is strong emphasis on the question of information superiority, both in terms of functionality of systems and of the prevailing content or narrative in the information sphere and the public perception. There is also discussion of using unconventional concepts like nano technology weapons, 'disorganization' techniques, affecting people's thought processes, etc. (See Thomas 2011 for more details) While it is unclear how much and which components of the unconventional approach are mere intellectual musings, it is a strong indication that Russia should be considered as a hybrid actor.

Another view of cyberspace is focused on the opportunities offered by cheap and easily accessible computing devices and global networking. Online shopping, social networks, strong public cryptography and (anonymous) real-time communication are examples of this. These solutions provide asymmetric advantages to actors who have limited resources. For example, it is possible to raise awareness of an issue on a blog, find people who are supportive of the cause through social networks and coordinate group actions on encrypted chat channels. On the other hand, the technology also allows for much greater control by those in power. For example, state (security) services might limit people's access to the Internet or specific services, eavesdrop unencrypted (or weakly encrypted) communications and even hack into personal computing devices to gather evidence against them.

The possibility to perform these activities with scarce resources enables sub-state actors. This is a big change compared to the Cold War and earlier times. The hacktivist group Anonymous has reported, for example, that its members recently hacked several hundred websites and published information on thousands of Israeli government officials as a response to Israeli efforts to shut down Internet in the Gaza Strip (see Figure 1). (RT.com 2012) This is a non-state actor attacking a state, as in the case with Hezbollah during the Lebanon war (although the scenario was quite different). Israel's finance minister declared in no uncertain terms that the government was now waging war on a "second front" [in cyberspace]. (RT.com 2012)

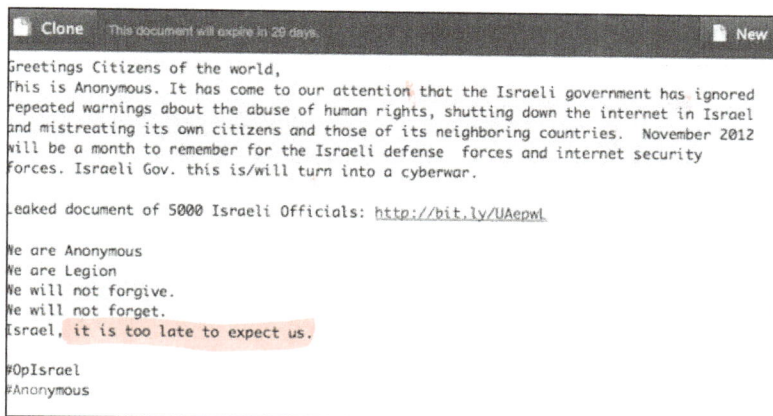

```
Clone   This document will expire in 29 days.                        New

Greetings Citizens of the world,
This is Anonymous. It has come to our attention that the Israeli government has ignored
repeated warnings about the abuse of human rights, shutting down the internet in Israel
and mistreating its own citizens and those of its neighboring countries.  November 2012
will be a month to remember for the Israeli defense  forces and internet security
forces. Israeli Gov. this is/will turn into a cyberwar.

Leaked document of 5000 Israeli Officials: http://bit.ly/UAepwL

We are Anonymous
We are Legion
We will not forgive.
We will not forget.
Israel, it is too late to expect us.

#OpIsrael
#Anonymous
```

**Figure 1:** A message from the hacktivist group Anonymous (RT.com 2012)

The war-like reference might seem a bit overdone, but cyber operations against a state are likely to get such reactions, depending on how serious the state thinks the problem is. A US state official has stated that "If you shut down our powergrid, maybe we put a missile down one of your smoke stacks". (Gorman and Barnes 2011)

Cyberspace is a contested environment. In recent years there have been many interesting developments to illustrate this point. The discovery of the StuxNet malware in 2010 created a lot of discussion about government malware and sabotaging critical infrastructure through cyber-attacks. (See, for example, Falliere, Murchu and Chien 2011, Sanger 2012, The Economist 2010a) In Germany, a debate sparked on the use of malware and hacking techniques for law enforcement purposes. (See, for example, Herkner 2007) The so-called Arab Spring demonstrated the dual use of information technology for both the people and the government. (See, for example, Afanasjev 2011)

The international community is trying to find consensus on some of these issues, but so far there is little success. There are efforts to shape or ana-lyze the legal instruments for this area, such as the Council of Europe Con-vention on Cybercrime (2001) or the Tallinn Manual on the International Law Applicable to Cyber Warfare (2013). In reality, however, state practice is developing the norms for tomorrow.

# 4 Overlap of cyberspace (operations) and hybrid threats

From the perspective of hybrid threats, cyberspace can be viewed in several ways. First, cyber capabilities in support of conventional forces. Second, as an asymmetric and unconventional attack vector on its own. Third, as an enabler or disabler of events and social movements.

## 4.1 Supporting conventional forces

Offensive cyber capabilities may one day be considered part of the 'conventional' toolkit. However, for now they are a rarity in military combat operations and can be safely categorized as 'unconventional'. This means that any military operation that includes offensive cyber operations as well as conventional capabilities is by definition a manifestation of hybrid threats. Potential targets of military cyber attacks include sensors, computer controlled systems (drones, guided missiles, etc.), command, control, and logistics systems, etc.

Remotely controlled or autonomous drones operating in air, land, sea or space domains, rely completely on computers and computer networks to function. As such, they also fall into the domain of cyber operations. An interesting example of a possible cyber attack against such systems occurred in 2011, when Iran was able to manipulate a US drone to land in Iran - in effect, performing a remote hijack of the drone. While technical details are not published, there is speculation that the event involved jamming the control signal (forcing the drone into autopilot mode), as well as jamming and spoofing the GPS signal (tricking the drone into landing at the wrong coordinates). (See, for example, Peterson 2011; Rawnsley 2011)

It is important to note that the cyber operation does not have to cause lasting effects. For example, a short disruption in adversary air defense sensors or control systems may be the only goal of a cyber operation that is preceding an air strike. A potential example of such an event is the Israeli air strike against the alleged Syrian nuclear site in 2007, where Israeli (non-stealth) planes flew the mission without being harassed by Syrian air defense. Potential explanations include built-in kill switches in the Syrian systems or advanced EW capabilities. (See, for example, Adee 2008; Fulghum 2007)

However, the most likely target for military cyber operations is not a drone or any other tactical weapon system. The modern military relies heavily on its logistics and communication systems. These systems are more vulnerable to cyber attack, since they are less mobile and less reliant on custom hardware and software (compared to a drone, for example). Consider the strategic and operational effects of a cyber attack that scrambles the data (in a way that is not easy to restore) in the information systems of a major logistics hub: which container is where, what is in that container, who needs what, when they need it, etc. At the very least there will be delays, which could translate into loss of tactical or operational momentum and lives.

The military must be able to protect their own systems from cyber attacks. However, in many instances the military is reliant on or sharing infrastructure (dual use systems) with non-military systems, such as civilian Internet Service Providers. Therefore, the military must also be concerned with the security of these enabling systems. The problem here is that the military is rarely in a position to actively contribute to their defense. The best approach is to map the dependencies and mitigate the associated risks through cooperation and duplication of service providers.

## 4.2  Non-military targets

A hybrid actor might also target systems that are not directly linked to the military. It is important to note that such attacks could be in violation of international law, depending on the circumstances. However, there are actors who are not (too) concerned with laws, so it makes sense to explore this from cyber hybrid threat perspective. While the military is typically not responsible for the protection of these systems, it is important to realize that attacks against them can significantly change the conditions that the military has to operate in. For example, an attack against civilian infrastructure could cause civil unrest or a mass evacuation in the area of operations.

If an actor wanted to influence the state or the population in general, then an obvious (although probably unlawful) target would be some Critical Information Infrastructure (CII) system. Our societies and economies are very dependent on CII, which are the information systems that enable and maintain our way of life. For example, systems that are used to control the power grid, water treatment plants, air traffic control and banks. In recent decades, critical infrastructure has become more and more automated in order to increase efficiency. Often this has also increased the attack surface of the information systems within.

CII attacks, if successful, could cause serious harm to human life, (critical) infrastructure, economy, ecology, etc. While most of this is hypothetical so far, it is within the realm of the possible. StuxNet is a great example of a cyber attack that causes physical damage against critical infrastructure. It is exceptional, because it exploits four zero-days (vulnerabilities that are only known to the attacker), disrupts industrial control systems and damages physical devices. While nobody has taken responsibility for the attack, there is general consensus that it was developed and deployed by a state or states. It manipulates the parameters of the variable frequency drives (programmable logic controllers - PLCs) that control uranium enrichment centrifuges. This causes the centrifuges to speed up and slow down repeatedly and rapidly. The two primary effects are that the enrichment process is no longer efficient (the isotopes mix again when the centrifuge slows down) and that the centrifuge may physically break due to mechanical stress (the discs inside the centrifuge may shatter). (See, for example, Falliere, Murchu and Chien 2011, Sanger 2012, The Economist 2010)

The same approach can be used against other types of CII, since PLCs are used everywhere, from elevators to nuclear power plants. However, this does not mean that physical damage is always possible. First, there could be alternative systems or safeguards (for example, brakes on the elevator). Second, the system may not involve destructive forces (for example, banking systems deal with information). It is also clear that physical destruction is not the only outcome that has national security implications. An attack against the banking sector that leads to bank runs can cascade into a serious economic problem for a state - more costly, perhaps, than a bomb.

However, CII is not the only concern when facing a cyber-enabled hybrid threat. Everyday life gets more and more entangled with information technology enabled services and devices. Consider, for example, that your smart phone 'knows' your location, schedule, contacts, etc. If soldiers take their smart phones to the field, they and their units can be tracked in real time by technologically savvy adversaries.

But information technology is becoming even more intimate. There are medical devices that are surgically implanted into people - pacemakers, insulin pumps, etc. The problem is that those devices are sometimes very poorly secured. Researchers have been able to remotely manipulate such devices (in lab conditions) in ways that could kill or harm a person. (See, for example, Halperin et al. 2008; Kirk 2012) While there are no known examples of lethal attacks against personal cybernetic enhancements, they should be considered in case a key person has one 'installed'.

With this in mind, it is clear why a hybrid threat actor might consider offensive cyber operations against non-military targets - the list of potential victims keeps growing and very often these systems are not hardened against dedicated attackers. While the military is not the right entity to provide security for these systems, they may be in charge of disabling or eliminating the source of the attacks. In addition, the military should be ready to provide assistance to local crisis management services, upon request and within the existing legal framework.

## 4.3   Environment

The third reason to consider cyberspace from the hybrid threats perspective is that it offers new ways of accomplishing tasks that were previously prohibitively expensive or complicated. For example, consider the challenges of global communications and self-organization under oppressive regimes before the widespread adoption of Internet.

While cyberspace did not provide the motivation for the so-called Arab Spring, it definitely had a role in the events. On one side, people used the Internet to gather and share information about their governments, and to self-organize using social media and instant communication tools. On the other side, several governments tried to limit access to the Internet or to specific services on the Internet in order to regain control and to quell the unrest. (Afanasjev 2011)

It is well known to the national security and intelligence community that terrorist organizations use cyberspace to facilitate their operations. The Internet provides accessible, cheap (free) and anonymous ways to spread propaganda, identify and shape recruits, share training materials, gather intelligence, plan and coordinate attacks, etc. (Bardin 2010) However, to date there are no publicly known cases of cyber terrorism - cyber attacks that aim to coerce a population or government through terror.

Criminals and criminal groups are also taking advantage of cyberspace. Identity theft (including theft of credit card information), fraud, money laundering, extortion (for example, by using ransomware that encrypts the victim's data, or by performing distributed denial of service attacks), sale of counterfeit goods, and breaking into bank and electronic currency accounts are just a few examples of criminal use of cyberspace. The relative anonymity and problems with international law enforcement cooperation foster a thriving underground community that operates on a global scale.

Cyberspace is also a useful medium for espionage. Since the vast majority of information is stored digitally, the cyber spy can usually operate remotely. This means that there is very little risk of getting caught (although one might be identified), especially considering that there is no international law prohibiting espionage. From the hybrid threats perspective it allows to even the playing field considerably by 'skipping' the research and development phase on new technologies or by getting advance warning of deployments and capabilities of adversaries.

Intelligence agencies are actively monitoring Internet in the interest of national security. This is a rather passive and defensive form of cyber operations compared with cyber attacks. Still, the signs are clear that many states are preparing for cyber conflict. What we can conclude is that cyberspace is an area of conflict where states act in an apparently more direct way than they would when it comes to conventional means. Getting peoples' and organizations' financial information or destroying uranium enrichment centrifuges in conventional ways would stir up a lot more controversy than it does in the cyber world – much because the problems with attribution. The old definition of hybrid threats that non-state actors wield state actor capabilities seems to be in reverse here, as state actors try to masquerade as non-state actors. There are most likely a host of reasons for this, but again – the lack of strong attribution is a key enabler.

Cyberspace in itself can also be attacked with rather conventional means. Consider the problem of supply side vulnerability. In recent years there have been numerous cases of counterfeit microchips and other hardware, which could also contain hidden flaws, back doors or remote kill switches.

National security is at risk as modern missiles, airplanes, and even munitions often have microchips in them. In the future one can imagine nanotechnology applied undercover on sensitive hardware, which might result in faulty or even changed functionality.

Once again, the military is not the primary actor in this field. However, it is very important to stay informed of the opportunities that information technology provides and to embrace them where applicable. In terms of social media, the military must practice good OPSEC on one hand, and STRATCOM on the other hand. For example, NATO homepage has links to the Alliance's presence on FaceBook, Twitter and YouTube, in order to reach the demographic that prefers this type of media. (Newsroom 2013)

# 5   Conclusion

The national security implications of cyberspace are growing. Many states have recognized the importance of being able to operate in cyberspace – if for nothing else, then to boost their economy. Some states have even started developing military capabilities to ensure freedom of action during military conflicts, while suppressing the adversary's capabilities. It is also widely believed that state actors are very active on the cyber espionage front, although this is done in a clandestine manner.

This new focus on cyber capabilities is mirrored by sub-state actors as well. From individual activists to organized crime to terrorist organizations, these actors are seeking ways to benefit from cyberspace. On the one hand this is about using the myriad services available: communication, information gathering, etc. On the other hand, it is about abusing the services – harvesting personal information, stealing money, disrupting other services, etc. Traditionally, this form of activity has not been of much interest for the military. On the modern battlefield, however, cyberspace enables both prospective allies and enemies, engages the global community with local operations, and creates new modes of operating for the military.

For (relatively) like-minded states, such as members of NATO and EU, it is important to develop a common understanding on the opportunities and risks posed by cyberspace. On the defensive side, international cooperation is required to deter or defeat serious cyber threats, whether military or not. Cooperation between military and civilian (government and private) sector sphere is also required, since most of the CII is not owned and operated by the military, but may impact the capability or operations of the military. Therefore, the military must be ready and eager to cooperate and share with various partners that also have 'cyber power' and can affect the mission.

## Acknowledgements

The authors would like to thank the Swedish National Defence College for funding this work.

## References

Adee, S. (2008) "The Hunt for the Kill Switch", IEEE Spectrum, May. Available at: http://spectrum.ieee.org/semiconductors/design/the-hunt-for-the-kill-switch/0. [Last accessed: 13.02.2013]

Afanasjev, M. (2011) Approaches to Avoiding Government Censorship, Blockade and Surveillance on the Internet. Master's thesis, Tallinn University of Technology.

Bardin, J. (2010) Cyber Jihadist Use of the Internet: What Can Be Done? Whitepaper.

Council of Europe. (2001). Convention on Cybercrime. Available at: http://conventions.coe.int/treaty/en/treaties/html/185.htm. [Last accessed: 13.02.2013]

Falliere, N., Murchu, L.O. and Chien, E. (2011) W32.Stuxnet Dossier. Available at: http://www.symantec.com/content/en/us/enterprise/media/security_response/whitepa pers/w32_stuxnet_dossier.pdf. [Last accessed: 13.02.2013]

Fulghum, D. (2007) "Why Syria's Air Defenses Failed to Detect Israelis", Aviation Week, Oct 3. Available at: http://www.aviationweek.com. [Last accessed: 13.02.2013]

Gorman, S. and Barnes, J.E. (2011) "Cyber Combat: Act of War. Pentagon Sets Stage for U.S. to Respond to Computer Sabotage With Military Force", Wall Street Journal, May 30. Available at: http://online.wsj.com/article/SB10001424052702304563104576355623135782718.html. [Last accessed: 13.02.2013]

Halperin, D., Heydt-Benjamain, T.S., Ransford, B., Clark, S.S., Defend, B., Morgan, W., Fu, K., Kohno, T. and Maisel, W.H. (2008) "Pacemakers and Implantable Cardiac Defibrillators: Software Radio Attacks and Zero-Power Defenses", Proceedings of the 2008 IEEE Symposium on Security and Privacy. Available at: http://www.secure-medicine.org/icd-study/icd-study.pdf. [Last accessed: 13.02.2013]

Herkner, L. (2007) "Hacken für den Staat", Zeit Online, May 16. Available at: http://www.zeit.de/2007/21/Sicherheitsplaene. [Last accessed: 13.02.2013]

Ho, J. (2005) "The Advent of a New Way of War: Theory and Practice of Effect Based Operations", Johan Elg (Ed.), Effektbaserade operationer, Stockholm.

Joint Publication 3-13. Information Operations. (2006) Chairman of the Joint Chiefs of Staff.

Kirk, J. (2012) "Pacemaker hack can deliver deadly 830-volt jolt", ComputerWorld, Oct 17. Available at: http://www.computerworld.com/s/article/9232477/Pacemaker_hack_can_deliver_deadl y_830_volt_jolt. [Last accessed: 13.02.2013]

Markoff, J. (2008) "Before the Gunfire, Cyberattacks", NYTimes.com, Aug 12. Available at: http://www.nytimes.com/2008/08/13/technology/13cyber.html?em&_r=0. [Last accessed: 13.02.2013]

Matthews, M.M. (2008) "We Were Caught Unprepared: The 2006 Hezbollah-Israeli War", The Long War Series Occasional Paper 26. U.S. Army Combined Arms Center, Combat Studies Institute Press, Fort Leavenworth.

Mattis, J. (2008) "Commander's Guidance for Effects-Based Operations", Joint Forces Quarterly, 51:4, Washington.

Newsroom (2013) North Atlantic Treaty Organization. Available at: http://www.nato.int/cps/en/natolive/index.htm. [Last accessed: 13.02.2013]

Peterson, S. (2011) "Exclusive: Iran hijacked US drone, says Iranian engineer (Video)", Christian Science Monitor, Dec 15. Available at: www.csmonitor.com/World/Middle-East/2011/1215/Exclusive-Iran-hijacked-US-drone-says-Iranian-engineer-Video. [Last accessed: 13.02.2013]

Rawnsley, A. (2011) "Iran's Alleged Drone Hack: Tough, but Possible", Wired, Dec 16. Available at: http://www.wired.com/dangerroom/2011/12/iran-drone-hack-gps/. [Last accessed: 13.02.2013]

RT.com (2012) "Anonymous leaks personal information of 5,000 Israeli officials", Nov 18. Available at: http://rt.com/news/anonymous-israel-officials-leaked-002/. [Last accessed: 13.02.2013]

Sanger, D. (2012) "Obama Order Sped Up Wave of Cyberattacks Against Iran", NYTimes.com, June 1. Available at: http://www.nytimes.com/2012/06/01/world/middleeast/obama-ordered-wave-of-cyberattacks-against-iran.html?_r=2&pagewanted=2&seid=auto&smid=tw-nytimespolitics&pagewanted=all. [Last accessed: 13.02.2013]

Tallinn Manual on the International Law Applicable to Cyber Warfare (to appear 2013). Cambridge: Cambridge University Press. Draft available at: http://www.ccdcoe.org/249.html. [Last accessed: 13.02.2013]

The Economist (2010a) "A worm in the centrifuge", Sep 30. Available at: http://www.economist.com/node/17147818. [Last accessed: 13.02.2013]

The Economist (2010b) "War in the fifth domain", Jul 1. Available at: http://www.economist.com/node/16478792. [Last accessed: 13.02.2013]

Thomas, T. (2007) Decoding the Virtual Dragon: Critical Evaluations in the Science and Philosophy of China's Information Operations and Military Strategy. Fort Leavenworth: Foreign Military Studies Office.

Thomas, T. (2009) The Dragon's Quantum Leap: Transforming from a Mechanized to an Informatized Force. Fort Leavenworth: Foreign Military Studies Office.

Thomas, T. (2011) Recasting the Red Star: Russia Forges Tradition and Technology Through Toughness. Fort Leavenworth: Foreign Military Studies Office.

Wiener, N. (1948) Cybernetics: Or Control and Communication in the Animal and the Machine. New York: John Wiley.

# Comparing Models of Offensive Cyber Operations

## Tim Grant[1], Ivan Burke[2] and Renier van Heerden[2]

[1]Faculty of Military Sciences, Netherlands Defence Academy (NLDA), Breda, The Netherlands
[2]Defence Peace Safety and Security department, Council for Scientific and Industrial Research (CSIR), Pretoria, South Africa
tj.grant@nlda.nl
iburke@csir.co.za
rvhheerden@csir.co.za

*Originally Published in the Proceedings of ICIW, 2012*

**Editorial Commentary**

Based on the idea that offensive cyber operations should be studied and emerge from the darkness in which they typically hide, Grant and his colleagues embarked on a research program to explore the potential answers to the question, "What resources would be needed by a Cyber Security Operations Centre in order to perform offensive cyber operations?" The analysis was performed, using as a springboard seven models of cyber-attack, and resulted in the development of what is described as a canonical model. Whether or not this model stands the test of time or evolves along unexpected lines, it is an important exploration of the structural needs for any organization wishing or needing to engage in offensive activities.

Because this is a short paper, several questions are unanswered which would need to be addressed in the event of the implementation of this model. These include definitional descriptions of what constitutes offensive activities in cyberspace and exactly what an attack might be comprised of. These two questions are enormously important and have attracted considerable intellectual effort. Readers are encouraged to consider these two aspects while reading this paper, particularly when reflecting on the question of staffing, training, and equipping an organization to implement the canonical model. Important questions, such as whether the attacker must be a member of a recognized armed force in order to conduct a legal attack and what provocation legitimizes offensive activities, are considerations that make the reading of this paper a valuable contribution to the developing sophistication of thought in this area.

**Abstract:** Cyber operations denote the response of governments and organisations to cyber crime, terrorism, and warfare. To date, cyber operations have been primarily defensive, with the attackers seemingly having the initiative. Over the past three years, several nations (e.g. USA, UK, France, The Netherlands) and NATO have published cyber security strategies emphasising national and international collaboration. Many strategies call for the establishment of a Cyber Security Operations Centre, as well as for a better understanding of attacks. In the scientific literature, Lin (2009) and Denning and Denning (2010) have argued that offensive cyber operations deserve a more open discussion than they have received to date. Research into cyber attacks would improve the scientific understanding of how attackers work, why they choose particular targets, and what tools and technologies they employ. This improved understanding could then be used to implement better defences. Moreover, research would enable governments and other organizations to take offensive action where justified against adversaries, whether these be criminals, terrorists, or enemies. This could include responding to an (impending) attack by counter-attacking or by proactively neutralizing the source of an impending attack. A good starting point to improving understanding would be to model the offensive cyber operations process. The purpose of this paper is to find, formalise, and compare models of the offensive cyber operations process available in the open scientific literature. Seven models were sufficiently well described for formalisation using Structured Analysis and Design Technique (SADT) notation. Finally, a canonical model has been constructed by rational reconstruction. Although the model has not yet been tested, it has been reviewed by subject matter experts. The paper describes the search methodology, the SADT analysis, the shortcomings of each model, rational reconstruction, and the canonical model. Further work will include elaborating the canonical model to identify the resources needed to set up a Cyber Security Operations Centre with offensive capabilities and to cross-compare the model with the literature on attack ontologies.

**Keywords**: offensive cyber operations; process model; rational reconstruction; canonical model; formalisation; SADT

# 1   Introduction

Cyber operations denotes the response of governments and organisations to cyber crime, terrorism, and warfare, and encompasses computer network defence, exploitation, and attack. To date, cyber operations have been primarily defensive, with the attackers seemingly having the initiative (Owens, Dam & Lin, 2008). Over the past three years, several nations (e.g.

USA, UK, France, The Netherlands) and NATO have published cyber security strategies emphasising national and international collaboration. Many strategies call for the establishment of a Cyber Security Operations Centre (TSO, 2009) (MinJus, 2011), as well as for a better understanding of attacks.

In the scientific literature, Lin (2009) and Denning and Denning (2010) have argued that offensive cyber operations deserve a more open discussion than they have received to date. Research into cyber attacks would improve the scientific understanding of how attackers work, why they choose particular targets, and what tools and technologies they employ. This improved understanding could then be used to implement better defences. Moreover, research would enable governments and other organizations to take offensive action where justified against adversaries, whether these be criminals, terrorists, or enemies. This could include responding to an (impending) attack by counter-attacking or by proactively neutralizing the source of the attack before it can begin. This paper makes a contribution to the literature on offensive cyber operations.

A good starting point to improving understanding would be to model the offensive cyber operations process. Although the literature is limited, nine models have been found, of which seven were sufficiently well described for analysis. Some models seem to be intuitive (Colarik & Janczowski, 2008), some are based on an analogy with similar domains (typically military Command and Control, e.g. (Veerasamy, 2010) and (Sorensen, 2010)), others are based on case studies of cyber operations (Croom, 2010) (Dreijer, 2011) (Van Heerden & Burke, forthcoming), while yet others are based on experienced attackers' own writings (Grant, Venter & Eloff, 2007).

There is an extensive literature on cyber attack patterns (Moore, Ellison & Linger, 2001), attack trees (Schneier, 1999), attack plans (Boddy, Gohde, Haigh & Harp, 2005), attack graphs (Sheyner, 2004, and Wing, 2005), attack taxonomies (Mirkovic & Reiher, 2004), attack ontologies (Simmonds, Sandilands & Van Ekert, 2004), and attack languages (Undercoffer, Joshi & Pinkston, 2003). These representations are predominantly aimed at modelling specific attacks to an executable level of detail. At a higher level, the question arises as to whether computer intruders follow a standard attack process, which they then tailor for each specific attack. Working together with subject matter experts from the University of Pretoria's Information and Computer Security Architectures (ICSA) research group, Grant, Venter and Eloff (2007) extracted a nine-phase process model for cyber crime from computer intruders' own writings, such as (Mitnick & Simon, 2005). Subsequently, Colarik and Janczewski (2008) described a model for a cyber terrorist attack. Dreijer (2011) benchmarked both models against five cases of cyber warfare, and proposed a refined model.

In the research reported in part in this paper, we posed the following research question (RQ):

*RQ1: What resources would be needed by a Cyber Security Operations Centre in order to perform offensive cyber operations?*

Corresponding to the likely organisation in a Cyber Security Operations Centre, the scope of our research is limited to the resources needed by a professional civil and/or military group under governmental control. The resources needed by mercenaries, volunteers, or individual hacktivists are outside the scope of our research. Moreover, we assume that the legal issues associated with offensive cyber operations will have been resolved, at least for cyber counterattack and for proactive cyber defence. Legal issues are not discussed further in this paper; interested readers can consult Owens et al (2009).

We decomposed RQ1 into two sub-questions:

*RQ1.1: Can a canonical process model be developed for offensive cyber operations performed by a professional group?*

*RQ1.2: Can the set of resources needed by a Cyber Security Operations Centre be extracted from this canonical process model?*

This paper addresses RQ1.1. Our strategy was to find existing process models, formalise and compare them, extracting a canonical model. In a subsequent paper we will address RQ1.2 by elaborating the canonical model to identify resource needs.

The purpose of this paper is to find, formalise, and compare models of the offensive cyber operations process available in the open (semi-)scientific literature. Seven models were found that were sufficiently well described for formalisation using the Structured Analysis and Design Technique (SADT) notation (Marca & McGowen, 1988). Analysis shows that the seven models assume penetration of the target system, few represent target selection, attack planning, and Denial of Service attacks, and none specifically represent attack coordination within distributed groups. Finally, a canonical model has been constructed by rational reconstruction (Habermas, 1976) to address these shortcomings. Although the model has not yet been tested, it has been reviewed by subject matter experts. The paper has five sections. Section 1 is introductory. Section 2 describes the search methodology and results. Section 3 describes the analysis and formalisation of the models using SADT, and summarises the key observations arising. Section 4 describes the canonical model developed by rational reconstruction from the seven formalised models. Section 5 draws conclusions and outlines further research planned.

# 2 Searching for process models

## 2.1 Search method
Existing process models were sought by consulting subject matter experts (University of Pretoria, CSIR, and the Royal Netherlands Army), by performing web searches, by following citation chains using Google Scholar, and by filtering the proceedings of appropriate conferences (including the International Conference on Information Warfare (ICIW) and the European Conference on Information Warfare (ECIW)). A limitation in our literature survey is that we have not yet filtered relevant scientific journals, such as Computers & Security or the Journal of Information Warfare (JIW). There are also other conferences, such as the Black Hat conferences, in which cyber attack process models may have been presented.

The criteria for selecting a candidate as a valid process model were as follows:
- It should describe a cyber attack or offensive cyber operations;
- It should describe the behaviour of the attacker, whether this be an individual or a group; and
- It should describe the attack process in sufficient detail for formalisation.

Following Dreijer's (2011) lead, we did not limit candidates to cyber warfare, but accepted models of cyber crime, - terrorism, and/or -warfare.

## 2.2 Models found

We found seven models, listed in Table 1 by chronological order of publication. Two additional models (Sorensen, 2010) (Veerasamy, 2010) were rejected because they did not describe a process model sufficiently clearly for formalisation.

**Table 1:** Models found and their key characteristics

| Model | Context | Basis | Attacker | DoS | Temporal aspects |
|---|---|---|---|---|---|
| Grant et al, 2007 | Crime | Hackers' writings | Lone | No | No |
| Colarik & Janczewski, 2008 | Terrorism | Analogy to cyber crime | Group | Fallback only | No |
| Damballa, 2008 | Crime | Case studies | Lone | No | No |
| Owens et al, 2009 | Warfare | Literature | Group | Yes | Yes |
| Croom, 2010 | Crime (APT) | Case studies | Group | No | No |
| Dreijer, 2011 | Warfare | Previous models and case studies | Group | Yes | No |
| Van Heerden & Burke, forthcoming | Crime & warfare | Case studies | Lone or Group | Yes | Yes |

All of the models describe a linear process representing an isolated attack by an individual attacker or a homogeneous group. None describe the co-ordination that would be needed by a geographically or functionally distributed group of attackers. While some of the models describe the installation of a backdoor or an advanced persistent threat (APT), none of them describe the behaviour involved in returning to a previously-penetrated target. All models identify (the equivalent of) Penetration, Action, and – apart from Damballa (2008) – Reconnaissance phases.

# 3    SADT analysis

## 3.1    SADT method

SADT notation has been chosen for analysing and formalising the process models. SADT is highly suited to specifying the behaviour of systems in terms of functional processes. The graphical notation represents the system as a network of boxes interconnected by arrows. Each box represents a process, and each arrow represents an interface between processes. Processes operate concurrently, with information passing over the interface arrows. Information is output by an information producer process and input to one or more information consumer processes. Arrows may enter a box from the left, from above, or from below. Arrows may only exit from a box from the right. Arrows entering a box from the left represent data input, and arrows exiting a box from the right represent data output. Arrows entering a box from above represent control inputs, constraining the process. Arrows entering a box from below represent the mechanisms or resources needed to perform the process. Control and resource inputs are neither consumed nor changed by the consumer process, while data inputs are transformed into data outputs. In this paper, we limit the SADT analysis to data inputs and outputs, with control and resource inputs being added to address RQ1.2 in a subsequent paper.

Processes can be decomposed into sub-processes. This is represented in SADT notation by enclosing a set of boxes within a larger box. The inputs and outputs of the larger process must match the free inputs and free outputs, respectively, of the network of sub-processes. A free input is a data input that has no producer process, and a free output is a data output that has no consumer process. A rule of thumb to aid the SADT user's understanding is that there should be three to seven sub-processes. Additional details of the rules and methodology of SADT, may be found in (Marca & McGowen, 1988).

## 3.2   Example SADT analysis

The value of SADT formalisation can be demonstrated by its application step by step to the Colarik and Janczewski (2008) model. Colarik and Janczewski describe the first phase as follows (p.xv):

> *"The first phase of an attack is reconnaissance of the intended victim. By observing the normal operations of a target, useful information can be ascertained and accumulated such as hardware and software used, regular and periodic communications, and the formatting of said correspondences."*

The first step is to give the process an appropriate name, taken from the authors' text. The obvious name is "Reconnaissance". The next step is to identify inputs from the text. The phrase *"By observing the normal opera-tions of a target"* yields two inputs: the intended target/victim, and its normal operations. In the third step, the sole output is identified as useful information, e.g. hardware and software used, regular and periodic com-munications, and its formatting. The resulting SADT process is shown in Figure 1.

**Figure 1:** Reconnaissance phase, Colarik and Janczewski (2008)

Colarik and Janczewski (2008) describe the second phase as follows (p.xv):

> *"The second phase of an attack is penetration. Until an attacker is inside a system, there is little that can be done to the target except to disrupt the availability or access to a given service provided by the target."*

The obvious name is "Penetration". Inputs are more difficult to find in the text. Clearly, one is the identity of the system to be penetrated. Although not stated in the text, the Useful information gathered in phase 1 is likely to be essential to achieving penetration, so this has been added. The out-puts are more easily identified: either penetration (violating integrity) is achieved, or – as the second sentence indicates – denial of service (disrupt-ing availability) is the "consolation prize" if (say) no suitable malware is to hand. The description suggests a sequence of sub-phases, as shown in the resulting SADT process in Figure 2.

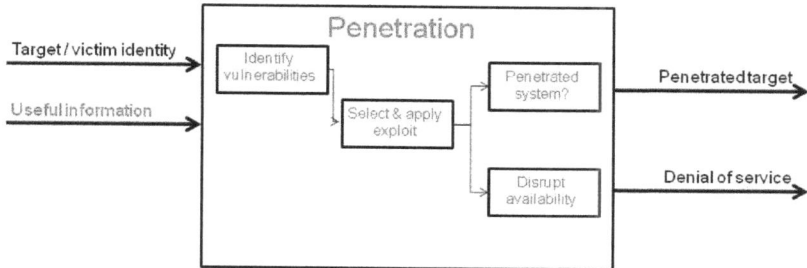

**Figure 2:** Penetration phase, Colarik and Janczewski (2008)

Colarik and Janczewski (2008) describe the third phase as follows (p.xv):

> *"The third phase is identifying and expanding the internal capabilities by viewing resources and increasing access rights to more restricted, higher-value areas of a given system."*

The obvious name would be "Identifying and Expanding the Internal Capabilities", but this is shortened to "Expanding Capabilities". No inputs are mentioned, but the output is access to the high-value areas of the target system. The target must be identified by an input, and hence "Penetrated target" and its associated "Useful information" have been added. The process also needs to know what constitutes "high value", and this is shown as a control input. The phrase *"by viewing resources and increasing access rights"* suggests two sub-phases (also implied by the "Identifying" and the "Expanding" in the long name), as well as possible resources needed. It is not clear whether the sub-phases are sequential or in parallel. The control input and resources are not needed for the purpose of this paper, but are shown for completeness. The resulting SADT process is shown in **Figure 3**.

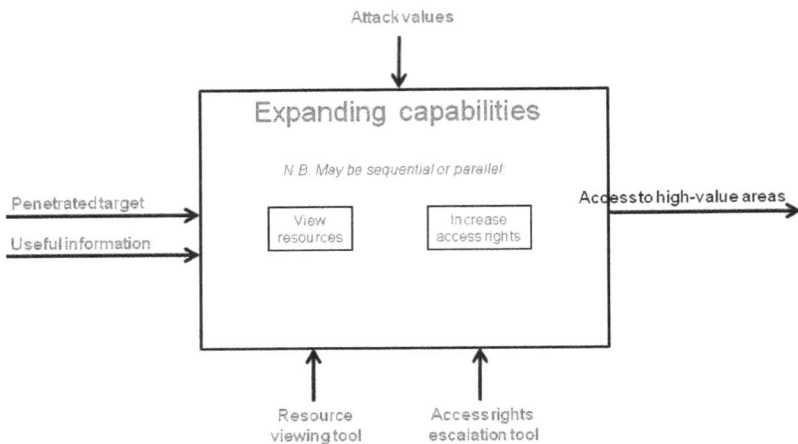

**Figure 3:** Expanding capabilities phase, Colarik and Janczewski (2008)

Colarik and Janczewski (2008) describe the fourth phase as follows (p.xv):

> *"The forth [sic] stage is where the intruder does the damage to a system or confiscates selected data and/or information."*

The obvious name is "Damage system". The sentence describes damaged hardware and/or software, modified information, or confiscation of data/information as the outputs. Although no inputs are mentioned, access to high-value areas is needed to damage the system. Moreover, the data/information to be damaged must be accessible, and Useful information gained in phase 1 could provide knowledge of the hardware and software configuration. Hence, these have been added as inputs. The resulting SADT process is shown in Figure 4.

**Figure 4:** Damage system phase, Colarik and Janczewski (2008)

The Log files output will be discussed in the context of phase 5.

Colarik and Janczewski (2008) describe the fifth phase as follows (p.xv):

*"The last phase can include the removal of any evidence of a pene-*
*tration, theft, and so forth by covering the intruder's electronic trail*
*by editing or deleting log files"*

The obvious name is "Removal of Evidence". The only output mentioned is the modified or deleted log files, but hiding the installed toolset has been added by example from Damballa (2008). These outputs imply as inputs Access to high-value areas, the Installed toolset, and the Log files. The latter input has to come from some preceding phase, else it becomes a free input. These files can be most easily captured immediately after the system has been damaged, in phase 4. It is for this reason that Log files has been added as an output to phase 4. The resulting SADT process for phase 5 is shown in Figure 5.

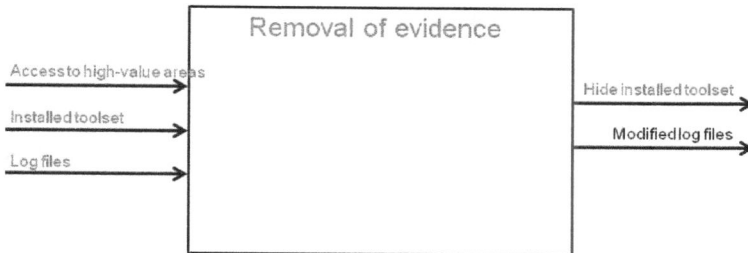

**Figure 5:** Removal of evidence phase, Colarik and Janczewski (2008)

The final step in the analysis of the Colarik and Janczewski (2008) model is to put the individual SADT processes for phases 1 to 5 together, making the links between inputs and outputs. The resulting SADT diagram is shown in Figure 6, with the dashed box showing the larger process representing the whole attack. As can be seen, the Useful information output of phase 1 is one of the inputs to phases 2, 3, and 4. The Penetrated target output of phase 2 is needed as input to phase 3, and phase 3's Access to high-value areas output is an input to phases 4 and 5. The Log files, output by phase 4, are input to phase 5.

Free inputs include which target system should be attacked (shown as Target id), which can be assumed to have been determined by governmental authorities. The Normal operations free input is obtained (from the target) by the Reconnaissance process. Phase 4's free input, Data to be damaged/modified, can be assumed to be determined as a part of the goals for the operation. Phase 5's free input Toolset is identical to the set of tool resources used in the preceding phases. For the purposes of this analysis, they can be assumed to have been provided before the operation began. Free outputs (e.g. that could go to the authorities, or used in lessons learned for future operations) include the Useful information about the target, the knowledge that the system has been penetrated or that a DoS attack has been executed, that access has been gained to the high-value areas, what damage has been achieved, and that as much evidence as possible has been removed.

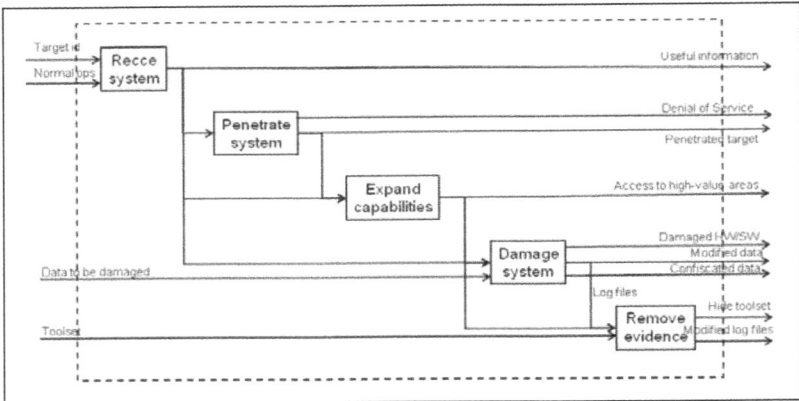

**Figure 6:** Overall process model, Colarik and Janczewski (2008)

# 4    Rational reconstruction

## 4.1    Method

In philosophy, rational reconstruction (RR) is defined as "a philosophical and linguistic method that systematically translates intuitive knowledge of rules into a logical form" (Habermas, 1976). RR has been applied in computing research to redesign a seminal expert system (Cendrowski & Bramer, 1984) and to formalise Boyd's (1996) Observe-Orient-Decide-Act (OODA) loop (Grant & Kooter, 2005).

In the research reported here, we used the SADT notation to represent the text describing each phase or step (i.e. sub-process) in the attack process.

Using a formalisation like SADT enforces systematic analysis, and the graphical notation is Habermas' (1976) "logical form". As we have seen, the source text often omits to specify completely the inputs and outputs of each phase. Moreover, terminology may be inconsistent between phases or steps in the same process model. For example, Colarik and Janczewski (2008) refer to an "attacker" in their second phase and an "intruder" in their fourth phase, but the knowledgeable reader realises that the two referents are identical. Such omissions and inconsistencies occur because the authors of the seven models were not writing with formal linguistic analysis in mind. In Habermas' terms, the source texts are "intuitive". By applying the SADT rules and methodology when linking the sub-processes into the overall process, many of these omissions and inconsistencies can be rectified.

## 4.2 Comparing models

The problems of analysis are magnified when we compare the process models. Although each model is formalised using SADT, there are still differences in terminology, this time between models. For example, three of the authors "penetrate" the target system (or the equivalent in Dutch: "binnendringen"), two "deliver malware", and one "launches" the attack. In describing copying data residing in or passing through the target system and exporting the copy to the attacker, Grant et al (2007) "extracts" it, Damballa (2008) "steals" it, Colarik and Jaczewski (2008) "confiscate" it, Dreijer (2011) "gathers" or "collects" it (In Dutch: "vergaren"), and Owens et al (2009), Croom (2010), and Van Heerden and Burke (forthcoming) respectively "compromise", "violate", and "breach" its confidentiality. Our analysis interprets all of these as the same sub-process. More insidiously, "target" can refer to an organization, a computer system or network, a hardware or software component or a piece of information residing in or passing through a system or network, or a vulnerability in a component. We distinguish target organizations, systems, and vulnerabilities.

A further complication is that the process models differ in their level of detail and where they draw the boundary around the process. For example, Colarik and Janczewski (2008) go straight from Surveillance (phase 1), in which "useful information" is gathered about the target, to Penetration (phase 2). Other process models first identify vulnerabilities in the target system, e.g. Grant et al (2007), Dreijer (2011), and Van Heerden and Burke (forthcoming). Dreijer then selects malware suited to exploiting those vulnerabilities, and Croom (2010) "weaponises" the exploit by coupling it with a remote access Trojan into a deliverable payload. Damballa (2008) goes straight into malware delivery, apparently without any reconnaissance, surveillance, or intelligence gathering. Only Dreijer is sufficiently careful to model planning the attack in advance and testing the plan before penetration. Only Van Heerden and Burke recognise that there might be unintended effects from the attack and to assess the damage by post-attack reconnaissance. Only Dreijer evaluates the operation, and only Grant et al disseminate the lessons learned to their colleagues. None of the process models caters for an attack that is geographically or functionally distributed. In short, there is no "best" process model.

## 4.3   Canonical model

Since each source model differs in terminology, level of detail, and functionality, our strategy has been to form the canonical model as the union of the source models. The (sub-)phases identified in the SADT analysis of each model are the starting point for bottom-up rational reconstruction. These (sub-)phases are then synthesized into the canonical model by SADT composition, grouping them top-down into phases by the following division of responsibilities within a professional group:

1    Governmental authorities would select one or more target organisations and (counter-)attack goals based on the nature and attribution of the incoming or impending attack.

2    Intelligence analysts would select and gather information about the target systems owned or used by the target organisations.

3    Planners would plan the counterattack in detail, obtain and prepare the resources needed, and test the plan and resources in a simulated environment.

4    Cyber operatives would rehearse and execute the tested plan, aiming to achieve the goals set by the authorities.

5    The whole group would evaluate the operation, archive related information, and identify and disseminate lessons learned.

The resulting canonical model has three levels of decomposition, as shown in Figure 7.

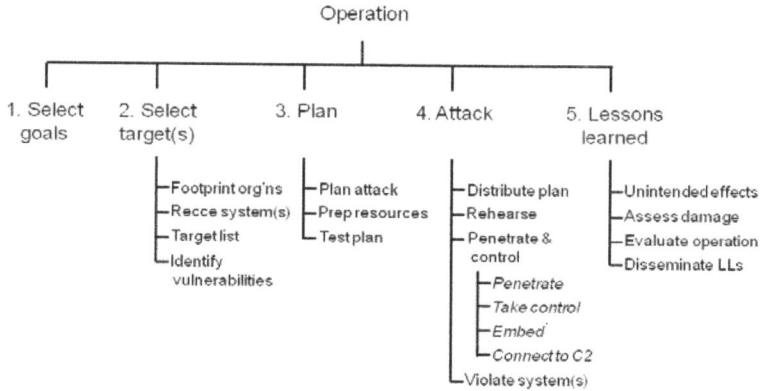

**Figure 7:** Canonical model: breakdown into phases and sub-phases

At the lowest level, the Penetrate and Control process – itself part of the Attack phase – composes the Penetrate, Take control, Embed, and Connect to C2 sub-processes, as shown in Figure 8.

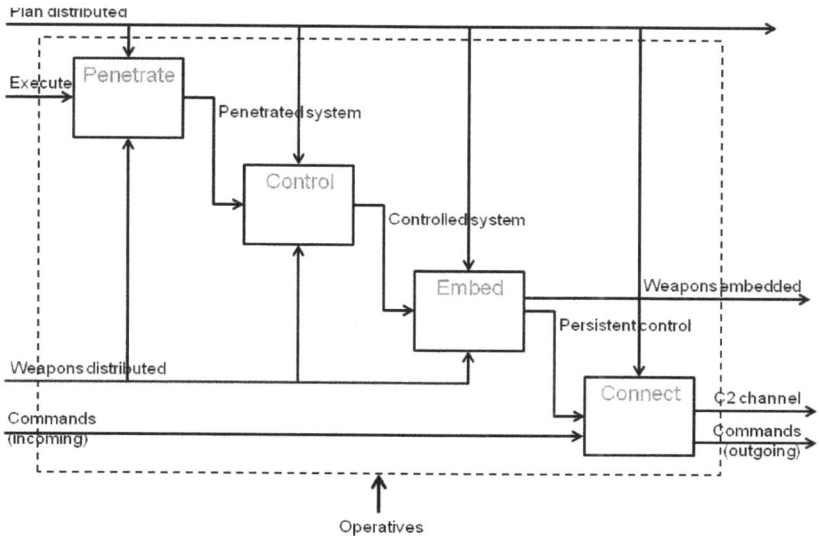

**Figure 8:** Canonical model: Penetrate and control sub-phase

49

At the middle level, there are five phases: Select goals (Figure 9), Select targets (Figure 10), Plan (Figure 11), Attack (Figure 12), and Lessons learned (Figure 13).

**Figure 9**: Canonical model, step 1: Select goals

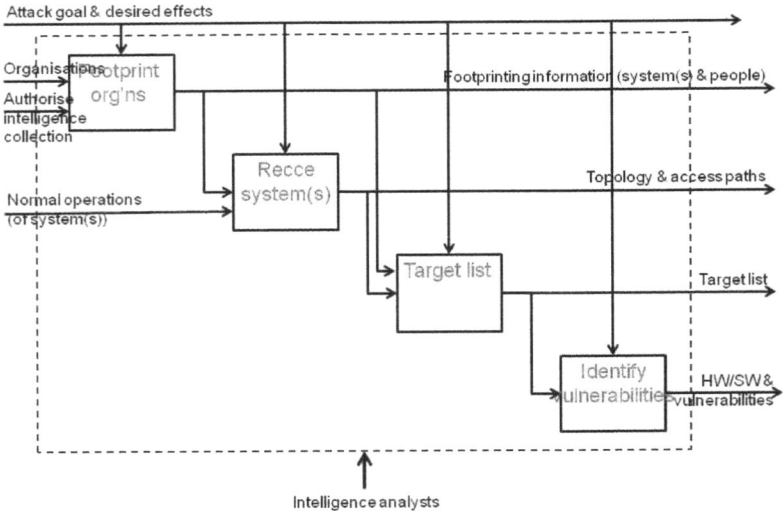

**Figure 10**: Canonical model, step 2: Select targets

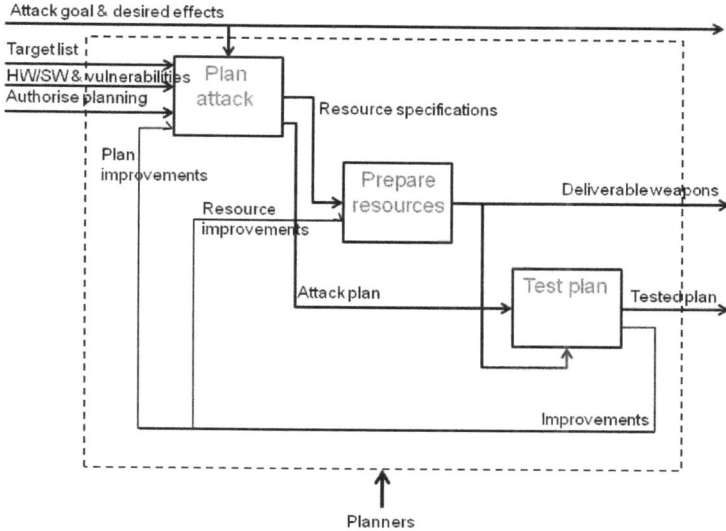

**Figure 11:** Canonical model, step 3: Plan

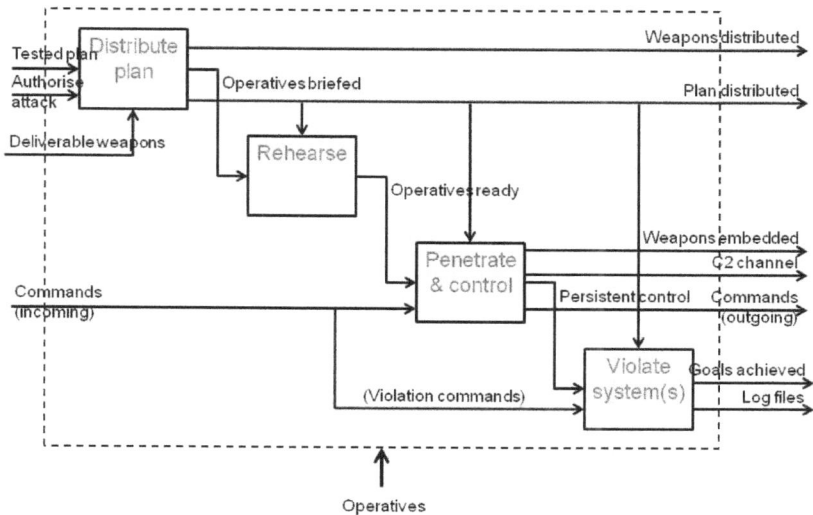

**Figure 12:** Canonical model, step 4: Attack

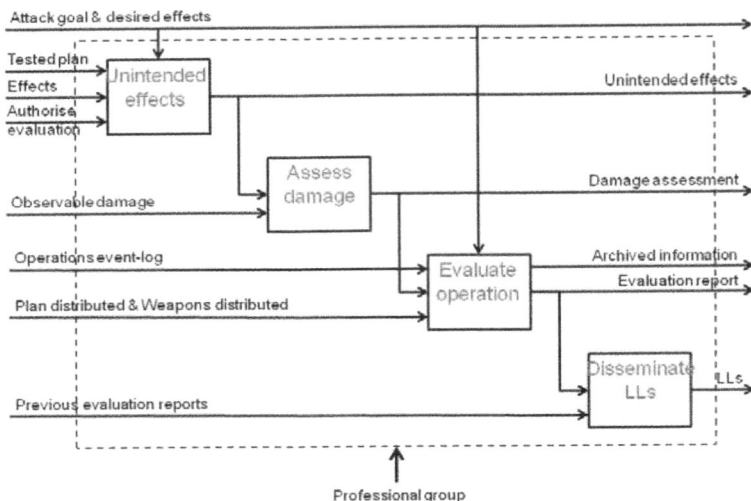

**Figure 13:** Canonical model, step 5: Lessons learned

At the top level, the Operation process composes these five phases, as shown in Figure 14.

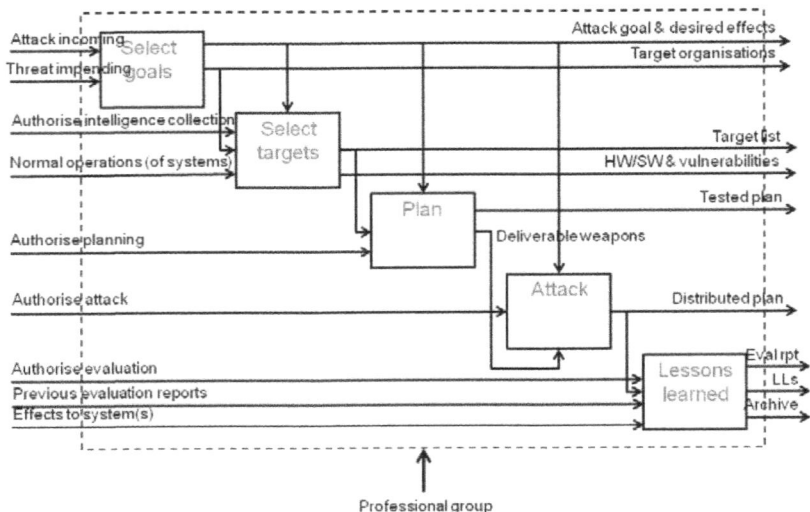

**Figure 14:** Canonical model, operation

# 5 Conclusions and further research

In the research reported in this paper, we found seven sufficiently well-described models of the cyber attack process in the open literature. Each model has been formalised from its textual description using the SADT graphical notation, permitting comparison of functionality and terminology. A canonical model has been constructed by forming the union of the formalised source models, taking into account the likely division of responsibilities within the professional group associated with a Cyber Security Operations Centre.

There are several limitations to this research. The SADT analysis and rational reconstruction have been done by a single analyst. Ideally, this should be done using a Delphi process involving multiple analysts working independently, followed by comparing the SADT diagrams and canonical models. Although the canonical model presented in this paper has been reviewed by subject matter experts, it has not been tested by simulation or use.

This paper contributes to the scientific body of knowledge by formalising, comparing, and rationally reconstructing existing models of the attack process in cyber crime, terrorism, and warfare. It also offers to make a practical contribution in that the authorities and Cyber Security Operations Centre personnel could use the canonical model to develop doctrine and Standard Operating Procedures, for training, and in simulations and operations.

Several areas for further research have been identified. Firstly, the canonical model needs to be tested before it could be used "in anger". It could be compared with case studies, with other approaches (including attack languages, taxonomies, and ontologies), with hacker tool functionality, and by using the model in a simulated environment. Secondly, the canonical model could be elaborated with control and resource inputs, enabling RQ1.2 to be answered. The tools and technologies needed by a Cyber Security Operations Centre could be identified from the resource inputs, while analysis of the control inputs would provide guidance on doctrine and governance. Thirdly, our research has not addressed the command and control aspects of offensive cyber operations. These aspects deserve deeper study once the resources, doctrine, and governance arrangements for offensive cyber operations have been clarified.

# Acknowledgements

We are grateful to Professor Hein Venter, Computer Science Department, University of Pretoria, South Africa, for bringing the authors into contact with one another.

# References

Boddy, M., Gohde, J., Haigh, T., and Harp, S. (2005). "Course of Action Generation for Cyber Security using Classical Planning". In Proceedings of International Conference on Automated Planning and Scheduling (ICAPS'05).

Boyd, J.R. (1996). The Essence of Winning and Losing. Unpublished lecture notes, Maxwell Air Force Base, AL.

Cendrowski, J. and Bramer, M.A. (1984). "A rational reconstruction of the MYCIN consultation system", International Journal of Man-Machine Studies, Vol 20, pp 229-317.

Colarik, A. and Janczowski, L, (2008). "Introduction to Cyber Warfare and Cyber Terrorism". In Janczewski and Colarik. Cyber Warfare and Cyber Terrorism. Hershey: Information Science Reference, pp xiii-xxx.

Croom, C. (2010). "The Cyber Kill Chain: A foundation for a new cyber security strategy". High Frontier, Vol 6, no 2, pp 52-56.

Damballa, (2008). Anatomy of a Targeted Attack. White paper, Damballa, Inc.

Denning, P.J. and Denning, D.E. (2010). "Discussing Cyber Attack". Communications of the ACM, Vol 53, no 9, pp 29-31.

Dreijer, D. (2011). Offensieve Cyberoperaties: Een onderzoek naar de fasering en uitvoering van offensieve cyberoperaties die plaatsvinden in de context van een internationaal conflict. Unpublished bachelor dissertation, Netherlands Defence Academy, Breda, The Netherlands [In Dutch: Offensive Cyber Operations: A study into the phases and execution of offensive cyber operations occurring in the context of an international conflict].

Grant, T.J. and Kooter, B.M. (2005). "Comparing OODA and Other Models as Operational View Architecture". In Proceedings of the 10th International Command & Control Research & Technology Symposium (ICCRTS'05) (McLean, VA, USA, June 13-16, 2005). US DoD CCRP, Washington DC, USA, paper 196.

Grant, T.J., Venter, H.S., and Eloff, J.H.P, (2007). "Simulating Adversarial Interactions between Intruders and System Administrators using OODA-RR". In Proceedings of the Annual Conference of the South African Institute of Computer Scientists and Information Technologists (SAICSIT'07), ACM International Conference Proceedings.

Habermas, J. (1976). Communication and the evolution of society. Beacon Press, Toronto.

Lin, H. (2009). "Lifting the Veil on Cyber Offense". IEEE Security & Privacy, Vol 7, No 4, pp 15-21.

Marca, D., and McGowen, C.L. (1988). SADT: Structured Analysis and Design Technique. McGraw-Hill, NY.

MinJus. (2011). De Nationale Cyber Security Strategie. Ministerie van Justitie en Veiligheid [Ministry of Justice and Safety], The Hague, Netherlands [In Dutch: The National Cyber Security Strategy].

Mirkovic, J. and Reiher, P. (2004). "A Taxonomy of DDoS Attack and DDoS Defense Mechanisms". ACM SIGCOMM Computer Communication Review, Vol 34, no 2.

Mitnick, K.D., and Simon, W.L. (2005). The Art of Intrusion: The real stories behind the exploits of hackers, intruders & deceivers, Wiley Publishing, Inc.

Moore, A.P., Ellison, R.J., and Linger, R.C. (2001). Attack Modeling for Information Security and Survivability. Technical note CMU/SEI-2001-TN-001, Software Engineering Institute, Carnegie Mellon University, Pittsburgh, PA.

Owens, W., Dam, K., and Lin, H. (2009). Technology, Policy, Law, and Ethics Regarding U.S. Acquisition and Use of Cyberattack Capabilities. Washington D.C.: The National Academies Press.

Schneier, B. (1999). "Attack trees: Modeling security threats". Dr Dobb's Journal.

Sheyner, O. (2004). Scenario Graphs and Attack Graphs. PhD dissertation, technical report CMU-CS-04-122, Computer Science Department, Carnegie Mellon University, Pittsburgh, PA.

Simmonds, A., Sandilands, P., and Van Ekert, L. (2004). "An Ontology for Network Security Attacks". Applied Computing, LNCS 3285, pp 317-323.

Sorensen, C.B.L. (2010). Cyber OODA: Towards a conceptual cyberspace framework. Masters thesis, School of Advanced Air and Space Studies, Air University, Maxwell AFB, AL.

TSO. (2009). Cyber Security Strategy of the United Kingdom: Safety, security and resilience in cyber space. The Stationery Office, Her Majesty's Government, London.

Undercoffer, J., Joshi, A., and Pinkston, J. (2003). "Modelling Computer Attacks: An ontology for intrusion detection". LNCS 2820, pp 113-135.

Van Heerden, R. and Burke, I, (forthcoming). "Network Attack Model". Submitted to ICIW 2012.

Veerasamy, N. (2010). A High-level Mapping of Cyberterrorism to the OODA Loop. In Proceedings of the 5th International Conference on Information Warfare and Security, Ohio, USA, pp 352-360.

Wing, J.M. (2005). "Scenario Graphs Applied to Security". In Proceedings of Workshop on Verification of Infinite State Systems with Applications to Security. (Timisoara, Romania, March 2005).

# DUQU'S DILEMMA: The Ambiguity Assertion and the Futility of Sanitized Cyber War

**Matthew Crosston**

Bellevue University, USA

matt.crosston@bellevue.edu

*Originally Published in the Proceedings of ICCWS, 2013*

### Editorial Commentary

The dilemma invoked by the title of this paper is that which stems from the existence of the variety of malicious software (malware) known as the Duqu family (or collection). The dilemma, which is a difficult choice between two (or more) alternatives, is fundamentally expressed as a control problem: "the reality of cyber-attacks and initiatives can be for information gathering or physical attack potentiality; they can be originated from a government effort but executed through major commercial assets; they can be aimed for political/military objectives yet facilitated by piggy-backing on civilian systems." The implication is that since the controls associated with the conventional laws of armed conflict only apply to about half of that list, adopting and enforcing that control would be less than effective in meeting the goals of such a control structure. The alternative, however, is equally bleak: accepting the ambiguity associated with the nature of cyberspace in both structure and usage, where ambiguity as a concept is rather foreign to international norms, blame-finding, and legal structures. Thus, truly, this is a dilemma.

Crosston does a masterful job in setting the stage in describing this dilemma. Starting with international law and moving through to the inevitable turf wars, he sets up a powerful argument for a new strategic approach that embraces the ambiguity. This, of course, has been tried in the past. One of the oft-quoted examples of integration of commercial assets and military might is the existence of "privateers": individuals given charters to engage in hostile activities on behalf of their countries. Operating as a privateer was not without risk: William Kidd, hanged for piracy in 1701, may

well have been operating as a privateer. (There are other similar stories for those who are interested in the checkered history of privateering.) The point, however, is that the use of private citizens or companies as agents of governments is as much a dilemma as not, and should be thought through carefully. One approach that may be useful to consider is the development of a private reserve force of citizens, such as is being done in Estonia. A discussion of this effort makes excellent ancillary reading for Crosston's paper: see Ottis, Rain. "From Pitchforks To Laptops: Volunteers In Cyber Conflicts." 2010. Available online at
https://ccdcoe.org/sites/default/files/multimedia/pdf/Ottis%20-%20From%20Pitchforks%20to%20Laptops%20Volunteers%20in%20Cyber%20Conflicts.pdf.

**Abstract:** There is an intense debate about the applicability of international law to cyber war and the need for a cyber-specific international treaty. The problem, however, might be that this debate is irrelevant. Both camps misread how the structure of the cyber domain likely precludes strategically 'piggy-backing' on conventional norms of war. There is a civilian/military ambiguity in the cyber domain that makes target differentiation unlikely if not impossible. Thus, Duqu's dilemma: with the focus on establishing legitimate targets and setting limitations on allowable action the United States and its allies are engaged in a futile endeavor that cannot lead to improved cyber governance and likely only exposes them to vulnerabilities. Greater effort should be spent on accepting this structural ambiguity by developing strategy that aims to instill preemptive fear and produce reluctance to action.

**Keywords**: cyber war, cyber deterrence, cyber theory, law of armed conflict, attribution

# 1 Introduction

The debate over the applicability or non-applicability of international law to cyber war and the need for a cyber-specific international treaty might be irrelevant. Both camps, pro and con, argue about the need for cyber war to have the Law of Armed Conflict or some new international legal project properly cover the cyber domain. Both camps, however, misread how the structure of the cyber domain precludes strategically 'piggy-backing' on conventional norms of war. International laws on conventional war are effective because of the ability to differentiate between civilian and military sectors. There is a civilian/military ambiguity in the cyber domain that makes such differentiation unlikely if not impossible well into the future.

Thus Duqu's Dilemma: with the focus on establishing legitimate targets and setting limitations on allowable action, the United States and its allies expose themselves to vulnerabilities while engaging a futile endeavor that does not lead to improved cyber control. Just like the Duqu virus that dominated global discussion in 2011, the reality of cyber-attacks and initiatives can be for information gathering *or* physical attack potentiality; they can be originated from a government effort *but* executed through major commercial assets; they can be aimed for political/military objectives *yet* facilitated by piggy-backing on civilian systems. The effort to establish cyber rules akin to conventional norms is therefore fruitless as these rules are not enforceable or logical in truly dealing with this military/civilian ambiguity. Current efforts simply handcuff lawful states. This means greater effort should be spent on creating pre-emptive strategy that accepts the military/civilian ambiguity problem. The tendency of scholars and policymakers to strive for 'sanitized' cyber war by constraining damage through explicit target classification means cyber strategy remains absent true deterring power. In short, cyber defense specialists are exacerbating the dilemma.

Whether one believes the Law of Armed Conflict can or cannot apply to the cyber domain, whether one pushes for an international cyber treaty or thinks such treaties will be meaningless, one aspect is constant: the desire for rules governing cyber war behavior. The problem is in attempting to create a code of cyber conduct that demands a distinct separation between civilian and military sectors. The cyber domain is not amenable to this separation as the aforementioned fusion, where participants, facilities and targets are hopelessly entangled between civilian and military institutions, has basically been a missing explanation as to why the global effort to enhance and clarify norms has remained uneven and inadequate.

## 2   The Ineffectiveness of international law

As the East-West Institute said in a 2011 report, "There is an urgent need for international cooperation on this most strategic of issues. If we fail on this task, global stability could be as threatened as it would be by a nuclear exchange."(Leithauser 2011) International norms established with the Geneva and Hague conventions were meant to be explicit lines of protection for civilian populations when states engaged in war. That respect and preservation of civilian life is now held to be sacrosanct, regardless of what form or delivery method war may take. As such, there is an expectation that cyberspace can be brought under the discipline of conventional rules of war.

Others argue establishing these customary understandings into the cyber domain is one of the most important geopolitical battles today, going so far as to say it is Ground Zero for global diplomacy, national security work, and intelligence.(Gjelten 2010) The goal is to bring the principles of arms control into the cyber domain. Indeed, the most optimistic want voluntary agreements that create constraints on the development of cyber capabilities and ostensibly ameliorate behavior in cyberspace. Some, however, have acknowledged that there are potential dangers in trying to reach this achievement. Stewart Baker, a former general counsel at the national security agency and assistant secretary for policy at the Department of Homeland Security under Pres. George W. Bush, declared the obvious fear: the United States and its allies would obey whatever was written down and agreed to while no adversaries would.(Gjelten 2010)

There may be a larger problem, however, than non-compliance: conventional war has the distinct advantage, historically, of being fairly explicit over target classification. Most military networks that would initiate and enact a cyber-attack depend upon and work within countless numbers of civilian networks. In addition, many of the actors that are part of the planning, initiation, and deployment of cyber-attacks are not necessarily formal military but civilian employees of government agencies. In other words, the world of cyber conflict and cyber war is not a world that can achieve such explicit classification. In fact, future trends only show this fusion growing deeper and tighter in time. As such, any attempt to introduce norms and rules that are predicated upon knowledgeable differentiation will likely end up confused and ineffective.

This 'ambiguity assertion,' for lack of a better term, has so far been relatively ignored in the various cyber debates. They tend to revolve around how loose or rigid, how informal or formal, how international or local such codes of constraint should be. Many of these proposed codes aim to constrain cyber behavior so as to protect banking, power, and other critical infrastructure networks 'except when nations are engaged in war.'(Sternstein 2011) Without addressing the ambiguity problem, however, states find themselves facing a quandary: where are the lines of distinction between civilian and military drawn? Perhaps the biggest dilemma, therefore, is not the problem of figuring out attribution (who was the true trigger man?) but rather this futile attempt to clear up the inherent and purposeful ambiguity that characterizes the critical infrastructure used to house, develop, and utilize a state's cyber capabilities.

Many of the current cyber discussions are flawed by the manner in which they implicitly want to analogize conventional conflict with cyber conflict, to make cyber-attacks equivalent to armed attacks. To do this, however, the conversation must turn to legal definitions and parameters: when does cyber conflict constitute the use of armed force or a formal act of war? What actions would constitute a war crime? How much damage triggers a necessary retaliatory response?(Liaropolous 2010) These questions are much more difficult to answer in the cyber realm because of the logistical nightmare provided by the ambiguity assertion. This fact is not emphasized to date appropriately and is not strategically addressed at all.

Up to now questions have focused more around comparable lethality, damage estimates, and the aforementioned attribution problem. To a certain extent, however, all of these legitimate problems are enveloped by the civilian/military ambiguity issue. The inability to establish that separation means lethality could potentially be more deadly by being more than just military casualties, damage could be more devastating by being more than just military facilities, and attribution might not even be relevant: defining the WHO of an attack is not a resolution of the problem if the HOW behind the WHO is inextricably fused between government, military, and civilian properties and people. In other words, many assume figuring out the WHO in cyber war will solve most problems. The ambiguity assertion reminds everyone to be careful what is wished for: in cyber war the WHO will never be conveniently distinct because of the HOW.

International law clearly does not alleviate the problem of civilian/military ambiguity in cyber conflict. Whether the discussion extends to codes of conduct, treaties, or international laws writ large, none of these potential documents attempt to address the inherent structural problem of modern societies and how they currently organize, conduct, and develop their cyber capabilities. Further confirming this is the equal amount of time, effort, and frustration in the sister projects of establishing terms and defining parameters. Examining that frustration will illustrate how impactful the ambiguity assertion is when contemplating how the world should deal with the rules for cyber war.

## 3   The frustration of setting terms

Part of the problem in getting international law efficiently covering the realm of cyberspace involves a long-standing failure to translate essential terms and parameters into something that would truly impact the cyber domain. Progress in moving beyond this problem has been extremely limited. Indeed, even a cursory glance across the literature over the past decade brings testimony to the fact that cyber war does not fit perfectly into the legal frameworks that already exist on war and use of force. (Anatolin-Jenkins 2005) Despite this reality these terminological and doctrinal difficulties have been continually investigated with the aim to forcefully coordinate existing terms and doctrines into the cyber arena. This article argues that their lack of success is attributable to the unwillingness to engage the civilian/military fusion.

The desire for explicit terms, parameters, definitions, laws, and treaties is based more on the worry that failure to produce such explicitness will leave cyber war outside the boundaries of rules that currently govern conventional war. The consequences are considered stark: critical civilian infrastructure could be targeted as well as basic necessities, such as agriculture, food, water, public health, emergency services, telecommunications, energy, banking and finance, etc. The ambiguity assertion, however, articulates the difficulty in establishing such explicitness: most if not all of a state's cyber capability utilizes and depends upon critical civilian infrastructure that also provides many important civilian functions. No state to date has created a cyber operations capability that is wholly distinct and separate from civilian networks and civilian infrastructure. In other words, go after the 'military' targets and you will also *de facto* be going after 'civilian' targets. The literature to date seems to bypass this fact. Consequently, much of the literature engages in a false riddle, trying to force a theoretically precise answer to an empirically ambiguous reality.

This is further confirmed by the number of respected scholars, diplomats, and policymakers that miss the relevance of the ambiguity assertion by demanding that the laws of cyber war should actually *forbid* the targeting of purely civilian infrastructure, indicating that cyber actors should try to respect the Geneva Conventions as much as conventional actors do.(Tennant 2009) The problem, of course, is that in cyber war purely civilian infrastructure is a category of diminishing returns. Indeed, given the obvious trend that sees only intensification and deepening of the civilian/military fusion, purely civilian infrastructure will end up more myth than reality.

The failure to address this structural riddle has been matched by an overemphasis on agency. This manifests itself namely in the focus on limiting and controlling potential cyber actions from adversarial states. James Lewis of CSIS emphasizes how a state can reduce risks for everyone by imposing common standards, like moving from the Wild West to the rule of law.(Fallows 2010) Eugene Spafford concurred, citing how cyber security is a process, not a patch, requiring continual investment for the long-term as well as the quick fix, without which states will always be applying solutions to problems too late.(Fallows 2010) These are some of the brightest and most respected names in the cyber discipline. Their warnings are not irrelevant but the emphasis on state actor agency, while failing to recognize the impact and importance of inherent cyber structure, leaves a vulnerability gap in cyber strategic thinking. Indeed, the contemporary failure to create explicit norm coordination should be seen as a demand to consider new strategy that can accept this structural incompatibility as inherent and not something to 'overcome.' For structural ambiguity is not only intrinsic: states are purposely deepening the ambiguity for its strategic advantage and economic efficiency. States, therefore, should not focus on how to force a distinct civilian/military separation but should rather develop new strategic thinking that accepts the ambiguity problem as a logistical reality that must be accounted for.

For empirical confirmation of the futility in trying to address these problems of conventional norms and explicit parameters, look no further than the United States military over the past half-dozen years. It is easy to produce a laundry list of frustration and unfulfilled hopes: Gen. Alexander of US Cyber Command mentioned that progress was being made but that the risks were still at present growing faster than the progress;(Curran 2012) Vice Adm. Michael Rogers, commander of the US Navy's fleet cyber command, admitted to Congress that no agreement had been reached amongst the various commands on ironing out the rules of cyber conflict but hoped there would be positive developments 'at some point in the near term';(Baldor 2012) and even the Pentagon produced a cyber document that ultimately said that the laws of armed conflict do apply in cyber-space as in traditional warfare, even while admitting the basic terms 'act of war' and 'use of force' were still somewhat *ill-defined* in the cyber do-main.(Gorman and Barnes 2011) This shows the real-term effects that the lack of new strategic thinking has when states do not address the ambigu-ity of civilian/military fusion.

## 4   Turf wars and tightropes: Military discussion on cyber parameters

Just as with scholars, policymakers, and diplomats, the military has been steadfastly committed to establishing strict rules of cyber engagement that are akin to the conventional rules of war.(Anonymous 2008) For several years there has been a pending revision of the military's standing rules of engagement in the cyber realm.(Nakashima 2012) It seems that while the military hoped the scholarly and diplomatic communities would be able to help define much of the needed clarification, the two latter communities were themselves hoping to see the military lead the way with its revision. This responsibility obfuscation, however, is not as relevant as many ob-servers and analysts might think: failure to address these issues is not so much a case of one community trying to pass the buck on to another but rather testimony to the confusion created when the ambiguity assertion about civilian/military fusion is not addressed.

Gen. Alexander stated that in debating the rules of conflict in cyber opera-tions the United States was trying to do the job right.(Nakashima 2012) Those debates, however, constantly oscillate back-and-forth between posi-tions that do not address the primary innate structural concerns of the cyber domain. Consequently, the military has spent half a dozen years promising imminent progress that does not materialize. The Pentagon's official report was itself described as 'ducking' a series of important basic fundamental questions, including defining such basic terms as 'war,' 'force,' and 'appropriate response.'(Nakashima 2011) This is pointed out not to poke fun at the military. Quite to the contrary, this article makes the argument that given the reluctance of all parties concerned to engage the ambiguity assertion, with an eye to develop new strategy that embraces it rather than hopelessly using old strategy to overcome it, the military has had no real chance of making substantive progress in its effort to concisely define the parameters of cyber action.

It is no coincidence that the American military has sincerely worked on issues such as administrative network control, cyber organization, force composition, cyber intelligence/operation differentiation, in addition to basic terminology parameters, without any major questions being considered definitively and comprehensively closed.(Andrues 2010) How, for example, can USCYBERCOM be expected to connect all the dots and be the competent arbiter in determining a case for action when it readily admits difficulty in even articulating who exactly makes up the fraternity of cyber warriors operating and defending home networks?(Andrues 2010) If the issues at hand were not so serious and not so far-reaching on the future of cyber conflict it would be almost comical. Only recently has it seemed possible that relevant military bodies have started to reach the epiphany discussed here:

> *"Although there are some noteworthy first steps toward establishing an international set of cyber norms - evident in bodies such as the Convention on Cybercrime - any global framework governing military response actions in cyberspace will surely materialize at an onerous pace. After all, how can the rules of war, built upon the tactile presence of combatants and weapons and sovereign territory, be retooled for a world where 'troops' can be dispatched in milliseconds from a multitude of states?"(Andrues 2010)*

At least the above quote begins to frame the discussion around the innate incompatibility between how war in cyberspace would likely be conducted and how that compares to all wars previous. It still, however, is emphasizing agency over structure: establishing an international set of cyber norms mainly to hallmark the division between civilian and military assets and mitigate action already undertaken. This might help explain why formal strategic documents about cyberspace end up being nothing but simple platitudes about how the United States intends to protect itself. Take for example the Department of Defense's Strategy for Operating in Cyberspace, released in mid-2011, and comprised of five 'strategic initiatives':

- Strategic Initiative 1: treat cyberspace as an operational domain to organize, train, and equip so that the DoD can take full advantage of cyberspace's potential.
- Strategic Initiative 2: employ new defense operating concepts to protect domestic networks and systems.

- Strategic Initiative 3: partner with other US government departments and agencies and the private sector to enable a whole-of-
  government cyber security strategy.
- Strategic Initiative 4: build robust relationships with US allies and
  international partners to strengthen collective cyber security.
- Strategic Initiative 5: leverage the nation's ingenuity through an
  exceptional cyber workforce and rapid technological innovation.

Take full advantage; employ new concepts; partner with others; build robust relationships; leverage ingenuity. All of these phrases are wonderful
slogans but they are not accompanied by any explicit new strategic thinking that could have the hope of actually establishing said initiatives. Trying
to adapt conventional strategy slightly and then force the cyber domain
into it is likely to remain a project bearing little to no fruit. Examining that
conventional strategy and proposing new strategy that engages the structural dilemma is the final section of this paper.

# 5 Engaging ambiguity: Strategic thinking for the civil-
ian/military cyber fusion

The need for a new strategic approach is best illustrated when the arguments of two highly respected strategic thinkers, one military and one legal and who happen to fall on opposite sides of the law of armed conflict
(LOAC) cyber debate, ignore the problem of civilian/military structural cyber fusion. Dunlap, while accepting the need for improvement, believes
the tenets of the law of armed conflict are sufficient to address the most
important issues of cyber war.(Dunlap 2011) The concern for distinguishing
between legitimate military and civilian targets does not seem to bother
Dunlap in its impact on the applicability of LOAC:

> *"LOAC tolerates 'incidental losses' of civilians and civilian objects so
> long as they are 'not excessive in relation to the concrete and direct
> military advantage anticipated.' In determining the incidental
> losses, cyber strategists are required to consider those that may be
> reasonably foreseeable to be directly caused by the attack. Assess-
> ing second- and third-order 'reverberating' effects may be a wise
> policy consideration, but it does not appear LOAC currently requires
> such further analysis."(Dunlap 2011)*

This distinction made by Dunlap is actually quite important given the current intellectual climate: he has introduced some much-needed realism

into the debates by reminding people that LOAC has never been a flawless strategy that perfectly protects civilians and civilian objects. The problem being highlighted here, however, is that his concerns over military/civilian differentiation are misplaced.

These pro-LOAC arguments are effectively built around the fact that cyber war does not have to have a perfect record in delineating and then protecting civilians because LOAC does not either. But these arguments take as given that such delineation is generally *possible*. The future of cyber war is unlikely to be able to create such possibility because it has been long-established how many of the military's critical functions, assets, service providers, and supply chains all rely heavily on civilian traffic and networks.(Mudrinich 2012) As such, new strategy needs to be positioned so as to prevent the use of cyber weapons in general, because once they are used the likelihood of incurring civilian risk, damage, and casualties will be *de facto*. 'Sanitizing' the impact of cyber weapons once they are used by trying to constrain targeting choices will not work.

The anti-LOAC camp makes the same mistake when discussing why the law of armed conflict does not bring clarity to cyber war:

> *"The laws of war are in place to ensure that parties to a conflict target combatants rather than civilians, and, if civilians are targeted, to ensure that such individuals have forfeited their protected status. To determine whether cyber-attacks properly distinguish between civilian and military targets, one must understand [the] distinction."(Gervais 2012)*

The opposition camp fails in the belief that such distinction can in fact be created in cyber. This camp does not see the strategic influence of the ambiguity assertion, focusing rather on the deficiencies within the law of armed conflict and other contemporary norms and treaties: in short, make better laws and the cyber world will come to heel. As such, this camp is even further from reality, ignoring a problem that is only going to deepen and intensify over time. The opposition camp, in essence, is a more liberal approach to conflict because the end goal is to create an atmosphere of trust that can minimize higher levels of violence and treachery.(Gervais 2012) This flies even more in the face of the current and future structure of cyber war.

Both of these camps believe in being able to monitor and regulate and circumscribe cyber war after it has begun, as done successfully with conventional war. This is a false hope. The ability to monitor, regulate, and circumscribe cyber action is best done through strategy that can inculcate preemptive fear and thereby induce caution and hesitation. *Current conventional strategies that aim for trust, target distinction, and minimizing noncombatant impact are simply inexplicably ignoring how cyber war is organized, structured, and operationalized.*

Liberal thinking also dominates the legal community that is heavily leaned upon for law projects and the strategic thinking meant to infuse said projects for the cyber domain:

> *"[An effective solution to the global challenge of cyber-attacks] cannot be achieved by individual states acting alone. It will require global cooperation. We therefore outlined the key elements of the cyber treaty - namely, codifying clear definitions of cyber warfare and cyber-attack and providing guidelines for international cooperation on evidence collection and criminal prosecution - that would provide a more comprehensive and long-term solution to the emerging threat of cyber-attacks."(Hathaway 2012)*

The above review shows yet another camp focusing on mitigating risk and limiting damage in the cyber domain *ex post facto*. Regardless of philosophical standing, political agendas, or theoretical acumen, every camp that examines the problem of parameters and definitions in the cyber domain seems to exclude considerations of preemptive strategies built upon fear and inducing reluctance to action. Gen. Alexander of US Cyber Command cited the need to establish the lanes of the road for what governments can and cannot pursue and that establishing those lanes was the necessary first step to addressing the challenge of cyber-attacks.(Hathaway 2012) What all of the camps examined here have in common is a tendency to give lip-service to strategy but then really focus exclusively on *ex post facto operations* to establish progress. If the focus continues to be on agency action and not on structural deficiency, then progress will not simply remain slow: it will become non-existent.

There has been a small beginning in the literature attempting to define this mindset-change and its strategic importance, focusing on how the goal for major powers should not be the futile hope of developing a perfect defensive system of cyber deterrence, but rather the ability to instill deterrence based on a mutually shared fear of an offensive threat. The United States is better positioned by expanding to an open, transparent policy that seeks to compel deterrence from the efficacy of its offensive cyber capabilities. (Crosston 2011) There has been an even smaller start trying to define how deterring pre-emptive cyber power works or what it strategically looks like. Ideally, this overt cyber strategy would create credibility in virtual weapons which employ disruptive cascading effects so powerful as to negate their use. The key would be in establishing plausible fear in the adversary. Given the recent revelations about Stuxnet and the effectiveness of the Duqu and Flame viruses—which quite possibly moved beyond Stuxnet capabilities—cyber weapons are rapidly obtaining that fearful reputation, and thus, deterrence via overt cyber strategy can no longer be considered pure fantasy. It is an important balancing argument for developing a fully encompassing strategy that allows for both covert and overt US cyber power.(Crosston 2012) In essence, adversaries need to be made to believe in rational self-interest that good behavior will avoid massive debilitation and bad behavior carries severe consequences. Ironic as it may seem, perhaps the key to developing this overt cyber strategy of pre-emptive deterrence is to rely on old-school realist strategy while simultaneously moving away from old-school realist norms of conventional warfare. This new literature impacts the ambiguity assertion because this mindset-change and strategic shift is arguably the best method to fighting Duqu's Dilemma: the only way to overcome the ambiguity is to avoid being put in a situation where the ambiguity has to be addressed. In other words, the current cyber reality and its foreseeable future make *ex post facto* strategies inherently inferior to pre-emptive ones.

## 6 Duqu's dilemma: Why it matters

This analysis has pinpointed flaws in the current thinking and efforts to establish clear definitions and parameters governing the rules and operations within cyber war. The emphasis placed here on inherent structural difficulties, namely the innate cyber civilian/military fusion, has shown the likely damaging and deadly consequences to societies when strategies do not focus on the effort to pre-emptively stop cyber action but instead focus on operational considerations after conflict has begun.

Only now are there beginning to be isolated legal analyses highlighting these problems:

*"It is unlikely that a state such as the United States could take pre-
cautions against the effect of attacks on military objectives by sepa-
rating military objectives from civilians and civilian objects in cyberspace. This is because of the interconnectedness of US government
and civilian systems in the near complete government reliance on
civilian companies for the supply, support, and maintenance of it
cyber capabilities... Proportionality assessments likely will prove
particularly precarious in cyberspace, where outcomes are more difficult to predict than in the physical world: physical attacks at least
have the advantage of physics and chemistry to work with. Because,
say, the blast radius of a thousand pound bomb is fairly well understood, one can predict what definitely lies outside the blast radius
and what definitely lies inside. Error bands and cyber-attacks are
much wider and less well-known... [Most reports do not explain
how] these public-private partnerships could be constituted in a
manner that adequately considers laws of war issues nor do [they]
address the likely use of active defenses by the private sector."(Lobel 2012)*

As illustrated above, this structural issue is more than just semantics. It
literally covers who engages cyber war, what can be destroyed in cyber
war, who can be a victim during cyber war, even the philosophical and
ethical questions meant to be asked about cyber war itself. Duqu's Dilemma is an entreaty to move away from unobtainable goals and idealistic
dreams in a futile hope to create sanitized cyber war. Cyber war will never
be sanitized. Consequently, contemporary strategic thinking about the
cyber domain must start treating the ambiguity assertion with the same
gravity that the more famous attribution problem receives.

# References

Anatolin-Jenkins, Vida CDR, "Defining the Parameters of Cyberwar Operations: Looking for
    Law in All the Wrong Places?" *Naval Law Review 51:132,* 2005.
Andrues, Wesley, "What US Cyber Command Must Do," *Joint Forces Quarterly, Issue 59, 4th
    quarter,* 2010.
Anonymous, "Syria's Secret War Against the Cyber Dissidents," *The Daily Star* (Beirut,
    Lebanon) Jul 12 2011.
Anonymous, "Cyber War Warning," *Derby Evening Telegraph,* (Derby UK) Feb 5 2011.
Anonymous, "Military Ponders Cyber War Rules," *Los Angeles Times,* (Los Angeles, USA) Apr 7
    2008.
August, Ray, "International Cyber-jurisdiction: A Comparative Analysis," *American Business
    Law Journal, 39:4,* Summer 2002.
Baldor, Lolita, "Cyber Warriors," *Army Times,* Aug 6 2012.

Clarke, Richard, "The Coming Cyber Wars," *Boston Globe* (Boston, USA) Jul 31 2011.

Crosston, Matthew, *"Virtual Patriots and a New American Cyber Strategy: Breaking the Zero-sum Game,"* Strategic Studies Quarterly, *Vol. 6, No. 4, Winter 2012.*

Crosston, Matthew, *"World Gone Cyber M.A.D: How Mutually Assured Debilitation is the Best Hope for Cyber-deterrence,"* Strategic Studies Quarterly, *Vol. 5, No. 1, Spring 2011.*

Curran, John, "Updated Rules for Cyber Conflict Coming Soon, Defense Officials Say," *Cybersecurity Policy Report* Mar 26 2012.

Department of Defense, "Strategy for Operating in Cyberspace," (Washington DC, USA) Jul 2012.

Dunlap, Charles, "Perspectives for Cyber Strategists on Law for Cyberwar," *Strategic Studies Quarterly,* Spring 2011.

Fallows, James, "Cyber Warriors," *The Atlantic Monthly, 305;2,* Mar 2010.

Fryer-Biggs, Zachary, "Turf War Slows New US Cyber Rules," *C4ISR, 12,* Jun 1 2012.

Gervais, Michael, "Cyber Attacks and the Laws of War," *Journal of Law and Cyber Warfare, 30;2,* 2012.

Gjelten, Tom, "Shadow Wars: Debating Cyber Disarmament," *World Affairs, 173;4,* Nov/Dec 2010.

Gorman, Siobhan and Julian Barnes, "Rules for Laws of War: US Decides Cyber Strike Can Trigger Attack," *The Australian,* Jun 1 2011.

Gross, Michael Joseph, "A Declaration of Cyber-war," *Vanity Fair, 53;4,* Apr 2011.

Gutmann, Ethan, "Hacker Nation: China's Cyber Assault, *World Affairs, 173;1,* May/Jun 2010.

Hathaway, Oona, et al, "The Law of Cyber-Attack," *California Law Review,* 2012.

Jarrett, Stephen, "Offensive Cyber Warfare," *Proceedings 137,* (United States Naval Institute), Dec 2011.

Jensen, Eric Talbot, "Sovereignty and Neutrality in Cyber Conflict," *Fordham International Law Journal, 35; 815,* Match 2012.

Leithauser, Tom, "Cyber War Rules Won't Cover All Situations, DoD Official Says," *Cybersecurity Policy Report,* May 17, 2010.

Leithauser, Tom, "Rules of War Should Apply to Cyber Conflict," *Cybersecurity Policy Report,* Feb 14, 2011.

Liaropoulos, Andrew, "War and Ethics in Cyberspace: Cyber-conflict and Just War Theory," *European Conference on Information Warfare and Security, 177-XI,* (Reading, UK), Jul 2010.

Lin, Patrick, "War 2.0: Cyberweapons and Ethics," *Communications of the ACM, 55;3,* March 2012.

Lobel, Hannah, "Cyber War Inc: The Law of War Implications of the Private Sector's Role in Cyber Conflict," *Texas International Journal of Law, 47;3,* Summer 2012.

Mavhunga, Clapperton, "The Glass Fortress: Zimbabwe's Cyber-Guerilla Warfare," *Journal of International Affairs, 62;2,* Spring 2009.

Mudrinich, Erik, "Cyber 3.0: The Department of Defense Strategy for Operating in Cyberspace and the Attribution Problem," *Air Force Law Review, 68,* 2012.

Nakashima, Ellen, "Pentagon: Cyber Offense Part of Strategy," *The Washington Post,* (Washington DC, USA), Nov 16 2011.

Nakashima, Ellen, "Pentagon Seeks to Engage Rules of Engagement in Cyber War," *The Herald,* (Everett, Washington, USA), Aug 10 2012.

Nye, Joseph, "Nuclear Lessons for Cyber Security?" *Strategic Studies Quarterly,* Winter 2011.

Schaap, Arie, "Cyber Warfare Operations: Development and Use Under International Law," *Air Force Law Review, 64,* 2009.

Schwartz, Matthew, "The Case for a Cyber Arms Treaty," *Informationweek,* Aug 24 2012.

Stanton, John, "Rules of Cyber War Baffle US Government Agencies," *National Defense, 84;555,* Feb 2000.

Stavridis, James and Elton Parker, "Sailing the Cyber Sea," *Joint Forces Quarterly, Issue 65, 2nd quarter,* 2012.

Sternstein, Aliya, "Experts Recommend an International Code of Conduct for Cyberwar," *National Journal,* Jun 10 2011.

Temple, James, "In Cyber War, Be Careful How the Worm Turns," *San Francisco Chronicle,* Jun 10 2012.

Tennant, Don, "The Fog of (CYBER) War," *Computerworld, 43;16,* Apr 27 2009.

Tsirigotis, Anthimos Alexander, "Cyber Warfare: Virtual War among Virtual Societies," *European Conference on Information Warfare and Security, 389-XII,* (Reading, UK), Jul 2010.

Zekos, Giorgios, "Cyber-Territory and Jurisdiction of Nations," *Journal of Internet Law, 15;12,* Jun 2012.

# Unrestricted Warfare versus Western Traditional Warfare: A Comparative Study

## G Commin and E Filiol

*ESIEA, (C+V)° Laboratory*
gcommin@et.esiea-ouest.fr
eric.filiol@esiea-ouest.fr

*Originally Published in the Proceedings of ECIW, 2013*

---

**Editorial Commentary**

Are we entering a period of unrelenting warfare? The context for this question is provided by the introductory discussion of a publication of two senior Chinese military officers, entitled "Unrestricted Warfare." In this text, the point is made *"that warfare is no more 'the use of armed force forcing the enemy to bend to our wishes' but rather use 'of all the ways, which the armed force or not armed, military or not military [...] to force the enemy to submit to its own interests.'"* This is an extraordinary change in definition of legitimate warfare from a Western perspective, which is based in the thought that has evolved from the influential work of Hugo Grotius in the early 1600s. Grotius is credited with developing a frame-work for international law in which states interacted as a society, mutually respecting and enforcing standards of behavior. His seminal work of 1625, "De jure belli ac pacis libri tres (On the Law of War and Peace: Three books)" is still studied to this day, and can be found online in many places, one of which is

http://socserv2.socsci.mcmaster.ca/econ/ugcm/3ll3/grotius/Law2.pdf.

This paper builds upon the themes touched upon in the previous papers. The inherent changes in how humans interact and how the boundaries of state interests have diffused and broadened require some reaction, some accommodation. The proposal that warfare would necessarily evolve to embrace all aspects of life, both traditionally military and non-military, is a notion that must be considered carefully, particularly because of the problems associated with integrating traditional military approaches with what can be called the "new warfare". The point is made that these efforts should "pass not only the physical borders, but also domains such as the economy, finance, religion and culture to attain the enemy." This is in some ways the perfect realization of the Clausewitzian concept of war as a continuation of politics by other means (the actual quote, translated, is "We see, therefore, that War is not merely a political act, but also a real political instrument, a continuation of political commerce, a carrying out of the same by other means." See http://oll.libertyfund.org/pages/clausewitz-war-as-politics-by-other-means for a translation of the first chapter of his book <u>On War</u>.)

Should this future be realized, changes would be required for all competitors. As noted by the authors, the principles of non-intervention, exclusionism, and free trade are all at risk at some level. The very notion of what constitutes a place of conflict — a battlefield — may soon be obsolete. While there may be dramatic reductions in loss of life and injury to persons, that may come with trade-offs we don't understand, which may come with unintended consequences. These challenges are somewhat similar to those that prompted the King of France in the early 1600s to ask Hugo Grotius to philosophize on war and peace. Although the technology has changed, human nature remains constant and revisiting history in the light of the potential of "unending warfare" is a useful exercise.

**Abstract**: The rise of the cyber dimension as well as the emergence of new strategic/economic leaders in the world, like China, is currently changing not only the face of the world but also threatens to upset the strategic balance in the world. In this context, the concept of warfare itself must be redefined. This paper seeks to analyse the concept of new warfare precisely, and then to discuss developments in the new art of warfare, and, finally, to establish a redefinition of the stakes.

**Keywords**: Warfare, Doctrine, Cyber Warfare, China, Qiao Liang, Wang Xiangsui, Modern Warfare

# 1 Introduction

The word 'warfare' draws its etymology from the inheritance of the Middle-East and the Latin name *'bellum'*. Over the course of many years, both the most abhorrent violence and the gloomiest stupidity have emerged from it. It is has been called both hideous and the mother of all crimes (Qiao & Wang 1999). It features in the preoccupations of statesmen, and it is considered sometimes as the continuation of politics by other means (Qiao & Wang 1999). Clear and obvious justifications for warfare were essentially made until the end of 19<sup>th</sup> century. Countries were fighting for territory or wealth. In the course of its evolution, warfare turned into demographic warfare, which had as its goal the massive destruction of people and commodities, as evidenced in, for example, cold warfare. Certainly, warfare takes all possible forms of confrontation, from espionage to technological competition in the domain of the conquest of space. (Indeed, the cold war of the 20<sup>th</sup> century took place in the entire world with indirect fights between two power states through their respective partners. It was characterized by a bipolarization of world.) This multiplicity of forms is part of the principle of traditional warfare. In the 21<sup>st</sup> century, warfare has assumed new forms; technology has become one of the crucial means of the conquest of the new space, which itself heightens a sense of globalization. The sense of time is also essential for this evolution, so the idea of acceleration becomes significant. In its old form, warfare has largely disappeared, but it has not been totally abolished.

In addition to this exponential multiplication of methods and techniques to improve warfare, peace must also be redefined in the face of the aforementioned changes. This jutting concept of absence of perturbation appears insufficient to Spinoza (1670) to define peace. (On the contrary, Spinoza defines peace as a virtue coming from the strength of soul.) This ideal is always considered, but the goal is almost never reached, except with the intervention of organizations such as the United Nations (an organization which has as its aim international peace and which seeks to facilitate cooperation among nations to achieve improvements in the fields of international rights, international security, economic development, social progress, and human rights) or the League of Nations (an international organization created to protect the peace in Europe at the end of World War I, which seeks disarmament and the prevention of warfare through the principle of collective security, and the resolution of conflicts through negotiation.)   In the vocabulary of traditional warfare, success toward a cool-down could be defined as a win, something usually achieved by the physical extinction of the enemy, by a renunciation of claims, and by surrender. This international agreement and harmony ignores borders but seems prone to difficulties in the coming years.

The concept of limit or borders during these showdowns, organized as a struggle between states, is a very controversial and sensitive issue and will be for years to come. The state is the organized society; it is endowed with a government and is considered a moral authority by other societies identically organized. Recently, two high ranking officers of the Chinese military, Qiao Liang and Wang Xiangsui, collaborated on the writing of a book entitled *Unrestricted Warfare.* A major general in the Chinese Army, Qiao Liang, has been a member of the Writers' Union of China and Assistant Director for the political department to the Army Air Corps.  Wang Xiangsui, another Chinese senior officer, was a political instructor and political commissar who served as a Major in the Army Air Corps. In *Unrestricted Warfare,* the two allude principally to cold warfare to describe Chinese strategy with regard to new conflicts and tensions in the world.

Moving forward, global powers will face the question of which form or forms warfare will take and what the consequences will be for different great powers.

## 2    On New Warfare

Chinese military officers Qiao Liang and Wang Xiangsui redefine warfare in their book *Unrestricted Warfare* vis-à-vis many hostile acts carried out in the upstream and downstream section of cold warfare. They demonstrate that warfare is no more "the use of armed force forcing the enemy to bend to our wishes" but rather "all the ways, which the armed force or not armed, military or not military...use[ ] to force the enemy to submit to its own interests" (1999).

Following many failures and having gone to the front and having been faced with U.S fire power on the battlefield, the Chinese military is trying to proceed differently. Indeed, everything started off with the revolution of weapons. The American military has demonstrated its superiority on the ground with military arms and advanced technologies capable of increasing precision. Americans appear willing to expend vast resources to stay at the forefront of technology. The increase in spending on development in favor of armies raises the question of whether societies want weapons to always be in the forefront of battle. For the U.S., military arms may be seen as evidence of its military lobby, whereas the Chinese adopt military arms as a means.  The consequence of this determination to be armed is illustrated by the United States' becoming 'slaves to technology'; in other words, continuous production and development of military arms can be  ruinous because of the costs involved of maintaining a certain level of technological prowess. Paradoxically, the development of military techniques aims toward weapon reduction in warfare. The prompt evolution of technology on the ground is thus described as the first objective, and states are on a constant quest for new techniques. In part, the weapons selected for development are chosen based on their ability to match weapons already in existence. Qiao Liang's insistence that the "new of today will become the old of tomorrow" (1999) is instructive here: the high technology of any current day is the low technology of its subsequent tomorrows. During the prehistoric time, the bow and the arrow combined to form a determinant weapon, like the sword during the time of barbarism and more modern weapons during civilized times. Qiao and Wang relativize the importance of high technology whatever the warfare domain might be.

Beyond the issue of technological advancements in weaponry, globalization, which is to say the notion of space, is another central issue to new warfare. The space available for occupation on the battlefield is limited. Inevitably, the battlefield will achieve its extreme limit. Qiao Liang and Wang Xiangsui envisage an evolution of the battlefield, an original dimension beyond all borders despite the real ones (sea-ground-space). From this perspective, the battlefield is 'everywhere'. Thus, the battlefield takes a one-dimensional aspect, the control of which requires the production of increasingly sophisticated strategies. From the moment the notion of warfare-without-limits is mentioned, societies must prepare for this cul-de-sac on the ground, and arms can be construed as binding the life of populations. According to the German general and military theorist Carl von Clausewitz (1832), warfare-without-borders includes the greater part of the problems "fog and friction", thus combining the once-distinct elements of ground and the map, strategy, and its concrete application to the real world. As Qiao and Wang (1999) summarize so well, "all the difficulty of the new warfare is to know how to plan and combine classic military arms and new military arms".

The key is to go over the borders, to pass not only the physical borders, but also domains such as economy, finance, religion, and culture to out-do the enemy. Such a combination will go over all the limits of traditional military conflicts. Two examples of this type of warfare can be found in the *Indignés* and *Occupy-Wall-Street* movements. *Indignés* is a non-violent movement that—to date—groups millions of people in a hundred cities to take a variety of actions. The name *'Indignés'* was inspired by the Stephane Hessel's manifesto *'Indignez-vous!'* ('Time for Outrage!') (2010).

One of principal goals of this movement is to transcribe political speech into reality, to put political theory into practice. *Occupy Wall Street* is a pacifist movement of protest against financial capitalism. The movement has been particularly inspired by the Egyptian revolution and the *Indignés* movement in Europe. The members of the Occupy-Wall-Street movement assert that they are the 99% that will not stand for the avidity and corruption of the remaining 1%. This assertion creates a heterogeneous character for the movement that exceeds the setting of Spain's *Indignés*; indeed some rich people have joined the Spanish movement. As a whole, it is concerned with the social inequalities as well as with the ultraliberal system. There is a phenomenal acceleration in the number of actions and growing politicization of these actions. Julien Assange, a member of the group Anonymous, is a perfect representative of this movement. He has gone from the logic of the technical to the logic of the journalist; "The technique is not an end, it is a way" (Bardeau & Danet 2012).

As warfare extends across new domains, it will no longer be an exclusively military concept; instead, "warfare wholly will become civil" (Qiao & Wang 1999). This reality raises two critical points. First, future warfare will enact fewer physical deaths but more 'deaths' of other types. And secondly, warfare is here to stay, permanently.

The nuclear age and the information age of the 20$^{th}$ century gave way to computer-science warfare and precision warfare, which are now yielding to a new type of warfare: cyber war. Back in the 1990s, John Arquilla and John Ronfeldt designed the pleasant concept of cyber war (Arquilla & Ronfeldt 1997). As they define cyber war, it is the major component of security strategy and power. In the current era of permanent instability, Chinese doctrine deals in depth with ways of directly affecting the neuralgic center of the enemy without damaging the rest. The best way is to control and not to kill.

Although the objective of 'zero deaths' suggested both by Arquilla & Ronfeld (1997) and Qiao & Wang (1999) is part of the current discussion, it is presently impossible. The United States' alleged use of micro nuke (or Directed Effect Weapons [DEW]) to take possession of the Baghdad airport illustrates the problem (May 2004). This thermonuclear bomb, which detonates with minimum explosion, gives out radiation that penetrates both buildings and tanks and is instantly fatal to humans. The Chinese, on the other hand, do not necessarily seek to inflict maximum civilian casualties on an enemy, but to create sufficient losses, other than human casualties, within the limits of what is tolerable to the public. They want to conceive discreetly a new art of warfare that combines all the ways to achieve their ends; they anticipate a dramatic change for the future of warfare on all continents. In such an environment, the United States, even with a perfect power on the ground during fighting, will be the most vulnerable: on 3 September 2007, "the Pentagon recognized that an computer network attack (CNA) targeted on its servers had made specialists have to disconnect for some days a part of the informatics network used by the Defense Department"; and Michael McConnell reported to the U.S. Senate that "if a cyber-war broke out today, we would lose it" (McConnell 2010).

Because of this perceived vulnerability, the United States' government has also created a commission to study economics and security in China. The commission's report, which was presented to the chief members of the Senate and of the House of Representatives, has sounded the alarm by explaining that Beijing has put in place specialized cybernetic combat units which have the objective of developing sophisticated computer viruses able to penetrate the defenses of the United States. The work of this commission of inquiry, related to cyber-security and cyber-threats, was initiated by Bill Clinton, former president of the United States (1993-2001), who wanted to eliminate the vulnerabilities of computer systems.

In the context of cyber warfare, the new protagonists on *terra incognita* are hackers, whose principal objective is to seriously threaten the safety of an army or a country. They neither receive vocational military training, nor do they exercise a military profession. (However a few of them work for existing cyber war units in countries like China, the USA, and Israel, for example.) Hackers stand alone in understanding and controlling relevant technology and have, therefore, extended the battlefield. In cyber warfare, the four strategies necessary in any conflict which are recognized by antiquity are: hide, know, delude, and persuade. These strategies can add new dimensions to the capabilities and implications of the new warfare and its techniques. To begin with, if a computer was out of control and incomprehensible, humanity might be at the mercy of an ace computer specialist and/or could be caught up in a huge net. Indeed, all notions of width, depth, and height of operational space have been transformed. Facing such threats, armies alone will be at a disadvantage. For this reason, national security can no longer rely on military strength only, according to Qiao Liang and Wang Xiangsui (1999). The hacker dimension is likely to become the key dimension in any country. There is also a cultural and sociological aspect to this change. The U.S. and the Western world prefer the individuality, which divides and weakens. In China, the group takes precedence over the individual and the State over the private sector. We are forced to admit that the modern concept undeniably favors the Chinese side.

Moreover, the Chinese doctrine recommends the controlled disruption of societies over the annihilation of humanity—a principle which leads to the dissimulated and hidden use of soft weaponry In connection with recent facts (Chinese attacks from the recent decade), this doctrine seems to be now fully applied: "Nowadays, the attacks which are considered as coming from China are evaluated as of necessary seriousness to constitute the other days of warfare" (Qiao & Wang 1999).

This high ranking officer of the Chinese Army, after an analysis of this phenomenon of warfare, sends us to a new question that is not clear: "Who is the enemy? Where is the enemy in the cyber-world?" (Qiao & Wang 1999). And if other countries join and follow China's doctrine, we would have created new forms of threat such as the cyber-terrorist.

## 3   A Discussion of New Methods of Operation

We are witnessing a metamorphosis because of this new form of warfare. This new image is seen as an art. The conduct of warfare is an art similar to that which auscultates its patient. J.F.C Fuller was an officer of British Army and a military historian; he has been the creator of *'artificial clair de lune'*, a battlefield technique which allows the attackers to localize the enemy during nocturnal attacks through the use of projectors (US Army 1945). According to Clausewitz (1832), a nation must now engage fully in any conflict, and the goal should be the complete destruction of the enemy. This idea involves combining all means (military and non-military) to achieve its purposes. The art of warfare will evolve because of the arrival of new players in the current conflicts. The expansion of the battlefield and the fact of conducting the fighting outside the limits are two of the main aspects that result in this change. According to Qiao and Wang (1999) increasing the scope of vision means "going to the other side of the hill to greet the rising sun"; this metaphor puts into practice the idea of a soldier that attacks the enemy face to face while using the strategy of surprise.

The emergence of new tactics and of new reference maneuvers greatly increases; in fact, the possibility of non-military actions threatens the security of nation states; "The international community, which is helpless when facing non-military threats of destruction no less serious than those caused by (conventional) warfare, lacks the least necessary and effective means to limit it" (Qiao & Wang 1999). This objectively accelerates the onset of a 'civil' war situation. Thus, each domain can, at any time, be the trigger of a fierce war between different groups. We can therefore say that the war of the past somehow dies under the trampling by a cooler future, but still remains a war because this results in the same damage as that of an in-fighting war... or even worse.

Therefore, mankind discovers again that peace efforts can be easily undone with a single strike; that is why we see that mankind never 'conquered the war'. The disregard of the rules of nation states induces a loss of legitimacy for the territories. Indeed, the visible (geographical) borders of nation states, the invisible space of the Internet, the international laws, the Ethics rules, and the ethical principles have no deterrent effect on a hacktivist or a terrorist group. Their very discreet movements and actions cause widespread damage. The Internet allows them to harm the social order exponentially. And, as we saw in the previous section, the facts suggest that wars will be permanent and will result in fewer deaths. The war will not even be war, but rather something that we have never considered as an act of war: an exchange of blows and strikes on the Internet, a battle between mass media, a conflict on the currency market which may well leave us speechless and stunned. This is the principle of games. The difficulty of locating the opponent or of understanding the rules of the game also shows the difficulty of localizing warfare.

Therefore, the sense of mistrust expressed by Qiao Liang and Wang Xiangsui (1999) invites us to understand that there is some sort of presumption regarding events but also regarding the thought of the Master of warfare: "Nothing is ever secure. The Only certainty is uncertainty" (Qiao & Wang 1999). Neither the enemy nor the weapons, nor the battlefields will ever be the same. In this situation with so many uncertainties, it must be necessary to define the new rules of the game.

After this famous denunciation, we arrive at the point where the 'addition' of ways would dominate this game. Indeed, it is interpreted according to the views of these high ranking officers of the Chinese military as the art of combination. It is obviously perceived as a lack of understanding from most warlords. It resulted in the failure to understand that crossing all boundaries and all borders is just the preliminary to a revolution in thinking and not the very final goal itself. When facing this entirely new conception of warfare, there is no doubt that the common vision of warfare to which we were accustomed will be shaken. Qiao and Wang (1999) point out "these men who only know to dispose of impressive numbers of troops... who also claim that warfare is to kill, that the art of warfare is the technique to kill". It is precisely in this vision that Qiao and Wang (1999) specify a concept which is however already well known but often forgotten: "If an army prepares too specifically against an enemy, it neglects what is outside of its scope of vision". They must get out of rut made over thousands of years by the conventional vision of warfare. But before doing this, they must overcome all obstacles (political, historical, cultural, and moral) and engage in thorough reflection.

Clearly, the development of techniques by the U.S. military is still insufficient regarding means and ways, especially in terms of military theory. We can see that the art of traditional warfare and combinatorial art are totally different but come closer to each to the other than any other variety of war. Indeed, the aim of the first one is the retreat of its enemy's army while the other aims at the total falling down of a state, while triggering social panic and a governmental crisis. China's strategy is based only on the combinatorial art, especially on the modified definition of the battlefield in which the notion of retirement/retreat is removed. There is nowhere where the opponent can take refuge. This is part of globalization. In addition, Yue Fei, a famous patriot who fought for the dynasty Song of South against the Jurchen's army of dynasty Jin, gives a detailed explanation of the exact use of the combinatorial method: "The excellence of its use comes from the existence of an exceptional will" (Qian 1995).

At this stage, Qiao and Wang (1999) expose a quest for the rule of victory where the idea is to bring the sword to the side of the opponent. Li Shimin, described it very succinctly (Qiao & Wang 1999): "When I make the surprise a rule, the enemy expects a surprise, and then I attack him according to the rule. When I make the rule a surprise, the enemy expects an attack by the rule, then I attack him by surprise" like the tragedy of September 11th, 2001. At this point, Qiao and Wang get into long unconvincing discussions: indeed, they hope to persuade readers that for need to balance the means of the warfare; they should refer to 'the golden ratio'. All nation states follow this rule secretly. During the search for Bin Laden, the U.S. military used enormous resources, but the most effective would have been a cyber-war. We conclude that warfare should affect all aspects of life in countries without us having to call for military action. They can use other means besides military means to complement and enrich, replacing military means to achieve goals which are unattainable by the force of arms only.

The goal is to lead to the full combination of anything off limits. The idea that 'the end justifies the means' is the most important spiritual legacy that warfare can give. However, using all available means to achieve one's goals is not the earliest source of 'thinking out of limits' but it is the clearest. It is precisely at this moment that we understand that limits have a relative meaning. Going beyond limits means precisely going beyond what is understood as limits (whether those limits are physical, spiritual or technical, scientific, psychological, ethical, or moral limits). The notion of overtaking limits is exposed by an outdated ideology. Warfare of the past, as we have seen previously, is the combination with a restricted view. In a few words, we could confirm that the recipe for victory does not exist but if we want to win in warfare, we must follow some rules of survival: "Combining all of the war resources - Requirements rules of victory - A hostile hand to pick the victory" (Qiao & Wang 1999).

The 'out of limits' combination results in various types of combinations. First, there is the 'supra-state' combination that uses a new paradox, where exceeding the limits consists of tolerating any restriction and of going over and above it. For China, the state is equal to the general concept which is equivalent to the entire civilized world. Then there is the 'out of area' combination, which falls somewhere between the concept of supranational combination and the 'out of means' combination. Then, the 'out of means [ways]' combination consists of going far beyond the conventional methods and tools necessary to achieve a goal. The supranational action describes a country as a means and the national action reads into the army as a means and the country as its goal. Finally, the 'out of degrees' combination shows the 'out of bounds [unrestricted]' war; the goal and the result override the method. This leaves us with a vague idea of the necessary basic principles to this type of warfare, as it noted by G. Kennan (1947), a diplomat, political scientist and American historian whose ideas got a big influence on the politics of United States. He became a model of loyalty in the Chinese culture—and for Sun Tzu. Sun Tzu describes the Chinese strategy: how to inquire, estimate, divide, and beat the enemy "without encountering any opposition"; he adds that "principles constitute a code of ethics, but it is not an absolute value", and he recommends "hitting the enemy where it does not expect it and taking him by surprise, avoiding the full and attacking the empty" (Tzu 1910).

The adoption of these principles does not guarantee victory, but not to comply with them would lead to defeat. Let us cite the most likely and the most efficient of those principles. Firstly, we formulate the concept of 'omnidirectionality', which is the main starting point for this ideology. The general principle is that all the factors related to or involved in warfare, such as natural and social spaces, are considered. The implementation of such synchrony controlled by computer science can lead to actions in the same space-time and in different places simultaneously, while considering limited objectives and unlimited resources. All objectives are inherently limited by the means and they should not be expanded. One thing is certain: as soon as the objectives are beyond the available means, defeat is inevitable. As for unlimited means that consist of fulfilling limited objectives, trying to expand the type of resources used and combined to achieve the goals does not mean the immoderate use of means or the use of absolute means. As a last principle, we appeal to the idea of imbalance. It consists of the research hubs of action in a direction opposite to the balanced symmetry, in other words to avoid the brutal face-to-face with the enemy but to exploit its weaknesses.

## 4  Redefined Stakes

The art of warfare requires the pooling of power between nations. This is the main rule to successfully defeat a state. Indeed, the only difference is that the combinations and alliances are made at several levels simultaneously: multi-, supra-state, and off-state. The Asian crisis in 1997 illustrates an ultra-modern battle.  The financial crisis of 2008 is a similar case. The United States interfered in imposing the IMF and laying down the conditions for its own interests. In all of the examples cited in this paper, the aim was to transform a weakness into a strength.

This is due to movements, such as those set out previously, that the Monroe Doctrine was born to address (Monroe 2012). This is summed up by a popular saying: 'America for Americans'. Monroe conceived his doctrine during conflicts between the Americas, the United States, and European powers. However, the Chinese vision does not share the same opinion and says that 'the world belongs to the Chinese'. The Monroe Doctrine was published after seeing the danger threatening the membership of a few states. Monroe translates it as a potential danger. According to Monroe, "It is only when one encroaches on our rights or when we are seriously threatened, that we feel insults and we make preparations for our defense"; then the states remain united and strengthened. We detect, through his doctrine, three fundamental principles: any American intervention into European affairs would be excluded; any intervention by a European power in the American continent would be considered an unfriendly demonstration against the United States; and the American continent must now be considered closed to any subsequent attempt to colonization by European powers. Nowadays, the last two points of the Monroe Doctrine are enforced by the USA, as far as the economic domain is concerned. They have put a strong economic protectionism in place. The Monroe Doctrine mentioned two dangers coming from Europe:

- Russian ambitions in North America, and
- The threat of intervention of the Saint Alliance on the old Spanish colonial empire.

This Doctrine was not put in place as soon as James Monroe was elected, but only at the mid-warfare of the 19th century. The Monroe Doctrine is still in place and retains a timeless dimension. The fears of Russia and of an emerging European power are still among the USA's main concerns. The Asiatic dimension is a more recent addition.

In fact, we are witnessing the exclusion of Europe. Thus, we have Jose Manuel Barroso's speech on the state of the European Union (Barroso 2010). Barroso, a Portuguese politician and the Chief of the European Commission, had identified a few spaces in which to manoeuvre that Europe must consider. On one hand, he considers Asia as an emerging continent and Europe as an overwhelmed country. This suggests that, despite all efforts, EU's responses have not convinced its citizens, markets, and international partners regarding these new challenges yet. On the other hand, Barroso argues that the EU also needs a pro-active trade policy to encourage the opening of new markets. Free trade is the DNA of the European Commission. Barroso's last point is the need for the creation of a federation of nation states, not a super-state, as a post-national step. Moreover, in this commission, German representatives recommended the convening of a convention to be composed of several hundreds of representatives to discuss the objectives and the institutional functioning of the European Union.

The stakes of cyberspace demonstrate the invisibility and the pervasiveness of warfare. Who-ever thinks about battle in (cyber)space, must think in fact in terms of global warfare, defense, and attack, between states or between non-state actors and in terms of sovereignty and rivalries. This virtual space is the subject of a strategy of control or influence, as seen with the laws on Internet and Information flow that are appearing in different countries. Multiple terms in cyberspace transpose the traditional terms of warfare: for example, 'cyberattack', 'cyberdefence', 'cybercops', 'cyberpolice'. The human dimension must not be obscured by a technical vision which is still prevalent today. The computer arm is only a tool and has no positive or negative effect on the human will that operates it.

One of the consequences is the rise of the image of a still very superfluous Occident which is perceived negatively by the non-Occidental world. Indeed, tensions between the United States and China following the Chinese cyber-attacks in 2009 are perfectly expressed by a comment from the Chinese press reported in *Le Monde* (Predoletti 2010): "The campaign of the United States by the free flow of uncensored information on an unrestricted Internet is a disguised attempt to impose their values on other cultures in the name of democracy".

An ultimate vision is described by Eric Przyswa (2010). Pryswa claims that cyber criminality has become a phenomenal world. Millions of people are tricked by cyber fraud or by identity theft. He considers the fact that weaknesses, in terms of expertise, are a problem of education. CNAC (National Anti-Counterfeiting Committee) does not have enough experts to monitor this traffic. It is feared that the analysis devices and control implemented by the majority of experts give priority to "strategizing about the daily dangers, an unreassured world where the risk is always read as a danger and not as an opportunity" (Przyswa 2010). The fight against counterfeiting can be seen as a new or a different type of warfare.

# 5   Conclusion

Finally, humanity is making progress, and it does not imagine that warfare could be a possible court of appeals. In fact, between the last trails of fog of the 19th century, the dawn of the 20th century, and the advent of the 21st century, we make our point about the opening of a new era. Humanity has no reason to be relieved, because we have done absolutely nothing except replace as far as possible bloody warfare by warfare that is not bloody. Traditional warfare has often resulted in several corpses and the blood flooding the different battlefields. The new image of warfare uses the civil technologies and Internet. Consequently, the notion of battlefield becomes out of date. It would explain the absence of blood trail through this virtual fight. The world has become a 'huge battlefield'. Military arms are more modern and, according to the means of each combatant, they have become more sophisticated. Warfare has come out of the domain of the military and has become the story of politicians, scientists, or ecologists. This is demonstrated by a relative reduction in military violence. The future will be accomplished with the technological union and apart from the unrestricted warfare, 'we cannot find the key the most appropriate for this new warfare'.

# References

Arquilla, J & Ronfeldt, D 1997. In Athena's camp: Preparing for conflict in the information age, viewed 24 Dec. 2014, < http://www.rand.org/pubs/monograph_reports/MR880.html>.

Bardeau, F & Danet, N 2012. Anonymous: Pirates informatiques ou altermondialistes numériques, FYP Publishing, Paris.

Barroso, J M 2010. Discours sur l'état de l'Union européenne, viewed 14 Dec. 2014, <http://staging.la-croix.com/Actualite/Monde/Discours-de-Jose-Manuel-Barroso-sur-l-etat-de-l-Union-europeenne-_NG_-2010-09-07-578206>.

Clausewitz, C 1832. On war, trans. M Howard & P.Paret 1989, Princeton University Press, Princeton, NJ.

Hessel, S 2010. Indignez-vous! Indigène éditions, Montpellier, trans. Damion Searls & Alba Arrikha 2011, Quartet Books, London.

Kennan, G 1947 "The sources of Soviet conduct". Foreign Affairs vol. 25, no. 4, pp. 566–582.

May, EH 2011. "Baghdad's neutron bomb and America's nuclear Obama", viewed 18 Feb. 2014, <http://www.veteranstoday.com/2011/04/09/baghdads-neutron-bomb-and-americas-nuclear-obama/>.

McConnell, M 2010. 'On how to win the cyberwar we are losing', Washington Post, 28 February, <http://www.cyberdialogue.ca/wp-content/uploads/2011/03/Mike-McConnell-How-to-Win-the-Cyberwar-Were-Losing.pdf>.

Monroe, J 1823. "The Monroe Doctrine". Basic readings in U.S. democracy. United States Department of State, viewed 24 Dec. 2014 <http://memory.loc.gov/cgi-bin/ampage?collId=llac&fileName=041/llac041.db&recNum=4>.

Pedroletti S 2010. "Washington et Pékin s'affrontent sur Google", Le monde, janvier 2010. Viewed 24 Dec. 2014 < http://www.lemonde.fr/technologies/article/2010/01/23/washington-et-pekin-s-affrontent-sur-google_1295600_651865.html>

Przyswa, E 2010. Cybercriminalité et contrefaçon, FYP Publishing, Limoges.

Qian, C 1995. General Yue Fei, trans. TL Yang, Joint Publishing, Hong Kong,

Qiao, L & Wang, X 1999. Unrestricted warfare. People's Liberation Army. Literature and Arts Publishing House, Beijing, viewed 25 Sept. 2012, <http://www.cryptome.org/cuw.htm >.

Spinoza, B 1670. Tractatus Theologico-Politicus, G. Bell & Son 1883, London.

Tzu, S 1910. The Art of War, Gutenberg Project, viewed 25 Sept. 2013, <http://www.gutenberg.org/ebooks/132>.

US Army Military Intelligence Corps 1945. 'Artificial Moonlight', Tactical and Technical Trends, vol. 57, viewed 25 Dec. 2014, <http://www.lonesentry.com/articles/ttt07/artificial-moonlight.html>.

Ventre, D (ed.) 2010. Cyberwar and information warfare, ISTE Ltd and John Wiley & Sons Inc., New York.

# Hofstede's Cultural Markers in Computer Network Attack Behaviours

## Char Sample and Andre' Ara Karamanian

Carnegie Mellon University, CERT, Cisco Systems, USA
charsample50@gmail.com,
akaraman@cisco.com,
andre377@me.com

*Originally Published in the Proceedings of ICCWS, 2014*

---

**Editorial Commentary**
Could differences in cultures affect how organizations approach and execute cyber operations? In this research study, the authors looked at a set of attacks and examined them to "determine the nature of the relationship between Hofstede's ... cultural dimensions" and the observed behavior patterns. The results indicated both a relationship between behaviors and cultural dimensions as well as a relationship between non-behaviors (those that were not observed) and cultural dimensions. Granted, this study was focused on website defacements that featured nationalistic or patriotic themes, which implies that the actors were probably at best loosely affiliated with each other and not professional warriors (although there may be some debate as to this conclusion). But the point is both interesting and important: the "software of the mind", as Hofstede dubbed culture, impacts how cyber attacks are performed. This could provide a framework for developing strategies for controlling or resisting such attacks. More importantly, taking this type of research further could provide interesting insights into issues associated with structural aspects of organizing, training, and equipping for cyber operations, as well as with the development of cyberwarfare engagement strategies.

---

**Abstract:** Culture, according to Hofstede, Hofstede and Minkov (2010) acts as "software of the mind". This mental software should logically extend into computer network attack (CNA) behaviours. Sample (2013), successfully inferred this relationship when examining the relationship between nationalistic, patriotic website defacements and Hofstede's cultural dimensions. However, Sample's study

(2013) dealt with a limited size data set, and only inferred the relationship between culture and CNA behaviours. This study advances the research by first, using a larger data set, and second, determining the nature of the relationship between culture and the number of these types of attacks. Geert Hofstede's cultural dimensions provide a framework for evaluating and understanding various behaviours. Hofstede's framework has been used in academia and business for research in order to better understand other cultures. Hofstede avails his data for researchers in all disciplines. The goal of this study is to determine the nature of the relationship between Hofstede's power distance index (PDI) and individualism versus collectivism (IVC) cultural dimensions as these behaviours relate to nationalistic, patriotic themed website defacements. The preliminary findings re-affirm the existence of a relationship between high PDI values, low IVC values, and nationalistic, patriotic themed website defacements. The analysed data displayed significant findings across these two dimensions, and a noticeable lack of activity on the opposite end of the dimensional pole was observed. The non-results also suggest a potential link between cultural dimensions and non-behaviours. The tests performed were quantitative and included means comparison tests. Additionally, a new relationship was identified across a third dimension, Long-Term Orientation versus Short-Term Orientation (LTOvSTO). The final analysis will contain both these results and the correlational testing results.

**Keywords:** computer network attack (CNA) behaviours, Hofstede, cultural dimensions, nationalistic, patriotic themed website defacements

# 1   Introduction

Culture according to Hofstede, Hofstede and Minkov (2010) acts as "software of the mind". Baumeister & Masicampo (2010) observed that the role of culture in thought is pervasive. Further Hofstede et al. (2010) identified unlearning habits or automatic thought processing is more difficult than learning the behaviour. Evans (2008) noted the inescapable and habitual role of culture in cognition. Horst (2007) observed that behaviour is oriented by culture, and individual members of a society internalize culture. Furthermore, Buchtel & Norenzayan (2008) said of cultural differences that they are "differences in habits of thought, rather than differences in the actual availability of information processing". This suggests that when a problem is being solved, the path to the solution, and possibly the solution itself, will vary by culture.

Guss (2011) along with Guss & Dorner (2011) determined through microworld simulations, that culture influenced problem perception, strategy development and the decision choices. This observation held even when all subjects had the same information available. Sample (2013), building on the previously mentioned research, inferred that culture influenced CNA behaviours.

When Sample (2013) related culture to CNA behaviours, a small dataset was used and compared against the distribution of Hofstede's dimensional data using a specific type of attack, specifically the nationalistic, patriotic themed website defacement. The original study (Sample, 2013) was unable to examine attack frequencies, in order to perform a correlational analysis. The researchers for this study seek to determine if a correlation exists between culture and CNA behaviours, and if the correlation exists, the nature of that correlation. The remainder of this paper discusses the scope of this study, relevant background information, research methods, hypothesis, results and interpretation of the results.

## 2    Literature review

Hofstede et al. (2010) identified personality as being associated with individual traits, and tied to an individual's psychology. They stated, "these individual traits are influenced by cultural programming, in addition to unique experiences". This study does not examine individual traits, which would be the prevue of psychology, but rather, examined the cultural programming of groups of people executing network attacks. Hofstede et al. (2010) identified cultural programming as one of the two components constructing the personality, and cultural programming as the uniquely identifying component which points to the group the individual is associated, and more powerfully, tendencies that person and the group have.

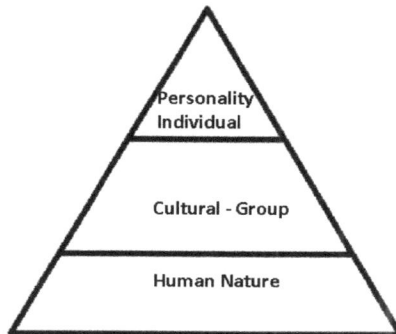

**Figure 15:** Relationship between culture and personality

*Note: This figure is adapted from Hofstede, G., Hofstede, G.J., and Minkov, M. (2010). Cultures and Organizations, McGraw-Hill Publishing: New York, NY.*

Hofstede et al. (2010) noted that the "software of the machines may be globalized, but the software of the minds that use them is not" (p. 391). Sanchez-Franco, Martinez-Lopez, and Martin-Velicia (2008) observed different usage patterns by culture with web-based training. Sample (2013) also observed evidence of the existence of a relationship between the dimensions power distance index (PDI) and individualism versus collectivism (IVC) and nationalistic, patriotic themed website defacements. However, Sample (2013) simply inferred the relationship instead of correlating the relationship.

Hofstede et al. (2010) defined certain behaviours associated with high PDI, such as loyalty, show of strength, preference to 'in group' persons and hostility toward 'out of group' persons. Guess (2004) and Hofstede et al. (2010) observed the relationship between PDI and IVC where they noted that high PDI occurs with low IVC. Sample (2013) also observed the presence of low IVC results in conjunction with high PDI scores.

## 2.1 Power distance index (PDI)

Hofstede et al. (2010) defined high PDI as the expectation and acceptance that "power is distributed unequally" (p. 61). Minkov (2013) noted that power distance is "about treating people differently" based on group membership (Minkov, 2013, p.414). There are several different behaviours associated with this dimension Hofstede et al. (2010) and Guess (2004

This differs somewhat from collectivism that also respects the group but does not necessarily require preferential treatment for the "in group" over the "out group". Hofstede et al. (2010) observed the exchange of protection for loyalty in the high PDI society. Sample (2013) inferred that this exchange would allow attackers to self-identify using the country flag or a similar symbol without fear of retribution.

## 2.2 Individualism versus collectivism (IVC)

Hofstede et al. (2010) identified the majority of people live in a collectivist society. A collectivist society values the betterment of a group, even at the expense of the individual. Hofstede et al. (2010) stated in a collectivist society, individuals associate with the larger group they belong to, up to and including the national level. IVC as a quantitative value is lower in a country with a high degree of collectivism, i.e. IVC increases as individualism increases. As such, a person in a low IVC country (low individualism) comes from a collectivist society. Hofstede et al. (2010) noted that the relationship between IVC and PDI are, in many instances, inversely correlated.

## 2.3 Masculine versus feminine (M/F)

Minkov (2013) defined a society as masculine where "emotional gender roles are clearly distinct" (p. 211). Minkov (2013) distinguished the feminine society when he defined that society as one where "emotional gender roles overlap: both men and women are supposed to be modest, tender, and concerned with the quality of life". In the masculine society men focus on achievement through aggressive means; in the feminine society both men and women focus on achieving success through cooperation.

## 2.4 Uncertainty avoidance index (UAI)

Uncertainty avoidance measures the response of a culture to the unknown or unexpected (Hofstede et al., 2010). High scoring UAI cultures tend to have highly structured processes. Interestingly, they may be less concerned with results ultimately, and more concerned with where they are in the process or roadmap towards a result (Hofstede, 2010). UAI is associated with how people respond to the human condition of ambiguity and the inability to ultimately control and predict all aspects of human existence (Hofstede et al., 2010).

## 2.5 Long-term orientation versus short-term orientation (LTOvSTO)

Hofstede et al. (2010) identified several elements of long-term orientation (LTO). One indicator of long-term orientation was deferment of gratification. Another identified by Hofstede et al. (2010) was humility. Cultures with higher LTO scores tended to consider humility an important cultural treat, while STO countries found it to be less assertive. Interestingly, Hofstede pointed out that countries that have LTO tendencies also tend to consider themselves in the flow of a larger purpose.

## 2.6 Indulgence versus restraint (IVR)

Hofstede et al. (2010) identified several characteristics of indulgence versus restraint. Cultures with high degrees of indulgence placed importance on leisure time, happiness and a sense of control of the choices one could make without cultural reprisal. A restrained society was identified as one that had several cultural norms against indulgent behaviours (Hofstede, 2010).

# 3   Methodology

This observational study relies on statistical analysis of Hofstede's dimensional values data and attributed nationalistic, patriotic themed website defacements from the website www.zone-h.org. The attributed defacements will be grouped by attack originating country, and the number of entries per country will be entered.  There are two tests that will be performed. Means testing of the control group of the full Hofstede set against the collected entries from the zone-h set represents the first test. In this case, means testing is performed on a group collected from a large sample and this test is designed as a second data point to the work done by Sample (2013) with a smaller data set.  All calculations will rely on the vassar-stats website that serves as the companion to Lowry's (2013) *Concepts & Applications for Inferential Statistics.*

The second test, determines if the independent variable, culture, and the dependent variable, the number of website defacements, a type of CNA behaviour, are correlated.  The Pearson correlation is the standard statistical test used to determine the existence of a relationship between variables, specifically in the case of a linear relationship (Cohen, 1988). Urdan (2010) pointed out that Pearson is not well suited for clustered or truncated data sets. For clustered data sets which have ordinal qualities, which the dataset in this sample resembles, Urdan (2010) identifies Spearman as a superior choice. Although upon inspection both correlation methods yield similar tendencies in their results.

This study relies on quantitative analysis involving a control group that is comprised of data found on Hofstede's website, www.geerte-hofstede.com, and two months of nationalistic, patriotic themed website defacements found at www.zone-h.org.  The zone-h data was collected and examined then categorized by country.  There were 1472 samples collected and sorted, in most cases they were all used. Some cases resulted in less usage due to the unavailability of cultural dimension information. Table 1 contains the list of countries represented in the attack set, along with the number of defacements and the six dimensional scores associated with each country. Hypotheses: $H_0$: There is no statistical relationship between culture and nationalistic, patriotic themed website defacements. The alternative hypothesis, $H_1$, states that there is a statistical relationship between culture and nationalistic, patriotic themed website defacements. $H_2$: There is no correlation between nationalistic, patriotic themed website defacements and PDI or any other cultural dimension.. Alternatively, $H_3$ posits: There is a correlation between nationalistic, patriotic-themed website defacements and PDI or any other cultural dimension.

**Table 2:** Attacking countries

| Country | Deface-ments | PDI | IVC | M/F | UAI | LTOvSTO | IVR |
|---------|--------------|-----|-----|-----|-----|---------|-----|
| Algeria | 102 | 80* | 38* | 53* | 68* | 26 | 32 |
| Argentina | 7 | 49 | 46 | 56 | 86 | 20 | 62 |
| Bangla-desh | 17 | 80 | 20 | 55 | 60 | 47 | 20 |
| Brazil | 235 | 69 | 38 | 49 | 76 | 44 | 59 |
| Chile | 1 | 63 | 23 | 28 | 86 | 31 | 68 |
| Ecuador | 9 | 78 | 8 | 63 | 67 | n/a | n/a |
| Egypt | 3 | 70 | 25 | 45 | 80 | 7 | 4 |
| India | 2 | 77 | 48 | 56 | 40 | 51 | 26 |
| Indonesia | 332 | 78 | 14 | 46 | 48 | 62 | 38 |
| Iran | 175 | 58 | 41 | 43 | 59 | 14 | 40 |
| Italy | 11 | 50 | 76 | 70 | 75 | 61 | 30 |
| Malaysia | 21 | 104 | 26 | 50 | 36 | 41 | 57 |
| Mexico | 45 | 81 | 30 | 69 | 82 | 24 | 97 |
| Morocco | 52 | 70 | 46 | 53* | 68 | 14 | 25 |
| Pakistan | 28 | 55 | 14 | 50 | 70 | 50 | 0 |
| Russia | 2 | 93 | 39 | 36 | 95 | 81 | 20 |
| Saudi Ara-bia | 84 | 95 | 20 | 60 | 80 | 36 | 52 |
| Sudan | 32 | 80* | 38* | 53* | 68* | 23* | 34* |
| Syria | 35 | 80* | 38* | 53* | 68* | 23* | 34* |
| Tunisia | 38 | 80* | 38* | 53* | 68* | 23* | 34* |
| Yemen | 241 | 80* | 38* | 53* | 68* | 23* | 34* |

Note: * indicates a value inherited by the Hofstede defined grouping a country belongs to, when a specific value for the independent country was not defined. For this data set the inherited values came for the grouping of Arab countries as defined by Hofstede et al. (2010).

When interpreting the results of a correlation study Cohen's effects size is the standard used to interpret the r score results (Cohen, 1988). According to Cohen (1988) an r score of 0.1 – 0.29 is considered a small correlation, 0.3 – 0.49 is considered a moderate correlation and an r score greater than 0.5 is considered a strong correlation. Since behaviour is being measured, Cohen's effect size will be applied.

# 4 Results figures and tables

The first test relied on a measure of central tendency comparison of the attackers to the control data group. This comparison was performed for each dimension, using the Mann-Whitney U test. When performing this test some countries in the Middle East only had scores for certain dimensions so they were collectively grouped as "Arab countries" for those dimensions. The test was run both with and without the generic Arab countries scores. The hypothesis tested stated that there is no relationship between culture and nationalistic, patriotic-themed website defacements. The initial results were plotted and visually inspected for activity cluster areas and they were compared against Hofstede's distribution for each dimension. The researchers looked for activity across the dimensional ranges. A lack of activity was considered as noteworthy as the presence of activity.

**Table 3:** Mann-Whitney U test results

| Dimension | Z Score | p-value | Hypothesis $H_0$: | Alternative Hypothesis $H_1$: |
|-----------|---------|---------|-------------------|-------------------------------|
| *PDI* | *-2.08* | *0.0188* | *Reject* | *Accept* |
| IVC | 1.34 | 0.0901 | Accept | Reject |
| MF | -0.6 | -0.2743 | Accept | Reject |
| UAI | -1.31 | 0.0951 | Accept | Reject |
| *LTOvSTO* | *1.84* | *0.0329* | *Reject* | *Accept* |
| IVR | 1.06 | 0.1446 | Accept | Reject |

Two dimensions, PDI and LTOvSTO, meet the 0.05 criteria for rejection of $H_0$ and alternative hypothesis $H_1$, acceptance; however, the IVC dimension is close enough to warrant further examination. The UAI dimension is of interest, thus suggesting possible influence, even though this dimension fails to show a statistically significant finding; however, the MF and IVR dimensions appear to have no influence at all on the behaviours.

A closer examination of the PDI dimension shows the range of behaviour that Hofstede recorded. The majority of countries had results in the 30 – 80 range with the greatest amount of activity clustered in the 60s. Figure 2 depicts the distribution that Hofstede recorded for the PDI dimension and Figure 3 depicts the actual attack distribution for the PDI dimension. Figure 2 presents a normal looking distribution with the mode clustering at 60-69. Figure 3 shows the mode of the attackers clustered in the 80-89 values range.

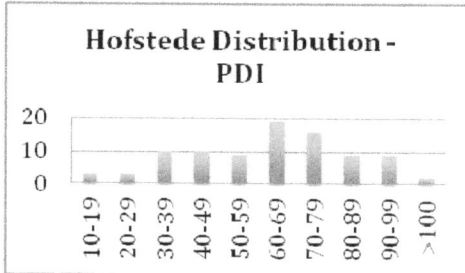

**Hofstede Distribution - PDI**

Figure 16: **Hofstede's Distribution - PDI**

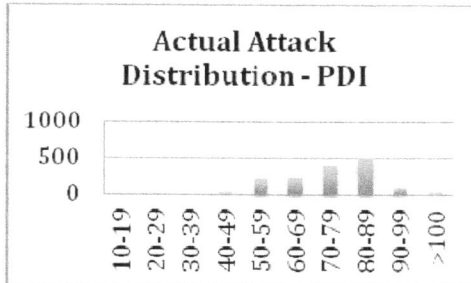

**Actual Attack Distribution - PDI**

**Figure 17:** Actual Distribution of Attacks - PDI

The IVC dimension in this study activity clustered near the collectivist pole of the dimension, values 30-39. Noticeably absent were entries on the individualist pole. Hofstede's distribution for this dimension is bi-modal with modes in the 20-29 ranges, and the second mode in the 60-79 ranges, this is depicted in Figure 4. Figure 5 shows the activity primarily in the 30-39 ranges and a second group in the 10-19 ranges. A lack of activity occurs above the 50 score line. Only one entry exists on the individualist pole, Italy (76). Figure 4 and figure 5 depict the differences between the full distribution, scored by Hofstede and the actual attacks.

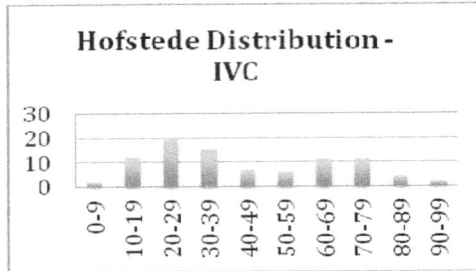

**Figure 18:** Hofstede's distribution - IVC

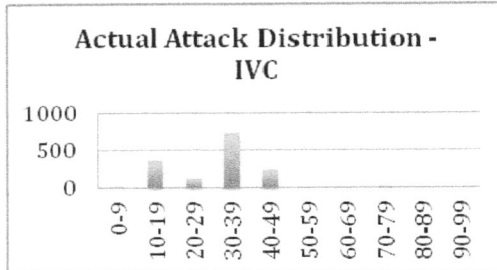

**Figure 5:** Actual distribution of attacks - IVC

The LTOvSTO dimension in this study activity clustered near the STO pole of the dimension, values 20-29. Noticeably absent were entries on the LTO pole. Hofstede's distribution for this dimension is bi-modal with modes in the 20-39 ranges, and the second mode in the 60-69 ranges as illustrated in Figure 6. Figure 7 shows a lack of activity occurring above the 70 score line. Figure 6 and figure 7 also depict the differences between the full distribution, scored by Hofstede and the actual attacks.

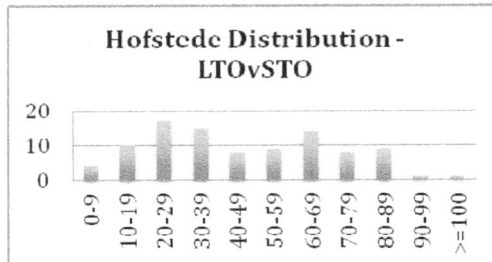

**Figure 6:** Hofstede's distribution - LTO

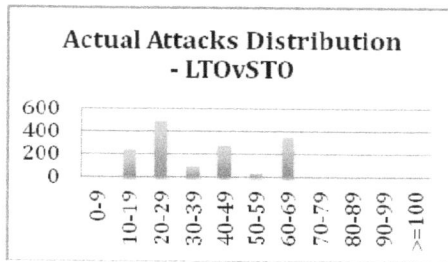

**Figure 7:** Actual distribution of attacks - LTOvSTO

The MF dimension in this study activity clustered near the middle of the dimension, values 40-59. Noticeably absent were entries on either pole. Figure 8 and figure 9 also depict the differences between the full distribution, scored by Hofstede and the actual attacks. While nothing significant was found in this dimension, the lack of activity on either pole suggests relevant non-behaviours.

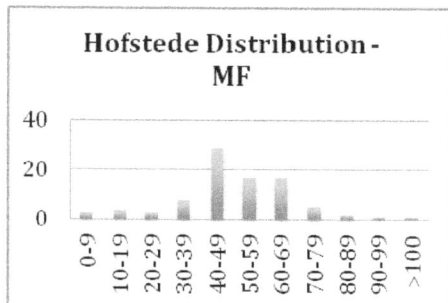

**Figure 8:** Hofstede's distribution - MF

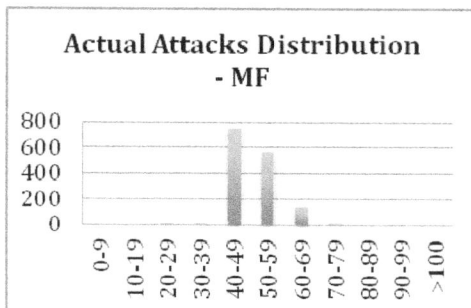

**Figure 9:** Actual distribution of attacks - MF

The UAI dimension in this study activity clustered near the middle of the dimension, values 60-69. Noticeably absent were entries on the low UAI end of the pole. Hofstede's distribution for this dimension is skewed to the high UAI end with the mode in the 80-89 ranges as illustrated in Figure 10. Figure 11 shows a lack of activity occurring below the 30 score line. Figure 10 and figure 11 also depict the differences between the full distribution, scored by Hofstede and the actual attacks.

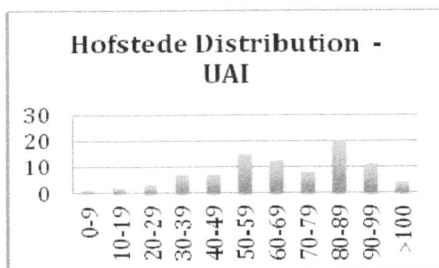

**Figure 10:** Hofstede's distribution - UAI

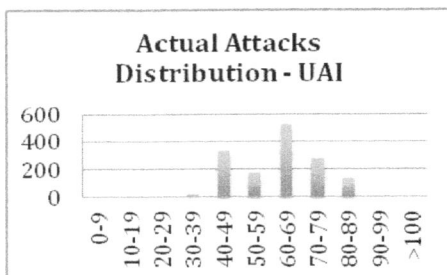

**Figure 11:** Actual distribution of attacks - UAI

The IVR dimension in this study activity clustered near the restrained pole of the dimension, values 30-39. Noticeably absent were entries on the indulgence pole, with the exception of Mexico (100). Hofstede's distribution for this dimension is slightly skewed toward the restrained pole the mode in the 40-49 ranges as illustrated in Figure 12. Figure 13 shows a lack of activity occurring above the 60 score line. Figure 12 and figure 13 also depict the differences between the full distribution, scored by Hofstede and the actual attacks.

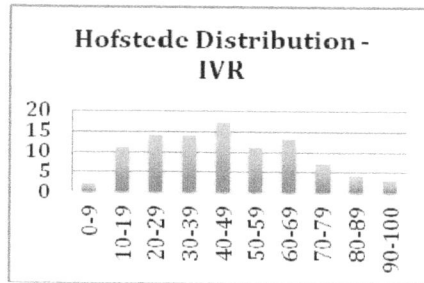

**Figure 12:** Hofstede's distribution - IVR

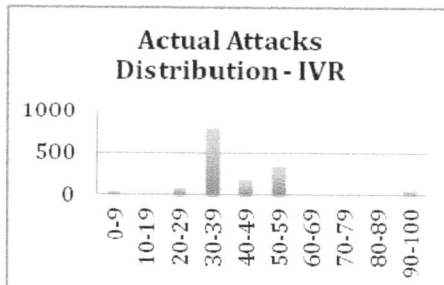

**Figure 13:** Actual distribution of attacks - IVR

The Spearman correlation is used to determine if the independent variable, culture, correlates with the dependent variable, CNA behaviours. For this analysis, the dependent variable is represented by number of attacks, and this number was compared against the six different cultural dimensions. When evaluating the Spearman's correlation, the Cohen effects size standard is used in determining the strength of the relationship. The data were grouped into intervals delimited by 10 and the pairs were set to these interval values. For example, a score of 16 would be part of the 10 scoring range. The x–axis was the interval representation and the y-axis was the number of attacks in the interval range. Table 3 shows the results of the Spearman correlation for each dimension.

**Table 3:** Spearman correlation results

| Dimension | T | r | Evaluation (Cohen) | $H_2$ | $H_3$ |
|---|---|---|---|---|---|
| *PDI* | *2.63* | *0.681* | *Strong* | *Reject* | *Accept* |
| *IVC* | *-2.53* | *-0.6669* | *Strong* | *Reject* | *Accept* |
| MF | -0.26 | -0.0858 | None | Accept | Reject |
| UAI | 0.89 | 0.2838 | Weak | *Reject* | *Consider* |
| *LTOvSTO* | *-2.45* | *-0.6331* | *Strong* | *Reject* | *Accept* |
| *IVR* | *-0.58* | *-0.2025* | *Weak* | *Reject* | *Consider* |

The results appear to show a strong positive correlation between PDI and the number of nationalistic, patriotic themed website defacements. A strong negative correlation was observed between IVC and nationalistic, patriotic-themed website defacements. Also a slightly less but still strong negative correlation was observed between LTOvSTO and nationalistic, patriotic themed website defacements. The weak relationships between the number of defacements and the UAI and IVR dimensions suggest the need for further studies. The remaining dimension, MF appears to have no direct influence on this behaviour, although an interesting observation is the lack of activity at either dimensional pole.

# 5   Conclusion

This study is observational in nature. Therefore, the use of correlation is an appropriate and common tool to that end. The resultant report shows that correlations have been identified between CNA behaviours and culture. The correlations between the number of defacements and high PDI and low IVC build on the findings from Sample (2013).

Hypothesis testing affirmed both inferential and correlational relationships between the defacements and the dimensions PDI and LTOvSTO for both $H_0$ and $H_2$ resulting in acceptance of $H_1$ and $H_3$ for these dimensions. Hypothesis testing for $H_2$ also affirmed a strong correlation between IVC and the defacements, resulting in acceptance of $H_3$ for IVC. Hypothesis testing for $H_2$ and the dimensions UAI and IVR suggested the existence of a weak relationship between variables; this resulted in rejection of $H_2$ and consideration of $H_3$ but not full acceptance. This suggests the need for further study in order to determine the nature of the relationship. Even the acceptance of $H_2$ on the MF dimension raises questions about further research due to the lack of activity on either dimensional pole.

While correlation does not imply causation this study can compel one to attempt to draw connections, and attempt to make predications. A predictive study preforming regressions is a suggested further study. In spite of the observational method of this study, the remainder of the conclusion will include some analysis beyond simple observation, and attempt to offer suggestions that might possibly explain the observations.

The tendency for individuals to associate themselves with the larger group in low IVC, high collectivist cultures (Hofestede, 2010) is consistent behaviour nationalistic self-identification of the attacker executing the defacement. Additionally the display of power of the in-group, i.e. the nation successfully executing the attack, is also consistent with high PDI behaviour (Hofestede, 2010). Furthermore, in the high PDI society, loyalty is rewarded (Hofstede et al., 2010). The relationship between the junior partner and the senior partner are one example of the "mutual and complimentary obligations" (Hofstede et al., 2010, p.80) between both partners. Sample (2013) suggested that the hackers performing nationalistic, patriotic-themed website defacements from high PDI countries do so as an expression of loyalty. The results of this study along with the strong results in PDI for all of the tests, appears to support that observation.

The correlation between STO and these website defacements was not anticipated, but was not surprising. Hofestede (2010) identifies several STO or opposite pole behaviours of LTO identified which could associate with the observed defacements. Of those behaviours, Hofestede (2010) identifies LTO as being identified as with humility. One might assert a statement of *'Your site has been rooted by country-x hackers'* with a large flag is arguably the inverse of humility and by transference, the inverse of LTO. Practically, this might suggest that a nationalistic website attack may be an end in and of itself, and not part of a broader cyber-attack campaign. Determining the motivations behind website defacements goes beyond the scope of this study, but provides a starting point for future studies.

This line of research is still very immature. Questions remain about multinational groups such as Anonymous. This study suggests that even in an organization that is as diverse as anonymous, those that identify with a high power distance may be more likely to engage in website defacements that are critical of the adversary and willing to show loyalty to the cause. This could be examined in further studies.

The other area that has yet to be explored is existence of groups within countries such as Sunnis and Shiites. The possibility that each of these groups will use similar tactics, techniques and procedures is very high, but has yet to find empirical support. This study could provide input for such a follow-on study.

This study, while limited in scope, offers insights that can be used to assist in building the foundation for additional research in the area of cross-discipline research into Cyber security and the behavioural sciences. Nationalistic, patriotic-themed website defacements and their strong relationship to culture provides an initial building block that may be compared against other behaviours. All of these must be considered in the context of related political events and activities.

The immediate short term use of this study details cultural characteristics of countries that engage in these types of attacks, and may provide context to attack victims, cyber defenders or other interested parties. While this area offers great promise, much more research is needed in order to draw specific conclusions. Other attack types will also need to be evaluated and longer-term studies both quantitative and qualitative may offer greater insights to the role of culture in CNA behaviours.

# References

Baumeister, R.F., and Masicampo, E.J., (2010) "Conscious Thought is for Facilitating Social and Cultural Interactions: How Mental Simulations Serve the Animal-Culture Interface", *Psychological Review,* Volume 117, No. 5, pp. 945-971.

Buchtel, E.E. and Norenzayan, A., (2008). "Which Should You Use, Intuition or Logic? Cultural Differences in Injunctive Norms About Reasoning", *Asian Journal of Social Psychology,* Volume II No.4, pp. 264-273. doi:10.1111/j.1467_839x.2008.00266.x.

Cohen, J. (1988). *Statistical Power Analysis for the Behavioral Sciences 2nd Edition,* Lawrence Erlbaum Associates, Publishers: New York, NY.

Evans, J.S.B.T. (2008). Dual-processing Accounts of Reasoning, Judgement and Social Cognition, *Annual Review Psychology,* Volume 59, pp. 255-278, doi: 10.1146/annurev.psych.59.103006.093629.

Geert-hofstede website (2013). Retrieved from http://www.geert-hofstede.com.

Guess, C.D. (2004). "Decision Making in Individualistic and Collectivist Cultures", *Online Readings in Psychology and Culture,* Volume 4, Retrieved from http://scholarworks.gvsu.edu/orpc/vol4/issl/3

Guss, C.D. and Dorner, D. (2011), "Cultural Differences in Dynamic Decision-Making Strategies in a Non-linear, Time-delayed Task", *Cognitive Systems Research,* Volume 12, No.3, pp. 365-376 Retrieved from http://dx.doi.org/10.1016/j.cogsys.2010.12.003

Hofstede, G., Hofstede, G.J., and Minkov, M. (2010). *Cultures and Organizations,* McGraw-Hill Publishing: New York, NY.

Horst, P. R. (2007). *Cross-cultural Negotiations,* Air War College, Air University. Retrieved from http://citeseerx.ist.psu.edu/viewdoc/download?doi=10.1.1.184.6790&rep=rep1&type=pdf

Lowry, R. (2013). *Concepts & Applications for Inferential Statistics,* Vassar College: Poughkeepsie, NY.

Minkov, M. (2013). *Cross-cultural Analysis,* Sage Publications: Thousand Oaks, CA.

Sample, C. (2013). "Applicability of Cultural Markers in Computer Network Attack Attribution", *Proceedings of the 12$^{th}$ European Conference on Information Warfare and Security,* University of Jyvaskyla, Finland, July 11-2, 2013, pp. 361-369.

Sanchez-Franco, M.J., Martinez-Lopez, and Martin-Velicia, F. (2009). "Exploring the Impact of Individualism and Uncertainty Avoidance in Web-based Training: An Empirical Analysis in European Higher Education", *Computers & Education,* Volume 52, pp. 588 – 598.

Urdan, T. C. (2010). *Statistics in Plain English 3$^{rd}$ Edition,* Routledge Taylor & Francis Group: New York, NY.

Zone-h website (2013). Retrieved from http://www.zone-h.org.

# Virtual NonState Actors as Clausewitzian Centers of Gravity: An Examination for Sensemaking, Elaboration and Discussion

## Larisa Breton

The University of the District of Columbia, Washington, D.C., USA
larisa.breton@gmail.com

*Originally Published in the Proceedings of ICIW, 2012*

**Editorial Commentary**

Building upon the previous paper's exploration of the cultural aspects of patriotic website defacements, Larisa Breton considers the problem of understanding the groups that are likely actors in those attacks. Intriguingly, the exploration is not just in and of themselves as entities, but through the lens of the Clausewitzian concept of centers of gravity (CoG).

As explained by Antulio Echevarria in his essay, "Clausewitz's Center of Gravity: It's Not What We Thought", (*Naval War College Review*, Winter 2003, Vol. LVI, No. 1, available online at http://www.au.af.mil/au/awc/awcgate/navy/art4-w03.htm) a "CoG is more than a critical capability; it is the point where a certain centripetal force seems to exist, something that holds everything else together." This is different than a strength: it is a unifying factor, one that inspires connectivity of though and actions. Conceptually, if the center were to be successfully attacked and destroyed, the system would collapse. Thus, it is a concept that is worthy of exploration.

Nonstate actors have increasingly used information technologies to create the connectivity, and thus the unifying motivation, for their community of influence. As IT-enabled connectivity has expanded in speed, multimedia aspects, and reach, the effect of this connectivity has become something of a force majeur. For example, the use of social media and websites by groups such as Al Qaeda and the self-named Islamic State is recognized to be a powerful recruitment and motivation mechanism. But these groups have a physical presence and are primarily operating as non-state actors in the real world.

Virtual non-state actors have emerged that exist in online venues and operate primarily in the information domain. A primary example is Anonymous: a global group of individuals, most of whom do not know each other, that (mostly) agree that action is needed, focused on what has been characterized as "Internet censorship is bad," although some element of group enforced social justice seems to also be a motivating factor. (Crenshaw, Adrian. "Crude, Inconsistent Threat: Understanding Anonymous, http://www.irongeek.com/i.php?page=security/understanding-anonymous). The intriguing aspect of Anonymous is that is exists as a group only as an online presence: it is truly a Virtual non-state actor, but one with impressive reach. That such a diverse and global group of people could self-organize online tends to lend support to the notion of a Center of Gravity, and thus is worth exploring.

In this analysis, Breton uses a geologic metaphor, that of islands, to explore how these emergent actors affect the rest of the environment. Her conclusions are that virtual non-state actors have the potential to affect both warfare and governance. The question that remains is how the life-cycle of a virtual non-state actor affects the perpetuation of the community, but this is a question that requires a lot more data. Conceivably, virtual non-state actors could be organized similarly to flash mobs, coming in and going out of existence relatively quickly, based on the emergence of a very large CoG with a short lifespan. Research into emergent behaviors may provide future insight into this possibility.

**Abstract**: Against traditional interpretations of Clausewitzian centers of gravity, we seek to examine the characteristics and behaviors of NonState Actors (NSAs) who operate in the virtual realm. These NSAs, such as leaked-documents repository Wikileaks, hacker group Anonymous, public-statements platform Twitter, and multinational corporations such as Google, create centers of gravity in cyberspace that may affect the entire political spectrum from diplomacy to kinetic warfare. Their aims may be disparate, but 'virtual NSAs' (VNSAs) increasingly affect the geopolitical battlespace. More specifically, we seek to examine the ways in which these VNSAs create spheres of influence, manipulate the public and the public sector, and are forming a hardened constraints-set for strategic and operational planning. Famously, many VNSAs are unaligned with geopolitical entities. How, then, may they be considered? What are some functional categories that may be applied to the creation of taxonomy when examining VNSAs? This paper is a qualitative examination, which is to say that it is not the examination of the less-tangible characteristics of a dataset in a Cartesian analysis. This paper attempts to examine the qualities of VNSAs themselves so that Center of Gravity (COG) analysis, when it is relevant, may be accurately applied.

**Keywords**: Clausewitz, Virtual NonState Actors, NonState Actors, Wikileaks, Twitter, Google, nonkinetic warfare, cyber, cyberwar, net-enabled warfare, center of gravity, qualitative analysis

# 1 Introduction: VNSAs and mountains

**From Joint Publication 3-0:**
**Center of gravity. The source of power that provides moral or physical strength, freedom of action, or will to act. Also called COG. (JP 1-02. SOURCE: JP 3-0)**

This paper begins with a question: Why pay attention to Virtual NonState Actors as potential Centers of Gravity from a Clausewitzian perspective? It may first be useful to examine Virtual NonState Actors (or VNSAs) from a taxonomic perspective and to use the widest possible lens. VNSAs occur in all realms of human activity: Governance, military, politics, social organization, economic, education, commerce, religion and communication all contribute to; transact with; and are affected by VNSAs.

Virtual Non-State Actors themselves are Internet-enabled entities comprised of commercial/non-commercial, governmental/nongovernmental, social [shared]/and social [private networked] entities and commercial/non-commercial entities, et cetera, in innumerable configurations (Turner, ed, p. 144-5). They are all organized around electronic and Internet-enabled activity and exist within and without the cyber realm. They may be considered within a whole-of-systems perspective as stakeholders with multiple stakeholding relationships and ties [as opposed to dyadic relationships within one society or one group of consumers] (Rowley, p. 888-890) and certainly they are actors within Actor-Network Theory (Brown, p. 5).

Before turning to how VNSAs may be considered Centers of Gravity (COGs), a different type of examination may be useful. Due to their relative recency (liberally considered; 100 years from the beginnings of an installed electro/communications grid in the United States), VNSAs could be considered new sprouts, new growths of the evolution of our human technological innovation. However: these organizations have deeper roots (brick-and-mortar, physical and profound social antecedents) than mere technological innovates. They are ubiquitous but in some cases of disproportionate influence and relevance to social life (Zúniga, 2008). They are of changing functionality and disposition. Therefore, it may be useful to consider VNSAs as mountains that protrude from the Earth's crust. This geologic analogy is of use so that VNSAs may be examined as physical entities in order to de-mystify them, and to place them in a physical frame for ease of examination with respect to their potential impact on strategic planning.

Generally, mountains are more recent than the rest of the landscape. Their creation comes from profound upheaval and a change-state occurring from powerful developmental forces. They dominate (Rockies) or cohere (Appalachians) our landscape. They evolve over time. They're subject to internal and external influences, get tunneled, dynamited, isolated by moving oceans into islands and eroded into sand. Similarly, VNSAs are more recent than the rest of the social landscape. Their creation comes from a profound upheaval and a change-state occurring from powerful developmental forces (the social change occurring as a direct result of the near-ubiquity of the Internet). They are evolving over time. They're subject to internal and external influences, though at this stage in their evolution, VNSAs are still quite protean.

Now, consider these direct analogues.
- Mountain-Islands and People. Peaky islands, isolated by oceans on which individual cultures thrive. Real world, real islands, real oceans, Hawaii. Virtual world, virtual islands, oceans of ideology, opinion and preference, SecondLife; but each mountain/island configuration supports real people and real culture, each subject to the same vicissitudes, joys and challenges.
- Mountains and Embedded Infrastructure. PayPal as the Alps: enormous, solid, bound by the constraints of the financial system as the Alps are constrained by year-round cold at their heights; moving slowly but with sudden jumps forward after enough pressure has been brought to bear [glaciers, Sarbanes Oxley regulation]; subject to sudden recursions in their usual state [avalanches; wild swings in currency exchange] and incursions [roadway tunnels; hackers].

- Mountains and Change. Wikileaks as the temporary rock peak of Mount Vesuvius-as-the-press; or pick your favorite active volcano that has an historic role in shaping the society around it [the free press construct]; smolders daily; and pukes occasional flaming chunks of magma as evidence of enormous conflict roiling within – to the detriment of those it strikes and watched closely by everyone else for signs of the next explosion. It's too-soon-to-say whether Wikileaks is here for good, adding several feet to the mantle of cognition about what the press is and what it's supposed to do (Breton&Pearson, 2010), or whether its explosion will create mini-vents around it [OpenLeaks and its ilk]. It's also too soon to predict whether an explosion will lay waste to the countryside [profound paradigm change]; or whether its effluvium will eventually become the compost for future generations' fruitful efforts. Perhaps all of these things will occur.

The author sincerely wishes to quickly, and concisely, treat VNSAs *physically* so that a common analytical presumption may be left by the wayside. VNSAs are not different, or special, because they are cyber-enabled. They are different and special because of their ubiquity, their asymmetric effect, their multi-functionality, and their direct relationship to *people* in a potential battlespace.

## 2 Considering influence; functionality; and asymmetry in recent examples

This extended metaphor attempts to describe Virtual NonState Actors as entities that exist and function for any number of reasons, organic or manmade; that may assume one or more states of being during their existence; and that may encourage or inhibit human activity writ large in any construct you can imagine. Not least, they are subject to elaboration, change, recursion, other destructive forces, and evolution. They're here, they're extremely relevant as systemic actors (Arquilla, p. 25) which are a source of deep and wide interconnectedness (Echevarria, p. 113) that may produce confluences of power (p. 112), and they may or may not be permanent. They also interact with each other. Latour writes, "It is an association between entities which are in no way recognizable as being social in the ordinary manner, except during the brief moment when they are reshuffled together" (p. 65). For purposes of sensemaking, Moore (p. 103-4) observes that synthesizing and interpreting partial answers as part of a multi-methodological approach that incorporates considering "issues from multiple points of view created from the intersections of action- and process-focused vantage points and the perspectives of the individual and the collective" is an effective way to make sense of extremely complex issues. How then shall we consider making sense of or applying Clausewitzian COG analysis to these extremely complicated entities?

Clausewitz writes, "The detailed knowledge of a few engagements is more useful than the general knowledge of a great many campaigns" (Principles of War, p. 68). Therefore, it may be useful to examine a few very recent events involving VNSAs and their valence in a potential battlespace due to their ability to wield political influence over populations; their functionality with respect to physical and social infrastructure; and not least, their asymmetric effect. These meet the Joint Publications definition of a COG as a source of power, moral strength and will to act; but they also possess an operational capability that may have strategic or operational effect as COGs based on their agency (Echevarria, 110).

In August 2011, Twitter users Gilberto Martinez Vera and Maria de Jesus Bravo Pagola caused public chaos in Veracruz, Mexico when they allegedly announced via Twitter that drug gangs and/or Mexican authorities had kidnapped children from school grounds and that a helicopter had opened fire on another elementary school's grounds (BBC). Mexican reaction was swift and draconian; the pair were arrested for terrorism and face exemplar criminal penalties of 30 years in prison (BBC). Here, we see a public-statements platform, Twitter, used as a vehicle for political influence and incitement by ordinary citizens. It is used as the *means* or the carrier, the kinetic object itself not subject to any curation or governance, in which a meme was loosed upon a body politic. The ordinary citizens achieved amplification of their meme with asymmetric effect upon the body politic and achieved, at least temporarily, one of the three "main objectives" of warfare, "to gain public opinion" (Clausewitz, Principles of War, p. 45). Twitter, itself, was more than the Lines of Communication (LOC) or the rails upon which the locomotive sat (Eikmeier, p. 5) – it was an operational COG. As a sub-example, Twitter's subsequent announcement in February 2012 that it will selectively censor in countries that find certain political expressions objectionable underscores Twitter's role as an operational COG (as opposed to a center of capability) for two reasons. First, by its announcement Twitter has firmly established its own political will with respect to global engagement. It is more than a high-volume platform for others' expressions. It is its own political entity. Second, Twitter users' need to resort to metonymic and synecdochic expressions in now-censored environments underscore, and amplify, the intrinsic politicization of message as a direct result of the political will expressed by the VNSA.

Turning to our second example, in April 2010, the Microsoft Corporation either accidentally or intentionally aided the government of the Republic of Kyrgyzstan during its revolution, by alleging a violation of Microsoft's Terms of Service and use of pirated software at an independent television station in neighboring Kazakhstan – not incidentally, the only media outlet providing coverage of the revolution; as all televised and online activity within Kyrgyzstan had been quashed (Farrell, 2010). Microsoft effectively took the television station offline thus rendering the main source of independent information about and into Kyrgyzstan unable to function. Unlike the more transparently State-encouraged shutting-off of the Republic of Georgia's Internet connectivity prior to the Russian incursion into Ossetia in 2008 as an actual war act; we have here a commercial actor, operating in the virtual realm, with fingers in equipment; software; and public communication; leveraging a utility it controls to influence baseline State functioning. Arquilla writes, "Indeed, the new paradigm for conflict implies that information dominance will win wars, as the uninformed may lose their ability *to* fight" (p. 26). Whether Russia itself played a part in leveraging Microsoft to leverage Kyrgyzstan is disputed (Carr, 2010).

It is also important to note that the brand identities of VNSAs and their intrinsic relationship to our human identities online (Palfrey&Gasser, 2008) means that, in addition to political influence, VNSAs may choose to wield and rely on *personal* influence. Taking Wikileaks as a third example, "Wikileaks frequently leverages its position by relying on the horizontal, emotional relationships that bind online communities, knowing that adherents and devotees will tweet, post, and blog about Wikileaks-offered topics. This has the effect of amplifying the reach, and the resonance, of Wikileaks' topics" (Breton&Pearson, 2010, p 11).

It is important to re-state that bodies corporate wielding as much or more political power than geopolitical entities is nothing new: think of the East India Tea Company and its trading power with a nascent modern China; or think of China's trading power with a nascent Google, as you prefer. Microsoft's action in Kyrgyzstan, motivated as it may have been by commercial and/or political considerations; *or by nothing at all*; certainly meets considerations of asymmetry by employing economy of force (Murdock, 88), political influence over a nation-state itself with subsequent consequence to a population; and infrastructural functionality. In this instance, the critical national infrastructure itself was the *mode* (target) of activity. In the first instance, Twitter was the *means* of activity. In addition to asymmetric, politically influential and infrastructural effects of VNSAs in a battlespace they also must be considered as a *means*, the vehicle, for activity and as a *mode*, the target itself, of the activity, on an offensive or defensive axis. (Figure 1)

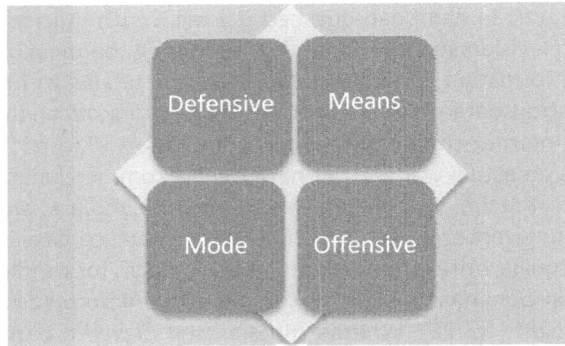

**Figure 1:** Quadrant of activity: Means and mode: Offense and defense

# 3   Key differences in VNSAs as COGs

What's different here is the essential quality of the actors more so than their cyber-enabled creation: VNSAs are protean, multipurposed, and may not possess single "critical capability" or "critical requirement" (Eikmeier, p. 4) that places them in to, or out of, any of the conditions to be met by COGs at any given time. (Figure 2)

| Actionability | Mass | Ideology/Opinion |
|---|---|---|
| Echevarria | Murdock | Smart |
| Arquilla | Arquilla | Brown |
| Eikmeier | Eikmeier | Latour |

**Figure 2:** Categories of functional consideration for VNSAs

Nor are VNSAs necessarily sources of ideological strength commonly viewed as COGs in counterinsurgent operations (Smart, 2005; Kilcullen, 2010) though they may be the repositories for ideology or platforms supporting the actions of ideologues. VNSAs also may be, knowingly or unknowingly, the attack vector by which malicious actors attack the people or critical infrastructure of a country in violation of international law (Lotrionte, 2012). However, their potential to be these things at various times; considered along with their necessity to people or to critical infrastructure functioning; as well as the voluntary relationship people have to VNSAs (Brown, p. 5-7) *make them actors in a system as opposed to elements that will remain knowable for planning purposes.*

# 4    Summary and conclusion

In summary, Virtual NonState Actors (VNSAs) are recent, but important, additions to the canon of human institutions. The author used a geologic metaphor in order to concisely express that due to their relative novelty as human institutions, VNSAs have a *human* constraints factor comparable to island-states; an *institutional* binding comparable to glacial activity; and a *dynamism* comparable to the potential destructiveness and fertility of volcanic activity. New or not, like all other human institutions, VNSAs effect, and are affected by, governance and warfare. To paraphrase Hammes, "If the enemy is going to strike across the spectrum of human activity" in fourth-generation warfare characterized by net-enabled warfare; military-civilian confrontation (Hammes); global insurgencies (Kilcullen); and full-spectrum engagements in resource-constrained circumstances (Arquilla); then the multiple potential roles and qualities of Virtual NonState Actors as Centers of Gravity in the battlespace are worth considering, naming, and including in planning scenarios.

It is important to articulate, in conclusion, some functional categories that may be applied to the creation of taxonomy when examining VNSAs. VNSAs' multiple potential roles include their ability to express their own political will; to serve as a communications platform; to be an intentional or a co-opted attack vector; to wield political influence; to affect key infrastructural functioning; to provide critical vending services and capabilities; to create and/or maintain horizontal-emotional relationships; to be effects multipliers; to be content and knowledge repositories; and others. It is important to note that some or all of these potential roles might be expressed simultaneously by a single VNSA at any given time. VNSAs are actors in a system, as opposed to static 'elements' upon which planners can rest assumptions. Therefore, it is essential for strategic planners to perpetually consider this multiple functionality *without respect to the VNSA's country of origin, its intended audience, or its stated commercial or political position.*

# References

Arquilla, J, 2004. "The Strategic Implications of Information Dominance," Strategic Review, Summer 2004, pp 24-30.

Breton, L and Pearson A, 2010. "Contextual Truthtelling to Counter Extremist-Supportive Messaging Online: Wikileaks and the Role of the Individual Interventionist," Small Wars Journal Blog. [online] <smallwarsjournal.com/blog/journal/docs-temp/595-bretonpearson.pdf> (Accessed on 09/01/2011)

Brown, J et al, 2007. "Word of Mouth Communication within Online Communities: Conceptualizing the Online Social Network," Journal of Interactive Marketing, Vol 21, No 3, Summer 2007, pp 2-19.

Carr, J, ed, 2012. Inside Cyber Warfare. Lotrionte, C, Active Defense for Cyber: A legal framework for covert countermeasures. Sebastopol: O'Reilly Media, Inc.

Carr, J, 2010. "Microsoft Denial On Kyrgyzstan Censorship Conflicts With The Facts," Forbes Magazine Online Edition. [online] <http://www.forbes.com/sites/firewall/2010/04/14/microsoft-denial-on-kyrgyzstan-censorship-conflicts-with-the-facts/> (Accessed on 08/15/2011)

Clausewitz, CV. Principles of War. Dover Publications, Inc., 2003.

Echevarria, AJ, 2003. "Clausewitz's Center of Gravity: It's Not What We Thought," Naval War College Review, Vol LVI, No 1, 2003.

Echevarria, AJ. "Center of Gravity Recommendations for Joint Doctrine," Joint Forces Quarterly, pp 10-17, Issue 35.

Eikmeier, DC, 2004. "Center of Gravity Analysis," Military Review, pp 2-5, July-August 2004.

Farrell, J, 2010. "Microsoft Denies Involvement in Kyrgyzstan Revolution," TechEye.Net Online Edition. [online] <http://news.techeye.net/software/microsoft-denies-involvement-in-kyrgyzstan-revolution> (Accessed on 09/01/2011)

Hammes, TX, 1994. "The Evolution of War: The Fourth Generation," Marine Corps Gazette, September 1994.

Hauser, M, Chomsky, N et al. "The Faculty of Language: What is it, who has it, and how did it evolve?" Science, Vol 298, No 1569, 2002.

Kilcullen, D, 2010. Counterinsurgency. Oxford: Oxford University Press.

Latour, B, 2005. Reassembling the Social: An Introduction to Actor Network Theory. Oxford: Oxford University Press.

Migliorini, J, 2011. "Mexico 'Twitter Terrorism' Charges Cause Uproar," BBC Online Edition. [online] <http://www.bbc.co.uk/news/world-latin-america-14800200> (Accessed on 09/13/2011)

Moore, DT. Sensemaking: A Structure for an Intelligence Revolution, Chapter 6. National Defense Intelligence College Press, 2010.

Murdock, P, 2002. "Principles of War on the Network-Centric Battlefield: Mass and Economy of Force," Parameters, Spring 2002, pp 86-95.

Palfrey, J and Gasser, U, 2008. Born Digital: Understanding the first generation of digital natives. New York: Basic Books.

Smart, CL, 2005. "The Global War on Terror: Mistaking Ideology as the Center of Gravity," Center for Strategic Leadership Issue Paper, Vol 08-05, July 2005.

Tecuci, G, Boicu, M et al. 2002. "Development and Deployment of a Disciple Agent for Center of Gravity Analysis," Proceedings of the Fourteenth Annual Conference on Innovative Applications of Artificial Intelligence, IAAI Press/The MIT Press.

Turner, BS, ed. 2009, The New Blackwell Companion to Social Theory. Law, J Actor Network Theory and Material Semiotics. Blackwell Publishing, Ltd.

Rowley, TJ 1997. "Moving Beyond Dyadic Ties: A Network Theory of Stakeholder Influences," Academy of Management Review, Vol 22, No 4, pp 887-910.

Zúniga, MM, 2008. Taking on the System: Rules for Radical Change in a Digital Era. New York: Celebra.

# On the Military Geography of Cyberspace

**Tim Grant**
R-BAR, Benschop, The Netherlands
tim.grant.work@gmail.com

*Originally Published in the Proceedings of ICCWS, 2014*

**Editorial Commentary**

One of the more important contributions to warfare has been the development of models of the potential battlespace, otherwise known as maps. Knowing where you are going, how to get there, and what you will find when you arrive is really valuable. Beginning as crude drawings of mountains and rivers, then with increasing details of terrain features, habitations, and weather patterns, maps have been refined and expanded for use in military planning, targeting, and manuever for hundreds of years. Current geographic information systems take the concept of maps even further, adding many layers of informational features over representations of a geographic space.

In his paper, "Military Geography in Cyberspace", Tim Grant explores the question: "Can existing representations of the battlefield, developed for the four kinetic domains, can be extended to cyberspace?" His approach to this question is to consider the emerging applications of human geography and physical geography in the context of cyberspace.

This is an important consideration with implications well beyond that of warfare operations. When cyberspace can be mapped as a geography, what does that mean in terms of governance and control of parts of that geography? We are used to thinking about governance issues in terms of real space: land, negotiated borders, population centers, etc. These are intuitively represented in physical models of terrain. A radically different approach to modeling cyberspace from the perspective of a cyber-geography might provide a very different perspective on collective groupings, governance, and control. To be sure, there will always be a physical geography component — places where electricity is generated, servers are located,

119

traffic is routed — but emerging cyber-geography visualizations may well birth an era where geopolitical relationships are less about physical colocation as they are about commonality of purpose.

**Abstract**: Military operations have traditionally been conducted in four domains: on land, at sea, in the air, and in space. Over the past few years, a number of nations have added cyberspace as a fifth domain of military operations. However, opinions vary widely on whether or not cyberspace is the same kind of domain. The four traditional domains are continuous, three-dimensional spaces, contain physical objects with inertia, and support kinetic action. By contrast, cyberspace is a discrete, multi-dimensional space, contains virtual, inertia-free objects, and supports cyber actions. This paper reports on research aimed at unifying the representations of geographically-related concepts in the five domains. The approach taken is to develop a layered ontology, ultimately intended to be the basis for developing software for simulating or supporting the military Command & Control process. The paper outlines the geographer's tasks of exploration, surveying, and cartography, applying them to cyberspace. It identifies the geographical concepts used in the military operations planning process. The core of the paper is a description of the informal semantics of a layered ontology incorporating these concepts. Finally, the paper identifies further research.

**Keywords**: military operations; cybergeography; ontology; layered network; planning

# 1    Introduction

For hundreds of years, military forces have been operating on land and at sea. They added air operations at the start of the 20th century and space operations towards that century's end. Land, sea, air, and space are regarded as the four traditional domains of military operation, often known as the "kinetic" domains because operations involve physical action,. Now, military forces are extending their area of operations to include cyberspace, in the form of Computer Network Defence (CND), Computer Network Exploitation (CNE), and Computer Network Attack (CNA). Opinions vary widely on whether or not cyberspace is the same kind of domain as the land, sea, air, and outer space.

This paper addresses the question as to whether existing representations of the battlefield, developed for the four kinetic domains, can be extended to cyberspace. In these domains, the space is geographical, the objects of interest are real, and military operations involve physical action. By contrast, cyberspace is networked, the objects of interest are virtual, and military operations involve cyber action. The paper focuses on the geography of the representations used in military Command & Control (C2), and in operation planning in particular. The aim is to find a way of unifying representations in all five domains, enabling the integrated planning of kinetic and cyber actions. We do this by means of an ontology, defined in the software engineering sense as a *"formal, explicit specification of a shared conceptualization"* (Gruber, 1993). Moreover, the ontology is layered.

Geography is the science that studies the lands, the features, the inhabitants, and the phenomena of the Earth (Dahlman & Renwick, 2013). There are two main branches: human geography and physical geography. Because C2 and cyberspace involve the interaction between humans and their natural and social environment our research integrates features of both. Common tasks include exploration, surveying, and cartography. A recent development is the application of geography to cyberspace under the heading of cyber-geography[24], concentrating on social interactions within cyberspace and on cartography. Military geography is the application of geographic tools, techniques, and information to solve military problems (Palka & Galgano, 2005). In planning a military operation, commanders first consider the geographical area within which operations will take place, and then the actors and other objects of interest likely to be encountered in that area. The subsequent planning process assesses the capabilities of these actors, generates possible courses of action, "war-games" own courses of action against those of other actors, and finally develops an Operation Order for own forces.

The unifying approach we adopt is to represent the five domains as a layered ontology, known as the Formalized Layered Ontology for Networked C2 (FLONC). Drawing from the C2 and cyberspace literature, we identify five layers representing the underlying geography, physical objects, information, cognitive models, and socio-organizational structures. Analysis results in an ontology of classes within each layer, together with the intra- and inter-layer relationships. Our ultimate goal is to develop software that simulates the network-enabled C2 process, that supports parts of this process or implements a complete C2 system. It is for this reason that we use the word ontology in its software engineering sense. FLONC has been

---

[24] See http://personalpages.manchester.ac.uk/staff/m.dodge/cybergeography/ (29 October 2013).

developed following the Ontology Development 101 method (Noy & McGuiness, 2001). We intend to encode FLONC in the Web-based Ontology Language (OWL) (Smith, Welty & McGuinness, 2004), making it both human- and computer-readable.

The purpose of this paper is to present the informal semantics of a unified ontological representation for the common concepts underlying the five domains of military operation. More formal details can be found in Grant (2014). The greatest challenge is in integrating cyberspace concepts with those in the other four, kinetic domains. The paper focuses on the representations used in military C2, and in particular the military operations planning process, enabling the integrated planning of kinetic and cyber actions. This paper is limited to aspects relating to the geographical area of operations, the objects of interest, and kinetic and cyber action. Other forms of information operations, such as strategic communication, civil-military interaction, and psyops, are outside the scope of this paper.

There are five sections in this paper. After this introductory section, section 2 summarizes the relevant theoretical background on geography, including military geography and cyber-geography, emphasizing the concepts of identity and place. Section 3 outlines the military operational planning process, discussing terrain and action in more detail. Section 4 describes the informal semantics of the FLONC ontology. Finally, section 5 draws conclusions and recommends further research.

## 2   Relevant aspects of geography

### 2.1   Geographer's tasks

Exploration is the process of travelling around or searching a geographical area for the purposes of discovering information or other resources. The explorer's aim is to develop an initial, rough understanding of the area. The product of exploration is the information obtained, usually recorded in the form of a sketch map. Nowadays, explorers may also bring back photographs, audio recordings, and possibly specimens. The area need not be terrestrial, because we also regard sending spacecraft to other planets as exploration of outer space. Likewise, exploration is not confined to dry land. Human history includes feats of oceanic exploration by people like Columbus and Vasco da Gama.

Surveying is the science and art of making measurements to determine the relative position of points or physical and cultural details on the Earth's surface. The purpose of surveying is to gather data for map-making or to determine the boundaries of geographical areas for governmental or legal reasons (e.g. establishing ownership). The process is more systematic than exploration and generally uses more precise instruments. Typically, positions are measured in the three spatial dimensions. In addition, these measurements are often time-stamped so that changes in position can be analyzed. The definition emphasizes that all positions are relative. This is because they are measured in relation to another point, which may be arbitrary (e.g. "the centre of London") or a widely-accepted origin, such as the equator and the Greenwich meridian. Surveying does not necessarily have to be done on-site. Surveys can be performed remotely, as when a terrestrial or space-borne telescope surveys the stars or when a map of the Martian surface is build up from multiple orbits by the Martian Observer spacecraft. Moreover, these examples show that surveying can be done by unmanned devices.

Cartography is the study and practice of making maps. A map is a visual representation of a geographical area, depicting objects, regions, and themes and their relationships symbolically. Maps may be thematic or general and typographic or topological. A thematic map is designed specifically to portray a particular theme, such as physical, cultural, social, political, or economic aspects. By contrast, a general map portrays a variety of themes together. A topographic map is a detailed and accurate graphic representation of cultural and natural features. Scales, distances, and directions are quantitatively correct in a topographic map. By contrast, a topological map is simplified, with scale, distance, and direction being relaxed, but maintaining the relationships (i.e. topology) between points. A good example of a topological map is the well-known map of the London Underground (the "Tube").

## 2.2   Cyber-geography

Before we can discuss cyber-geography, we must be clear what cyberspace is. There are many definitions of cyberspace. Some focus exclusively on the computing and telecommunications hardware, often emphasizing the role played by networks. For example, the American Heritage Dictionary defines cyberspace as "the electronic medium of computer networks, in which online communication takes place". There are definitions that equate cyberspace with data-spaces, with some adding the requirement that the data must be digitalized. For example, the Collins English Dictionary defines cyberspace as "all of the data stored in a large computer or network represented as a three-dimensional model through which a virtual-reality user can move". Note that this definition includes the human users. Other definitions are more concerned with the users' shared social experience. For example, Slater (no date) defines cyberspace as "the sense of a social setting that exists purely within a space of representation and communication ... within a computer space, distributed across increasingly complex and fluid networks".

Many definitions assign cyberspace a spatial quality. The Collins English Dictionary definition, quoted above, is one example. Strate (1999, p.383) states that "cyberspace can then be defined as the diverse experiences of space associated with computing and related technologies". The Zero Geography blog[25] goes further in saying that "the cyberspace metaphor is an inherently geographical concept". It notes that the metaphor is paradoxical because it is "both an ethereal alternative dimension which is simultaneously infinite and everywhere ... and fixed in a distinct location, albeit a non-physical one". Principia Cybernetica[26] adds that the cyber in cyberspace "connotes both the idea of navigation through the space of electronic data, and of control which is achieved by manipulating these data". Cyberspace is more than a space of passive data, such as a library. Its communication channels connect to the real world, allowing cyberspace navigators to interact with that world.

Several authors have come up with the idea of splitting cyberspace into layers. Principia Cybernetica states that "cyberspace's substrate is precisely the joint network of all existing communication channels and information stores connecting people and machines". If this network is a substrate, then there must be another layer above it. According to "SD" of the Alliance Géostratégique[27], cyberspace is composed of layers based on the historical sequence of the discovery of language, writing, printing, global communication, and man-machine convergence. Each layer is linked to a set of telecommunication technologies. Strate (2006) identifies three build-

---

[25] See http://www.zerogeography.net/2011/11/cyberspace.html (16 October 2013).
[26] See http://pespmc1.vub.ac.be/CYBSPACE.html (16 October 2013).
[27] See http://alliancegeostrategique.org/2010/10/04/une-ebauche-apocryphe-et-anthropocentrique-du-cyberespace/ (30 October 2013).

ing blocks: the *physical cyberspace* of the computer itself, the *perceptual cyberspace* based on users' interaction with computer interfaces, and the *conceptual cyberspace* that users create mentally by representing cyberspace in logical, metaphysical, and rhetorical terms. Libicki (2009) distinguishes three layers. The *physical* layer consists of computing hardware, the *syntactic* layer contains the designer's and users' instructions, and the *semantic* layer contains the information held in the computing hardware. We adopt and extend this idea of layering in defining the FLONC ontology.

Between 1997 and 2004, Martin Dodge at the University of Manchester, UK, led an investigation into the spatiality of cyberspace, which they defined as "the electronic 'places' that exist behind our computer screens". The main research questions of this cyber-geography project were:

- Does cyberspace have a geography?
- What do we know about the nature, shape, size, distribution, and geography of the Internet, the World Wide Web, and cyberspace?
- What needs to be mapped?
- What techniques can be used in visualizing information structures of the Web?

As the titles of their major publications (Dodge & Kitchin, 2001; 2002) show, the project emphasized cartography, mostly as topological maps of information, social, and cultural spaces. While some of the entities mapped were located in the physical world (e.g. undersea cables, routers, etc), cyberspace was not specifically related to the other four domains of military activity. Nevertheless, they have comprehensively covered the geographer's task of cartography for cyberspace.

Finding a cyber process equivalent to exploration is easy. Web users term this *surfing*, *browsing*, or *searching*, depending on how goal-oriented the process is. Computer crackers talk about *footprinting* (Beaver, 2007), and intelligence analysts might name this *reconnaissance*. Just as the traditional explorer used a donkey, a sailing ship, or a spacecraft to travel through physical space, so the cyber explorer travels along communication links and hyperlinks using software tools such as browsers and search engines. Moreover, as in outer space or underwater, unmanned devices may do the work of exploring on behalf of humans. In cyberspace, these devices are known as *bots* or *crawlers*. Like his/her terrestrial counterpart, the cyber explorer may build up the cyber equivalent of a sketch map (e.g.

browsing history) and bring back cyber snapshots (e.g. cached or saved web-pages and files).

A cyber equivalent of surveying can also be readily found. As the Cyber-Geography project shows, this largely involves the systematic gathering of accurate and representative data for mapping purposes. Data may also be gathered to determine the boundaries of cyberspaces or to establish the ownership of cyberspace entities or the jurisdiction into which they fall. The entities for which data is collected may be the Internet infrastructure, connections, IP addresses, information items, routes that data packets take through a network, web-pages, the architecture of an ISP's network, user paths through a website, etc. Unlike exploration, there is no common web user's term for surveying. Intelligence analysts may talk about *surveillance* or *computer network exploitation* (CNE).

## 2.3   Place and identity

Geographers make a distinction between locations and places (Dodge & Kitchen, 2001). A place is a special location that provides people with a sense of belonging, e.g. someone's home or office. The sense of place derives from shared heritage or commitment to social institutions such as family, neighbourhood, tribe, or community. Thus a place joins a location and a person in their social context.

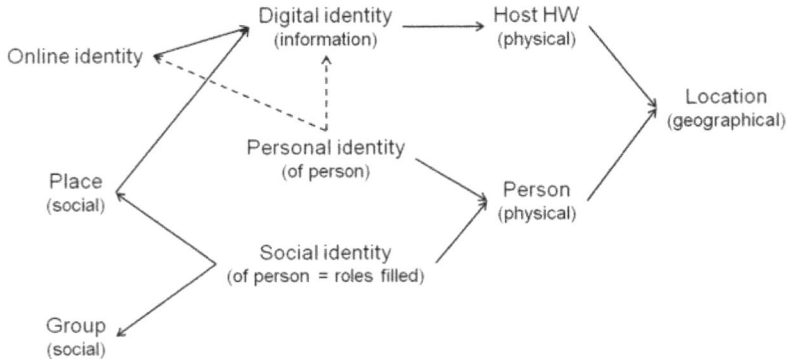

**Figure 19:** Relationship between identity and location

Identity is a more complex concept, as Figure 19 shows. In psychology, identity is a person's self-conception and expression of their individuality. Part of this identity is derived from the person's membership of social groups. For example, a person has a unique personal identify based on distinguishing features of his or her physical body and personality, but may have several facets of social identity (e.g. from nationality, as an inhabitant of a region, as a father or mother, in a team, as an employee of a company, etc) derived from membership of a set of groups. Since the person is embodied, he or she has a single, specific, geographical location.

In cyberspace, a person may have several online identities, each of which will be recorded digitally, i.e. as data or information held in one or more computers. The location(s) of the computer hardware may not correspond with the person's bodily location. Moreover, it may be difficult to relate their personal identity to the online and digital identities (see dashed arrows). The person's social identity is a set of joins between the person and the groups of which he or she is a member. These groups may have one or more social places, e.g. locations where the group habitually meets, the group's website, the chat channel they share, etc. If these places are in cyberspace, then they too will have a digital identity. It is this indirect relationship between a person's multiple online identities, personal and social identity, and geographical location that make the attribution of cyber action so difficult.

# 3 Military geography

## 3.1 Operational decision-making process

In the Royal Netherlands Army, the operational decision-making process is divided into four phases and nine steps (AFM 1, 2000):

- Phase 1: Mission Analysis
- Step 1: A new situation?
- Step 2: Analysis of mission
- Step 3: Commander's guidelines
- Phase 2: Evaluation of Factors
- Step 4: Intelligence preparation of the battlefield
- Step 5: Friendly assets
- Phase 3: Consideration of Courses of Action
- Step 6: Development of Courses of Action
- Step 7: Consideration of Courses of Action
- Phase 4: Commander's Decision
- Step 8: Commander's decision

- Step 9 (in parallel): Development of operation order, and Contingency planning

In Phase 1, the commander and his/her staff officers analyse the mission that they have been given by their superiors. Phase 2 is devoted to evaluating the battlefield environment and their own assets. Military geography is involved in the fourth step, the intelligence preparation of the battlefield (IPB). In Phase 3 the command team develop possible courses of action (COAs), i.e. sequences of action. Own and enemy COAs are developed independently, and then "war-gamed" against one another in the seventh step. In Phase 4, the commander decides which of his/her own COAs is best, and then this decision is worked out into detailed operation orders for his/her subordinates.

## 3.2    Geographical information used

AFM 1 (2000) was used as source material for an hierarchical task analysis (Annett, 2003) of the IPB in an unclassified four-nation Western European Union research project named "Military Applications foR Virtual Environments in Logistics and intelligence" (MARVEL). The analysis results (Van den Bosch & Martellini, 2001) can be used to identify what geographical information the commander and his/her command team take into account when planning an operation. For analysis purposes, the IPB was split into three parts: mind-setting (i.e. getting a global idea of the situation), battle area evaluation, and threat evaluation. We focus on the aspects of terrain and military action.

Terrain-related aspects can be found in the following parts of the IPB process:

- **Mind-setting:**
  - *What is the area of operations*
- **Battle Area Evaluation:**
  - *Evaluation of the influence of climate and weather:*
  - *Inventory of current weather: lighting, clouds, precipitation, minimum and maximum temperatures, wind force and direction, air pressure and humidity.*
  - *Evaluation of the terrain:*

- Relief of the land.
- Properties of overgrowth.
- Description of soil and its condition.
- Determine properties of natural obstacles.
- Determine properties of artificial works.

- **Threat Evaluation:**
  - Determine position of enemy forces (disposition) from reports.

Aspects relating to military action can be found in the following parts of the IPB process:

- **Mind-setting:**
  - What kind of operations are involved (offensive, defensive, delaying)

- **Battle Area Evaluation:**
  - Determination of the influence of weather on military aspects: mobility, troops, air support (fixed wing, rotary), visibility, C2, NBC warfare.
  - Military (tactical) aspects of terrain:
  - Determine slow-go and no-go areas for vehicles and groups.
  - Determine slow-go and no-go areas for formations and units (brigade / division)
  - Determine mobility corridors:
  - Mobility on road.
  - Mobility in third dimension (i.e. air support)
  - Determine strong lines of defence.
  - Determine fields of observation / fire in direction of approach:
  - Determine tactically important areas (TIAs).
  - State distances for fields of observation / fire for TIAs.

  o   *Indication for use of weapon or sensor systems.*

  o   *Determine observation and fire coverage.*

- **Threat Evaluation:**

  o   *Determine activities of opponent from reports*

These tasks are performed by drawing a fixed sequence of overlays, extracting information from a pre-existing topographical map of the area of operations. Information about height and the natural features that form obstacles is used to determine the corridors through which a military force could move (*mobility corridors*). Height information is also used to determine fields of view. The mobility corridors, fields of view, and doctrinal information are combined to obtain possible courses of action. Knowing the enemy's current position, the command team can then assess which of these possible courses of action the enemy is likely to take.

## 3.3   Geography in cyber warfare

Information in the open literature on the use of geographical concepts in cyber warfare is sparse. White Wolf Security's white paper[28] on offensive operations in cyberspace claims that:

1   Cyberspace is a terrain like land, sea, air and space.
2   Like a terrain, cyberspace has definite geographic limit and boundaries.
3   The attack planning and execution sequence is the same in both physical and cyberspace.
4   The problems of attack attribution are the same in both physical and cyberspace.
5   The range of attacks; from nuisance to mass damage is the same in both physical and cyberspace.
6   The range of responses; from reporting a grievance to mass damage is the same in both physical and cyberspace.
7   The range of actors is the same in both spaces with identical responsibilities.

While claims 3 to 7 are outside the scope of this paper, the cyber-geography literature indicates that White Wolf Security's claims are highly

---

[28] See http://www.whitewolfsecurity.com/publications/offensive_ops.php (30 October 2013).

simplistic. Moreover, claim 1 does not allow for the discrete spatiality of the network substrate of cyberspace.

A more authoritative reference is the US Department of Defense's Joint Concept for Cyberspace (US DoD, 2011). Interestingly, this too uses a layered representation. The *physical layer* consists of the geographic and physical network components. The *logical layer* consists of the connections between the network nodes. The *social layer* comprises the human and cognitive aspects, including *persona* and *cyber persona* components (equivalent to humans and their online identities, respectively). There is no explicit representation of information, social or organizational entities.

# 4   FLONC ontology

In this section, we describe the informal semantics of each of the five layers in the ontology. Figure 20 shows the ontology depicted using Chen's (1976) Entity Relationship Diagram notation. More details of its formalization can be found in Grant (2014).

## 4.1   Geographical layer

The purpose of the geographical layer is to represent the five spaces in which military (and civilian) activities can occur: land, sea, air, (outer) space, and cyberspace. These spaces may be conveniently represented as two-dimensional (2D, e.g. land and sea), as three-dimensional (3D, e.g. air and outer space), or as multi-dimensional (MD, e.g. cyberspace). Time will be an additional dimension. Operations may be concentrated in one of these spaces, but more often it involves multiple spaces (i.e. operations are *joint*). In particular, virtual actions in cyberspace may be integrated with real (or "kinetic") actions in one or more of the other four spaces. Hence, the ontology must be capable of representing all five spaces and any combination of them.

Geographical concepts that must be represented in the geographical layer include the idea of a space, with points embedded in this space. One or more frames of reference allows points, distances, and directions to be determined. Land, sea, air, and (outer) space are real spaces, with cyberspace being virtual. Real spaces are continuous, while virtual space is generally discrete. Points may be connected to one another by paths running through the space. The distance along these paths and the direction in which they run can also be determined from a suitable frame of reference.

We are particularly interested in locations, i.e. the subset of points where physical objects can be located.

## 4.2   Physical layer

The purpose of the physical layer is to represent the physical objects of interest involved in military (and civilian) activities, together with the physical links between them. While the full detail of all types of objects and links are not included in the ontology presented here, high-level abstract classes are provided which future ontology authors and software developers can extend as their needs dictate.

Objects have one or more locations in the geographical layer, and links run along a geographical path. An object can have multiple locations only if each location is in a different space. For example, an airfield has one location on land and another location in the air. Objects and links in the physical layer are tangible, and may be natural (typically humans) or man-made (known here as devices). An additional form of link is an interface between devices and humans. We make no distinction whether the interface is an input (from human to device), or an output (from device to human), or both.

Devices may be part of another device. Moreover, one device may act upon itself or another device, causing it to move (i.e. change location), to change an attribute, or to create or delete a part-of relationship. For illustrative purposes, three types of device are distinguished: a facility with a fixed location, a transport that can change its location, and an ICT device (i.e. a piece of computing hardware) that can create, sense, store, copy, process, display, and/or delete information. An ICT device may also sense information about other devices. Note that an ICT device will generally have two locations: one in real space (i.e. on land, at sea, in the air, or in outer space) and the other in virtual space (i.e. cyberspace).

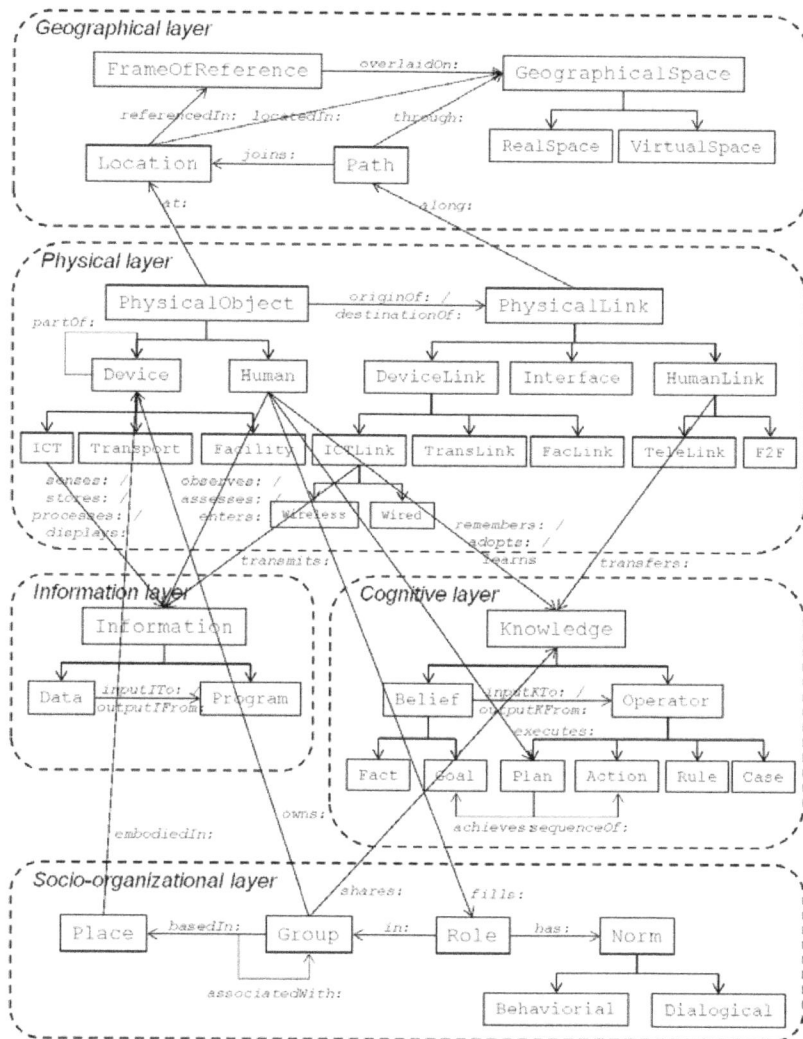

**Figure 20:** FLONC – entity relationship diagram

There are three corresponding types of link between devices, with an ICT link (i.e. telecommunications hardware) being able to transmit information from one ICT device to another. ICT links can be wired or wireless. Links between humans may be face-to-face or technology-augmented (e.g. typically telephone or radio, but also including older technologies such as pen and paper). Where it is necessary to represent digital communications between humans (e.g. email, chat, etc.), then this could be done by combining a (human-to-ICT device) interface at the sending end, with an ICT link, and with another (ICT device-to-human) interface at the receiving end. Note that ICT links will generally run along two paths, one in real space and the other in virtual space.

## 4.3   Information layer

The purpose of the information layer is to represent data and information used in military activities. We make no distinction between a piece of information and how it is encoded (e.g. as software or as a mark on a piece of paper). Information can only exist if it is stored in an ICT device or transmitted over an ICT link. The set of all information, together with the set of ICT devices and links in the physical layer, constitute the technical substrate (the "infostructure") of cyberspace.

Information is separated into data (typically representing a simple or complex variable, such as a sensed parameter of an object of interest, a set of such parameters, or a message to be transmitted across a link) and programs that process input data to obtain output data. Information has no inherent geographical location, but a location may be derived from the current location of the device in which it is stored. Since software can be readily copied, a piece of data or a program may be stored in multiple devices (and therefore in multiple locations) simultaneously.

## 4.4   Cognitive layer

The purpose of the cognitive layer is to represent pieces of knowledge held in the minds of humans engaged in military activities. This knowledge may be tacit or explicit, true or false, more or less certain, and based on direct observation, on messages from other humans, on information displayed by devices, or on inference or learning from other pieces of knowledge. Knowledge can only exist if it is carried in the mind of a human or transferred across a human-to-human link. Like information, knowledge has no inherent geographical location, but a location may be derived from the current location of the human whose mind is carrying it. Knowledge may be copied by transferring it to another human. Hence, a piece of knowledge may be known to several humans, and therefore in multiple locations simultaneously.

Just as information is separated into data and programs, so knowledge is separated into beliefs and operators. Taking our clue from the traditional definition of knowledge as "justified true belief" (Chisholm, 1982), we use the term "belief" to denote a piece of knowledge because this is more general than another term like (say) "assertion". Beliefs may be qualified by a degree of truthfulness, with justification for a belief being represented by the set of other beliefs that support it. We use the term "operator" in its mathematical sense to denote the equivalent in the cognitive layer to a program in the information layer.

Humans may create knowledge in other ways than receiving knowledge transferred from other humans. In particular, new knowledge may be created by learning. A new belief may be learned by observing or assessing information displayed by an ICT device. A human may also deduce new knowledge by combining other pre-existing beliefs using an operator. Using induction (an operator for learning from examples), a human may create a new operator from a set of beliefs.

For C2 purposes, beliefs are sub-divided into facts and goals. Facts are beliefs that the human regards as being currently true or were true in the past. Typically, facts represent some element of the state of an object of interest. Goals are beliefs that the human intends to make true at some time in the future. Operators are sub-divided into cases, rules, actions, and plans. A case is the record of using an operator successfully in the past, together with the beliefs used as input and generated as output. A rule is an IF-THEN operator for deriving support for beliefs in the THEN part, given that all the beliefs in the IF part are true. An action is an operator that, when executed, will change information in the information layer that will in turn result in a change in the physical layer. A plan is a sequence of one or more actions, designed logically so as to achieve a goal.

## 4.5  Socio-organizational layer

The purpose of the socio-organizational layer is to represent the social and organizational relationships between humans engaged in military (or civilian) activities. Social relationships are more informal, while organizational ones are more formal. Whether formal or informal, these relationships are based on the membership of a group. A human becomes a member of a social or organizational group by filling (at least) one of the roles within the group, and thereby gains a social identity. Membership requires the human to comply with the norms associated with his/her role. The literature on organizational norms distinguishes structural, functional, behavioral, and dialogical norms (Hübner et al, 2002). Compliance with these norms may be rewarded, and violation may lead to punishment or even expulsion from the group. We need only to represent the behavioral and dialogical norms here, because we model structural and functional norms in other ways (as groups and roles and as goals and plans, respectively). Behavioral norms constrain the autonomy of group members by imposing obligations and prohibitions on their behavior. Dialogical norms constrain with whom group members may communicate and the message formats and protocols they should use in doing so. For example, a dialogical norm may stipulate that group members must share all their knowledge with other group members, i.e. imposes the "need-to-share" principle. Alternatively, the norm may require that knowledge should be shared with another group member only when that group member has a demonstrable need-to-know.

One group may be associated with another. If this association requires the subgroup necessarily to adopt some or all of the roles and norms of the parent group, then the association is formal. When the requirement is optional, then the association is informal. When each subgroup has a single parent, then the set of associations models an organizational hierarchy. However, a set of associations generally forms a network. When the complete set is a network but some sub-networks are hierarchical, then this could represent a coalition of (hierarchical) organizations.

Some groups may attain the status of a community, characterized by social cohesion, personal intimacy, and moral commitment (Dodge & Kitchen, 2001). Such a group is regarded as being based in a place, where places are locations that are uniquely designated by shared social ties. In the geographical literature a place is implicitly assumed to have a fixed location. However, military operations are characterized by mobility. The place of work of a ship's crew is the ship, whose location can change. The same applies to aircrew, whose place of work is an aircraft. For this reason, instead of associating places directly with locations, we will say that a place is embodied in a device. This yields a synergistic effect for ICT devices. In everyday terms, a place that associates a group with an ICT device is known as a (computer-based) system, and the group is its set of users. In particular, we are interested in C2 systems and their users. Moreover, the group may be simultaneously based in one place (fixed or mobile) in real space and in another place in cyberspace.

# 5  Conclusions and further research

The purpose of this paper was to find a unified representation for the geographically-related concepts underlying the five domains of military operations. The approach taken was to develop a layered ontology, ultimately intended to be the basis for developing software to simulate or support the military Command & Control (C2) process. This paper presents the informal semantics of the ontology; details of its formalization can be found in Grant (2014). The geographical concepts relating to the military operations planning process were sought by focusing on the geographer's tasks of exploration, surveying, and cartography. These same tasks can be found in cyber-geography, although the literature tends to emphasize how to make maps depicting cyberspace, i.e. the cartography task. NATO nations all use similar processes for planning military operations. Using an hierarchical task analysis of the planning process described in the Royal Netherlands Army doctrinal manual on C2 (AFM 1, 2000) as our source material, we identified the geographical concepts needed to plan a military operation. These concepts are incorporated in the Formalized Layered Ontology for Networked C2 (FLONC), with the informal semantics being presented here.

The main contribution of this paper is to show that it is possible to unify the representation of geographical concepts underlying all five domains of military operation using a layered ontology. The work presented here is limited in that FLONC is currently only a conceptual ontology, lacking attributes and constraints. Software developers would have to extend the stubs provided to represent a full set of physical objects and links found in military operations and to create instances to represent a particular operational scenario. In on-going research, the ontology is being represented in version 2 of the Web-based Ontology Language (OWL2) using the Protégé ontology editor.

More fundamental research is also needed. In particular, the cyber-geography research needs to be extended to the exploration and surveying of cyberspace, drawing parallels with CNE and cyber intelligence analysis. Cyber action should also be widened to encompass other kinds of information operations. An intriguing possibility is to use FLONC to shine more light on the attribution problem.

# References

AFM 1. (2000). Army Field Manual 1, Command & Control. Director of Policy & Planning, Royal Netherlands Army, The Hague, Netherlands.

Annett, J. (2003). Hierarchical Task Analysis. In Diaper, D. & Stanton, N.A. (eds). Handbook of Task Analysis in Human-Computer Interaction. Lawrence Erlbaum, Mahwah, NJ, USA.

Beaver, K. (2007). Hacking for Dummies. 2nd edition, Wiley Publishing Inc., Indianapolis, IN, USA.

Chen, P.P-S. (1976). The Entity-Relationship Model - Towards a unified view of data. ACM Transactions on Database Systems, 1, 1, (March) 9-36.

Chisholm, R. (1982). Knowledge as Justified True Belief. In The Foundations of Knowing, University of Minnesota Press, Minneapolis, USA.

Dahlman, C.H. & Renwick, W.H. (2013). Introduction to Geography: People, places & environment. 6th edition, Prentice Hall.

Dodge, M. & Kitchen, R. (2001). Mapping Cyberspace. Routledge, London, UK.

Dodge, M. & Kitchen, R. (2002). Atlas of Cyberspace. Pearson Education, London, UK.

Grant, T.J. (2014). Formalized Ontology for Representing C2 Systems as Layered Networks. In Grant, T.J., Janssen, R.H.P, & Monsuur, H. (eds). Network Topology and Military C2 Systems: Design, operation, and evolution. IGI Global, Hershey, PA, USA.

Gruber, T.R. (1993). A Translation Approach to Portable Ontology Specifications. Knowledge Acquisition, 5, 2, 199-220.

Hübner, J.F., Sichman, J.S. & Boissier, O. (2002). A Model for the Structural, Functional, and Deontic Specification of Organizations in Multi-agent Systems. In Proceedings, 16th Brazilian Symposium on AI (SBIA 2002), LNAI 2507, Springer, 118–128.

Libicki, M.C. (2009). A Conceptual Framework. In Cyberdeterrence and Cyberwar, Rand Corp, chapter 2, 11-37.

Noy, N.F. & McGuiness, D.L. (2001). Ontology Development 101: A guide to creating your first ontology. Stanford Knowledge Systems Laboratory Technical Report KSL-01-5 and Stanford Medical Informatics Technical Report SMI-2001-0880, March,

Palka, E.J. & Galgano, F.A. (2005). Military Geography: from peace to war. McGraw-Hill, Boston.

Smith, M.K., Welty, C. & McGuinness, D.L. (2004). OWL Web Ontology Language Guide, W3C recommendation, 10 February 2004.

Strate, L. (1999). The Varieties of Cyberspace: Problems in definition and delimitation. Western Journal of Communication, 63, 3, 382-412.

Strate, L. (2006). Eight Bits About Digital Communication. Razon y Palabra, 11, 49.

US DoD. (2011). Joint Concept for Cyberspace. Version 0.7, US Department of Defense, Washington DC, USA, 25 October 2011.

Van den Bosch, J.J. & Martellini, L. (2001). User Requirements: Virtual Environments for Military Decision Making. Technical Note 1.3.1, issue A(5), EUCLID RTP 6.14 project, MARVEL consortium.

# Intelligence Preparation of the Cyber Environment (IPCE): Finding the High Ground in Cyberspace

**Antoine Lemay[1], Scott Knight[2] and José Fernandez[1]**
[1]Département de génie informatique et génie logiciel, École Polytechnique de Montréal, Montréal, Canada
[2]Department of Electrical and Computer Engineering, Royal Military College of Canada, Kingston, Canada
antoine.lemay@polymtl.ca
knight-s@rmc.ca
jose.fernandez@polymtl.ca

*Originally Published in the Proceedings of ICCWS, 2014*

**Editorial Commentary**

Just as understanding the geography of cyberspace is critical to being able to formulate military plans in cyberspace, developing a comprehensive approach to the underlying intelligence data needs, analytical structures, and applications is important. Some work has been done in this area; one of the most cited papers is that describing the concept of the intelligence value of a "kill chain" (Hutchins, Cloppert, and Amin, 2011, "Intelligence-Driven Computer Network Defense Informed by Analysis of Adversary Campaigns and Intrusion Kill Chains; available online at http://papers.rohanamin.com/?p=15). In that paper, the authors proposed the concept of indicators, which were defined as "any piece of information that objectively describes an intrusion". Other approaches to characterizing what is becoming to be known as cyber-intelligence are incrementally being developed, so there is an expectation that in the next several years, significant advancement will be made.

This paper provides an important framework for such advancements. By taking two existing, proven methodologies, Intelligence Preparation of the Battlespace (IPB) and Intelligence Preparation of the Operating Environment (IPOE) and analyzing the limitations for application to the cyberspace environment, the authors create a definable space for developing a new model. This new model, Intelligence Preparation of the Cyber Environment (IPCE), is meant to be complementary to existing approaches, providing insight into the domain of cyberspace from an intelligence perspective.

The findings of their analysis are illustrated by a simple example applying the IPCE method to a postulated attack on a Supervisory Control and Data Acquisition (SCADA) system. The demonstration shows that "the IPCE process generates products that can be used to inform operations" within the context of the "cyber terrain." As noted in their conclusion, this level of knowledge could be used to develop tactics resulting in the reshaping of the battle space, changing the dynamics of the conflict. Combined with the previous paper on the "Military Geography in Cyberspace", the notion of being able to treat cyberspace as a real domain, rather than something that is hard to comprehend, is progressing apace. This capability is particularly important when considered in view of the ideas presented in the previous papers, including that competition in cyberspace may become unending, as mentioned in the paper on "Unrestricted Warfare", and the rise of virtual non-state actors as forces to be reckoned with in cyber operations.

**Abstract**: The tool most commonly used in the planning phase of cyber defense, i.e. risk analysis, provides only limited guidance for adequate information collection and operational decision making. For example, while scenario-based risk analysis might identify vulnerabilities as sources of risk, it does not describe the actions typically taken by a particular adversary. It thus becomes difficult to produce indicators (required for guiding the collection and monitoring process) and decision guidance matrices for operational personnel (or automated processes) to act in accordance with the system owner's intent. To overcome these shortcomings, we propose a more comprehensive and deliberate process of intelligence planning: the Intelligence Preparation of the Cyber Environment (IPCE), an adaptation of the IPB (Intelligence Preparation of the Battlespace/Battlefield) and IPOE (Intelligence Preparation of the Operational Environment) processes employed by military forces in conventional and unconventional conflicts. In the IPB, intelligence planners study the adversary (capabilities, intent and history) and analyse the effects of the environment (terrain, weather, etc.), in order to identify likely enemy Courses of Action (CoA) and indicators that will help determine which CoA he is pursuing. The outputs of the IPB are then used to guide information collection and analysis, and can help support timely operational decision-making. In this paper, we describe how to adapt the IPB to intelligence support to Computer Network Operations (i.e. defensive cyber operations). The IPCE is complementary to and increases the value of traditional risk analysis techniques, by providing a more deliberate and rigorous framework for applying them. We highlight how some of the military concepts used in the IPB correspond to similar terms in cyber security. In particular, we describe how "weather" and "terrain" map onto the concepts of "user", "traffic", "network environment", etc. Then, we demonstrate the IPCE methodology with a case study: the defense of a SCADA system. The IPCE illustrates how SCADA systems have widely different "environmental" features from enterprise systems, and consequently warrant different surveillance and defensive postures. We also describe how the analysis of likely CoA's for a nation-state adversary targeting the SCADA infrastructure leads to the identification of important indicators of impending attack. Finally, we highlight how, unlike in the physical world, the defender has an important advantage in that he "owns" and can partially control the terrain. Applying certain engineering principles, such as "design for observability" could help the defender shape the cyber environment to his advantage by forcing the enemy into unfavourable CoA's.

**Keywords:** cyber intelligence support, cyber operation planning, cyber defense

# 1    Introduction

Warfare planning has steadily evolved and the great conflicts of the 20th century have brought a high degree of maturity to the operational art for conventional conflict. However, because the introduction of IT technology has been fairly recent, the planning of cyber operations does not show the same maturity, relying on planning processes more commonly used in the public sector such as risk analysis. In that sense, we can ask ourselves if tools used in conventional planning could not be adapted for the planning of cyber operations.

One of the tools which could benefit the cyber operation planning process is the Intelligence Preparation of the Operating Environment (IPOE). This tool enables military planners to build a better understanding of the environment and, based on that understanding, create a model of the adversary that can be used in the planning process. The products of IPOE can be used to validate the effectiveness of the proposed plan and can also be used to create contingencies for any dangerous adversary movements. In the cyber realm, where attacks and defenses can occur at the speed of electrons, the ability to pre-plan and automate responses is highly desirable. So, in this paper, we propose the Intelligence Preparation of the Cyber Environment, or IPCE, an adaptation of the concept of the IPOE to a cyber operation.

The paper is divided into five parts. In the first part, we describe the IPOE process in more detail and explain how the IPOE process is linked to the planning process. The second part covers the adaptation of the concepts of IPOE to the cyber environment and the third part applies the IPCE process to the defense of a SCADA network to illustrate how the process might be used to create actionable intelligence that can be used to help computer network operations. Then, a brief discussion about the findings is offered. Finally, we conclude the paper by presenting a brief summary of what was learned and by providing what we see as promising areas of research.

## 2  IPOE and the planning process

To fully understand the need for a new framework, we must understand the limits of the current paradigm in the planning process. The planning process, using the American government process as an example, takes as input information about the current state of the system coupled with a risk assessment. The risk assessment is informed by security countermeasures deliverables and, in turn, areas identified as lacking by risk assessments are improved by integrating more risk mitigation deliverables. In this mode of operation the primary driver for resource allocation is risk assessment: countermeasures are applied until the risk reaches an acceptable threshold or to produce the best reduction for the available budget.

In order to assess risks, a number of methods can be used. One example is the NIST guide for conducting risk assessment (Ross, 2012).  However, there is a significant overlap in terms of methodology. In his paper, Syalim (Syalim, et al., 2009) identifies three basic steps:

- Identify scenarios;

- Evaluate if a vulnerability exists for each scenario;

- Attribute a value to the risk.

One problem with a scenario-based approach is that the limit is imagination. While a trained analyst is unlikely to miss a scenario with a high probability of occurrence and the penalty for passing over a low probability/low impact scenario may not be significant, a gap exists for low probability/high impact scenarios, which may still present non-negligible risks. Because a typical military planning process is rife with such scenarios, the planning process for operations typically eschews scenario-based analysis and replaces it with a more meticulous actor-based analysis.

The military operational planning process (Department of Defense, 2011) follows seven steps to transform the policy maker's intent into a plan:

142

1. Planning Initiation
2. Mission Analysis
3. Course of Action (COA) Development
4. COA Analysis and Wargaming
5. COA Comparison
6. COA Approval
7. Plan or Order Development

In broad summary, the decision maker, in this case the military commander, interprets the policy maker's intent to produce a desired end state, develops a number courses of actions (CoAs) and analyses these CoAs to find the one(s) most suited to achieve the desired end state. According to the joint planning doctrine, "the operational approach is based largely on an understanding of the operational environment and the problem facing the [force commander]" (Department of Defense, 2011). The tool used by military forces to achieve this understanding of the operational environment is called the (joint) intelligence preparation of the operational environment, or (J)IPOE, but the terms intelligence preparation of the battlefield/battlespace, or IPB, are also used.

The general methodology for IPOE is described in joint doctrine (Department of Defense, 2009) and summarized in four steps:
1    Define the operational environment
2    Describe the impact of the operational environment
3    Evaluate the adversary
4    Determine adversary courses of action

First, the mission statement is analyzed in order to circumscribe the area of operation and detail its characteristics. For example, for a land forces perspective, this step would include the drawing of topographical maps. The second step requires an analysis of the operational environment (OE) to describe the impact it has on the mission. Of particular interest, is the description of how the OE affects friendly and enemy capabilities, and how it might constrain possible courses of action. The third step is an evaluation of the adversary. A model of the adversary is built based on a number of factors (for example, his doctrine, the commander's intent, his forces' center(s) of gravity, his forces' vulnerabilities, etc.) to predict how the adversary will react to various stimuli. For example, the evaluation might reveal that, when ordered to advance, his doctrine indicates he should form a line and follow a road. The fourth and final step is the determination of the enemy's courses of action (CoAs). Based on the adversary model, all potential adversary CoAs are detailed and are scored to determine their likelihood. These CoAs reflect how the adversary might adapt his doctrine to the particular operational environment that has been defined and described in Steps 1 and 2. In addition to the CoAs, several deliverables are produced that will help conduct operations, such as an Intelligence Collection Plan (ICP) including collection requirements necessary to be able to determine, once the operation has begun, which CoA the adversary is pursuing. In our example, the spotting of a certain vehicle along the road could be identified as an indicator. The ICP thus generated becomes a deliverable of the Planning phase of the Intelligence cycle, and an input to the Collection phase. In addition, the adversary CoAs and list of indicators are then fed into the operational planning process that in turn produces other deliverables such as an Intelligence, surveillance, target acquisition and reconnaissance (ISTAR) plan that actually tasks collection assets to particular areas, periods and indicators, an event matrix and an attack guidance matrix, that places in time and space the likely events that will be observed depending on the adversary COA and what adequate responses might be if these events become reality.

## 3    Intelligence preparation of the cyber environment

Just as various armed forces branches produce their own versions of IPOE adapted to their operating realm, there is a need for an IPOE process adapted to the cyber realm, which we dub Intelligence Preparation of the Cyber Environment or IPCE. After all, as Liles & al. (Liles, et al., 2012) remind us, cyber space, even though it is a new area of conflict, can still be considered a terrain and we must learn to use that terrain for maximum advantage.

Because IPCE is a form of IPOE, the same general steps are followed. First, we define the environment, then we describe the impact of the environment, follow with an evaluation of the adversary and end with the determination of enemy CoA. However, each step might present some differences. For example, if cyberspace is a terrain, what would be its features? Ultimately, the features of interest will depend of the type of operation that is being run. The type of rock on a particular hill might be relevant to a land forces operation but irrelevant to a navy operation. Because of this and in order to facilitate the understanding of the methodology, we will not provide an exhaustive list of characteristics, but will instead focus on providing a few examples that illustrate each point

The first IPCE step is to define the operational environment. IPOE Joint doctrine (Department of Defense, 2009) lists the required sub-steps. Of these sub-steps, the transition to cyber has a major impact on the determination of significant characteristics of the operational environment only. The "significant" characteristics typically include the weather and terrain components of the WET (Weather-Enemy-Terrain) triad. We must create cyber equivalencies for these concepts.

Ultimately, the mission of any computer network operation is to deliver a certain number of critical bits of information from point A to point B (and only to point B) in a timely manner. We will dub those important bits "signal". Any other bits produced by friendly forces or neutral forces transiting through our network, such as protocol headers, signaling traffic, personnel sending email at home, third parties visiting our website, etc., form a background traffic through which our signal is run. This background traffic, because it does not directly contribute to the mission and because it makes it more difficult to focus on the "good bits" will be dubbed "noise". While it is possible to control the noise under a certain set of circumstances, it is often the case that the "blue forces", i.e. the forces defending the network, have little control over the general population, or "grey forces", in their operational environment. These grey forces are made of typical end users over which the commander in charge of network defense seldom has any real authority. As such, they generate traffic in an arbitrary manner, but one that still follow a pattern. In this light, we can assimilate this behaviour to weather patterns over a physical area of operations. So, in our case, *Traffic*, i.e. the characteristics of the signal and the noise in the network, would be the feature of the operational environment that most resembles *Weather*.

If we pursue our equivalency where grey forces in an operating environment correspond to our user base, the "terrain" on which they reside is the material and logical infrastructure. For example, the type of computer software they use, the network topology, the access control rules, and so on. The exact characteristics of relevance may vary, but must remain focused on what has an impact on the enemy capabilities of "traversing" cyber terrain. Just as the enemy from our previous example could have trouble climbing a hill because the slope is too steep, a network might be impossible for the enemy to traverse because the adversary does not possess the means required to exploit it. In particular, features that strongly constrain the "shape" of red traffic are highly valuable. For example, the knowledge that a firewall rule prevents outgoing traffic except web traffic reveals that any exfiltration will be required to either use port 80 or bypass the firewall. This creates the cyber equivalent of the *Terrain* part of the WET triad. i.e the *Network*.

The second IPCE step is to describe the impact of the environment. The first sub-step is aimed at identifying mobility corridors that can be used as avenues of approach. Similarly, in a cyber environment, we can identify the potential infection vectors and command and control (C2) channels an adversary can use, based on the terrain in the first step. The second sub-step, where a systems perspective of the environment is developed, can be useful in understanding the underlying systems supporting the mission. In particular, the identification of any underlying pre-requisites to the fulfillment of the mission. For example, while Active Directory authentication traffic might not be mission critical, perhaps it is impossible to fulfill the mission if users cannot log on their computers. Finally, the third sub-step requires us to evaluate the impact on the capabilities. In a cyber evaluation, we can see how both offensive and defensive technologies are affected by network characteristics. For example, the presence of a firewall might constrain offensive forces to use reverse tunnels to maintain C2 or a high level of noise might prevent the effective use of an IDS.

The third and fourth IPCE steps consist of the evaluation of the adversary and the determination of adversary CoAs. These steps are conceptually similar to the equivalent steps performed in IPOE. In these steps, the first order of business is to identify the mission of the adversary. For example, does he want to steal secrets or create a denial of service? Once we establish the goals of the adversary, we can look at the doctrine and tactics, the psychology or the historical patterns the adversary has followed to attain these objectives. In terms of cyber operation, doctrine documents like *Unrestricted Warfare* (Liang & Xiangsui, 1999) can provide insight. We can also turn to documented incidents, such as the Mandiant report (Mandiant, 2013) or Stuxnet (Falliere, et al., 2011), to find commonalities that allow us to create a *modus operandi* for our adversary. Using this analysis we construct a number of courses of action for our adversary to reach his desired goal. We then list these CoAs and evaluate how the CoA would unfold over our cyber terrain to obtain a final description of the steps an attacker would take on our terrain to achieve his goals for each CoA. This normally represents the results of the fourth and final step of the IPCE process.

To be able to convert the CoAs into directly actionable intelligence, we have to process the various descriptions of the enemy CoAs and integrate the findings into the operational planning process and the intelligence cycle. The creation of enemy CoAs is invaluable to the development and war gaming of blue CoAs, however the products of IPCE can also be used in order to directly support operations. Using the detailed description of adversary CoAs and an analysis of possible "concealment" based on the Traffic-Adversary-Network (with the memorable acronym "TAN") analysis of our cyber environment, we can create a data collection plan that will enable us to generate indicators for the various enemy CoAs. This data collection plan can then be used to inform deployment decisions, such as IDS and other sensor placements. Finally, once sensors are correctly deployed, we can task the various sensors to look for specific events. These events match the indicators we created for various CoAs. As part of the planning process, we can prepare CoAs to respond and thwart enemy CoAs. If tasked sensors observe the prescribed set of events, we can automatically put into action the contingency CoA. The product containing these actions, called the Attack Guidance Matrix, can then be used to implement automated responses to expected enemy CoAs. In the case of defensive cyber operations, immediate actions in that product would most likely be deployment of defensive countermeasures such as port blocking, traffic shaping or other changes to system configuration, i.e. reshaping the "terrain" (i.e. network), something that the military commander has seldom the advantage to do in land, sea and maritime operations.

## 4    Theory to practice

In order to illustrate how IPCE would work, let us walk through a simplified example. Because the goal of the example is to visualize each step of the process and not to provide comprehensive advice for defense, we will consider only two CoAs. We will apply the proposed model to the case of defending a SCADA network from attack by a nation state. The analysis we present here is obviously not a complete review of the defense of a SCADA network or a complete set of indicators of compromise, but can provide a clear insight into how IPCE might be used to obtain actionable intelligence that can be used a guide for the (possibly automated) defensive operations of the network.

This example is inspired by our own technical research which shows that anomaly-based intrusion detection is very effective in SCADA networks. This is explained by the fact that the *Traffic* component of the *TAN* acronym is very regular because most of the traffic is driven by automated processes. This makes concealment for attackers very difficult and allows defenders to pursue a surveillance based strategy. However, surveillance alone does not help secure the network, it only alerts defenders to the presence of an attack. In this case, the integration of IPCE in the planning process for network defenses allows us to generate indicators, in the context of our surveillance strategy, that will not only alert us to the presence of an attack, but also guide the defensive response.

The first step is to define the operational environment. The implied mission of a SCADA network is to control a factory plant, a water supply system, and electrical grid, or any other remotely operated industrial control system. SCADA networks are made of a collection of special purpose built machines that are using custom software. Outside of maintenance, there is virtually no human users on the network (with the exception of visualisation software). The production network is often isolated from the Internet both for inbound and outbound connections by a firewall, but is linked to the internal network which can act as a bridge and is still linked to the outside by "sneaker net" (i.e. USB peripherals and outside laptops). Because virtually all the traffic is generated by automated systems performing mission critical tasks, the noise volume is low and the signal follows well ordered traffic patterns. For example, two field units (RTUs or PLCs) will never talk to each other during normal operation because the master-slave architecture requires them to talk to the master unit (MTU) only. However, there is (typically) no internal controls that prevent traffic from going outside of these well defined paths.

Next, for the second step of IPCE, we need to evaluate the impact of these cyber environment characteristics. In terms of mobility, we could describe the environment as an "open" terrain even if there is no direct, outgoing connection to the Internet and our scenario requires an internal compromise for the attacker's communications to be bridged on the Internet:

once the adversary is inside the network, there is little that can prevent him from hopping from one node to the next. However, there is a relative lack of concealment in the SCADA network because of the logical tree pattern created by the master-slave architecture. If an attacker wishes to remain stealthy, he has few choices to pivot.

Adversary capabilities are also impacted by cyber characteristics. For example, the use of reverse tunnels requires more support (e.g. a pivot point in the enterprise network) in a SCADA networks than in an enterprise network because an outbound connection to the Internet may not be allowed on SCADA production networks. This restriction on reverse tunnels severely constricts C2 channels for the adversary. These channels are vital to cyber operations, even if the "cyber weapon" is automated. Even automated cyber threats require regular updates (bug fixes, introduction of new attack vectors) and some level of C2 (necessity for assessing damage and weapon effectiveness, changing payloads based on changing mission requirements) if they want to sustain their usefulness.

In the third step of IPCE, we evaluate the adversary. As our example, we will consider a nation state adversary. Their mission would be to attack our SCADA network to disrupt the controlled system. Their ultimate goal is therefore to send commands to the logic controllers. Using our previous analysis of the system, we know there are two ways to do so: the adversary can either compromise the MTU or send commands locally to the RTUs or PLCs. We can look at historical cases for likely *modus operandi* of an adversary and evaluate if our adversary could perform such attacks. Looking back at previous targeted attacks events (Mandiant, 2013), we can identify a scenario starting with a phishing email designed to gain a foothold, then a pivot from the enterprise network to the target of interest in the SCADA network. In terms of USB infection, we can look at Stuxnet (Falliere, et al., 2011) as guidance for how a USB malware can bridge an "air gap". We see that the malware is introduced in the isolated network, then spreads "laterally" until it finds a node that has access to outside to establish C2. The goal is to establish a hold in the targeted network and maintain C2 until a payload needs to be delivered, i.e. what Applegate (Applegate, 2012) calls *positional cyber manoeuvre*. Once C2 is established, the malware is updated to perform its final mission. To insert the malware, an agent (willing or coerced) could simply insert the malware on the local control network in a SCADA substation which would send commands directly to the RTUs or PLCs, bypassing the MTU.

The fourth and final step is the development of adversary CoAs. Tables 1 to 4 will guide us through all the sub-steps of the development of adversary CoAs, from the development of CoAs to the generation of response guidance matrices for pre-planned responses. Each of these tables are also representative of the kind of products these sub-steps contribute to the overall planning process. For example, the Adversary CoAs product might be used for wargaming, the indicators product might be used to derive indications and warnings, the sensor tasking product might be used for ISTAR planning and the response guidance matrix might be used by operational commanders to respond to attacks.

Based on the study of historical cases and the capacity of the adversary, we might consider that our adversary could not adopt a supply chain attack CoA, but could use traditional cyber exploitation or bribe an employee to plant a USB device. We rule out a supply chain attack CoA but find that he might employ a targeted attack or a USB infection. We start our process by listing the likely adversary CoAs in Table 1.

**Table 1:** Adversary CoAs

| Adversary CoA |
|---|
| CoA 1: Injects a USB malware, spread laterally until C&C is established and then attack master controller |
| CoA 2: Infect a node in the enterprise network then pivot and attack SCADA master controller |

Based on these CoAs, we can develop a number of events which would be strong indicators of the occurrence of a particular CoA. For example, we know, based on our analysis of the environment that traffic between endpoints is not observed in normal operation. However, when the USB malware spreads laterally in the first CoA, we will observe this kind of traffic. We can consider that event to be an indicator of the USB malware CoA. Table 2 updates the matrix of table I by adding indicator columns and marking indicators seen in each CoA.

**Table 2:** Indicators

| Adversary CoA | Indicators | | | |
|---|---|---|---|---|
| | I-1: Communication between RTU/PLC nodes | I-2: Outbound traffic from SCADA network | I-3: Malicious document in a phishing email | I-4: Inbound traffic from enterprise to SCADA |
| CoA 1 | Y | Y | | |
| CoA 2 | | | Y | Y |

Once indicators are assigned to each CoA, based on our analysis of the cyber terrain and the likely enemy avenues of approach, we can position sensors (for example IDSs, system logs, HUMINT, etc.) and provide a tasking for each sensor to look for a specific observation that would match with the indicators. This is similar to the production of the ICP in conventional operations. While the IPCE process *per se* ends with the production of an ICP, like an the IPOE and IPB, we now provide examples of how its deliverables can be turned into further products within the operational planning process. For example, if indicators in the ICP are tasked to particular sensors, we obtain a sensor tasking (i.e. ISTAR plan). Table 3 provides a possible sensor tasking for our example.

In the event a sensor reports an event (or combination thereof) that is identified by the matrix, we infer that we are dealing with a specific CoA. We can now act directly on that intelligence to take the course of action that thwarts the specified enemy CoA in the most efficient manner. The planning process can identify (using war gaming or incident response preparation) actions that need to be taken to react to a CoA. A commander can list these automatic responses in the planning process in an "attack guidance matrix", or more appropriately in this case a *response guidance matrix* (RGM), that clearly conveys the commander's intent in terms of response to adversary CoAs.

**Table 3:** Sensor tasking

| Adver-sary CoA | Indicators | | | | Sensor tasking | | | | |
|---|---|---|---|---|---|---|---|---|---|
| | I-1 | I-2 | I-3 | I-4 | Tasking 1: SCADA network Firewall Logs | Tasking 2: Mail server logs | Tasking 3: IDS command center (MTU node location) | Tasking 4: IDS Substation 1 | Tasking 5: IDS substation 2 |
| CoA 1 | Y | Y | | | Out-bound C2 traffic | | Attack traffic from SCADA | Inter RTU or PLC traffic | Inter RTU or PLC traffic |
| CoA 2 | | | Y | Y | In-bound recon traffic | Phishing email | Attack traffic from enter-prise | | |

Table 4 builds on Table 3 by adding a response guidance matrix for automated responses.

The actions identified by the response guidance matrix can be considered orders representing the commander's intent and be followed immediately in the event of a report from the tasked sensors identifying a CoA. This enables a timely response because there is no need to check back with the higher levels of the chain of command. In the cyber realm, this is particularly important because the chain of command is affected by the human response time which is orders of magnitude greater than the reaction time of an automated process.

**Table 4:** Response guidance matrix

| | Indicators | | | | Sensor tasking | | | | | Attack guidance matrix |
|---|---|---|---|---|---|---|---|---|---|---|
| Adversary CoA | I-1 | I-2 | I-3 | I-4 | T-1 | T-2 | T-3 | T-4 | T-5 | Automated response |
| CoA 1 | Y | Y | | | Outbound C&C traffic | | Attack traffic from SCADA | Inter RTU or PLC traffic | Inter RTU or PLC traffic | Use IPS to block outbound traffic from SCADA |
| CoA 2 | | | Y | Y | Inbound recon traffic | Phish email | Attack traffic from enterprise | | | Use IPS to block Inbound traffic to SCADA |

# 5   Discussion

Looking back at traditional risk analysis, the main sub-products are the list of scenarios and their estimated likelihood and the benefit-cost analysis of countermeasures. In terms of informing a commander planning computer network operations, this guides him to install the countermeasures with the highest benefit-cost ratio until no budget is left. If the commander requires additional guidance, for example wanting to devise a response plan to a compromise that was just discovered, he is expected to re-iterate on the risk analysis process based on this new information. This lengthens the decision making process at the critical moment when contact with the adversary has occurred. In this light, while the risk analysis approach provides some guidance for planning, it does not provide any insight for operations.

On the other hand, the IPCE process generates products that can be used to inform operations. The focus of the IPCE methodology is to deny adversary CoAs and, as such, focuses efforts on contingency planning and surveillance aimed at finding the adversary's intent and CoA. To do so, during the course of IPCE, commanders are required to formally reason about the expected enemy CoA and about the indicators revealing the pursuit of those CoAs by an adversary in the context of the strengths and weaknesses of their "cyber terrain". This leads them to create surveillance requirements (sensor tasking) and indicators of compromise. These sub-products can be used to inform commanders about daily operational needs, such as staffing levels, and provide metrics allowing to gauge success. For example, a command that routinely fails to monitor all indicators might be understaffed or inappropriately trained. In addition, the generation of the response guidance matrix forces commanders to identify events that require an immediate response and prepare the appropriate contingency plans. These plans can then be activated in the event of a compromise quickly, because they do not require additional analysis by the commander. This moves the requirements in terms of information processing to the planning process instead of operations. This allows commanders to react faster to threats.

Ultimately, the sub-products of IPCE are providing commanders with tools that guide their operations rather than only informing their planning. It also helps commanders take a more proactive approach in interacting with the adversary by actively pursuing surveillance where the cyber terrain is advantageous rather than only monitoring his own operations. This leads to intelligence-driven computer network operations where the focus is on collecting intelligence that is directly actionable without the need for a lengthy analysis process in the critical moments where contact with the adversary is achieved.

# 6   Conclusion

As we have seen, by acquiring a deep understanding of the operating environment and of the relationship between the adversary and the environment, we can create a matrix linking an enemy's likely CoAs, indicators of those CoAs, sensor tasking and a response guidance matrix for automated response. That matrix can inform both countermeasure planning, such as IDS placement, and operations, such as the automated activation of incident response actions. In that sense, even if the cyber realm does not present the traditional Weather-Enemy-Terrain (WET) characteristics triad, it was possible for us to adapt it to the IPOE methodology to the cyber realm with the Traffic-Adversary-Network (TAN) triad, in order to be able to inform the intelligence cycle and the cyber operations planning process.

Using this process for the defense of a SCADA network, we have demonstrated how the environmental particularities of SCADA networks, such as the regularity of the traffic, the master-slave network relationships and the relative isolation from outside networks, force adversaries to maintain complex command and control channels as part of their attack CoAs. Depending on the exact CoAs, the channels will take different forms. By creating indicators that fingerprint each CoA, it is possible to determine the exact CoA the enemy is pursuing. This allows us to better plan our defenses both in terms of preparing contingencies, but also in terms of placing sensors to observe the appropriate indicators. These sub-products of IPCE, which are not available in traditional risk analysis processes, allow commanders to make sure actionable intelligence is collected and enables intelligence-driven computer network operations.

Naturally, we could do much more with the results of the IPCE. One of the most obvious applications would be in the realm of battlefield shaping. Just as an army commander might attempt to force an enemy commander to use certain avenues of approach by planting obstructions and laying minefields, a cyber commander might want to modify his terrain to force his enemy into certain CoAs. This cyber battlefield shaping might be even more efficient than in the physical realm because re-plugging cables is often easier than moving mountains. This is especially true for computer network operations where we own the infrastructure. In that sense, researching network design principles, such as the creation of chokepoints or the design of networks for observability, could yield interesting results.

## References

Applegate, S. D. (2012) The Principle of Maneuver in Cyber Operations, Paper read at 4th International Conference on Cyber Conflict (CYCON), Talinn, Estonia, June.

Department of Defense (2009) " Joint Intelligence Preparation of the Operational Environment", [online], Department of Defense, http://www.fas.org/irp/doddir/dod/jp2-01-3.pdf.

Department of Defense ( 2011) "Defense Technical Information Center", [online], Department of Defense, http://www.dtic.mil/doctrine/new_pubs/jp5_0.pdf.

Falliere, N., Murchu, L. O. and Chien, E. (2011) "W32.Stuxnet Dossier Version 1.4",[online], Symantec Security Response, http://www.symantec.com/content/en/us/enterprise/media/security_response/whitepapers/w32_stuxnet_dossier.pdf.

Liang, Q. and Xiangsui, W. (1999) Unrestricted Warfare, PLA Literature and Arts Publishing House, Beijing.

Liles, S., Rogers, M., Dietz, E. J. and Larson, D. (2012) Applying Traditional Military Principles to Cyber Warfare, Paper read at 4th International Conference on Cyber Conflict (CYCON), Talinn, Estonia, June.

Mandiant (2013) "APT1 - Exposing One of China's Cyber Espionage Units", [online], Mandiant, http://intelreport.mandiant.com/Mandiant_APT1_Report.pdf.

Ross, R. S. ( 2012) "NIST SP - 800-30rev1 Guide for Conducting Risk Assessments", [online], NIST, http://www.nist.gov/customcf/get_pdf.cfm?pub_id=912091.

Syalim, A., Hori, Y. and Sakurai, K. (2009) Comparison of Risk Analysis Methods: Mehari, Magerit, NIST800-30 and Microsoft's Security Management Guide, Paper read at International Conference on Availability, Reliability and Security 2009 (ARES '09), Fukuoka, Japan, March.

# Strategies for Combating Sophisticated Attacks

## Chad Arnold[2], Jonathan Butts[1], and Krishnaprasad Thirunarayan[2]

[1]Department of Electrical and Computer Engineering, Air Force Institute of Technology, Wright Patterson AFB, Dayton, Ohio, USA
[2]Department of Computer Science and Engineering, Wright State University, Dayton, Ohio, USA
Arnold.102@wright.edu
Jonathan.Butts@afit.edu
t.k.prasad@wright.edu

*Originally Published in the Proceedings of ICCWS, 2013*

**Editorial Commentary**

Having touched on the geography of cyberspace and preparing intelligence analyses for the cyberspace environment, this next paper looks at how sophisticated attacks might be dealt with. The focus of this analysis is industrial control systems (ICS), which are used to control various utility functions, such as mining operations, electrical grids, and multimodal transportation systems. (A specific type of ICS is a SCADA system, which was the focus of the analysis in the previous paper.) ICSs are increasingly connected to the internet and are also increasing interconnected with each other. These trends enable efficiencies that make life easier and better. They also enable systemic vulnerabilities and the potential for unmitigated disaster, particularly if an attack on one section is able to cascade to other components and cause wide-spread failures that might make the Northeast Power blackout of 2003 look tame by comparison. The New York Times published a retrospect of that event in 2013, entitled "The Blackout That Exposed the Flaws in the Grid", which is available online at http://www.nytimes.com/2013/11/11/booming/the-blackout-that-exposed-the-flaws-in-the-grid.html?_r=0. It does a very nice job of explaining the effects and implications of that event at the personal level, exploring the relationship between power, water, food supplies, and social services. Thus the notion of ICS as a target for a cyber attack is one that should indeed be taken seriously.

In this paper, the authors describe the components of a generic ICS and then explore the current defense strategies. After exploring the limitations of those strategies, using real world examples, they propose that an inside-out analysis of the system from a security perspective is just as critical as having effective defense-in-depth strategies. This is very complementary to the conclusions derived in the IPCE paper but from a civilian operator perspective. It also is complementary to the next paper, Replication and Diversity for Survivability in Cyberspace: A Game Theoretic Approach", which analyzes defense in depth effectiveness. The three papers taken together combine synergistically to describe the knowledge needed for both civilian and military organizations to effectively confront cyber challenges.

**Abstract**: Industrial control systems (ICS) monitor and control the processes of public utility infrastructures that society depends on—the electric power grid, oil and gas pipelines, transportation and water facilities. Attacks that impact the operations of these critical assets could have devastating consequences. Yet, the complexity and desire to interconnect ICS components have introduced vulnerabilities and attack surfaces that previously did not exist. Cyber attacks are increasing in sophistication and have demonstrated an ability to cross over and create effects in the physical domain. Most notably, ICS associated with the critical infrastructure have proven susceptible to sophisticated, targeted attacks. The numerous communication paths, various ingress and egress points, diversity of technology and operating requirements provide myriad opportunities for a motivated adversary. Indeed, the complex systems enable both traditional and nontraditional attack surfaces. Current defense strategies and guidelines focus on defense-in-depth as a core component to protect critical resources. System security relies on multiple protection mechanisms to present an attacker with various challenges to overcome. This strategy, however, is not adequate for safeguarding critical assets against sophisticated attacks. This paper analyzes current ICS defense strategies and demonstrates that defense-in-depth alone is not a successful means for preventing attacks. Findings indicate that a paradigm shift is required to thwart advanced threats. As an alternative, cyber security for ICS is examined from the notion of weakest link as opposed to the current recommended strategies. Recent examples, including Stuxnet, are examined to shed light on the next-generation targeted attack in the context of current defensive strategies. The results demonstrate that current defense-in-depth strategies are necessary but not sufficient.

**Keywords**: ICS security, defense-in-depth limitations, critical infrastructure protection

# 1   Introduction

As industrial control systems grow in complexity and are connected to business and external networks, the number of security issues and the associated risks grow as well (US-CERT, 2009). Cyber attacks are increasing in sophistication and new guidelines are required to adapt to next generation attacks. A single security product, technology or solution alone cannot adequately protect an ICS. Indeed, a multiple layer strategy involving two or more overlapping security mechanisms, a technique known as defense-in-depth, has been recommended to minimize the impact of a failure (Rebane, 2001). Defense-in-depth uses multiple layers of defense and diverse strategies to prevent an attacker from successfully penetrating an ICS network. The strategies implement subsequent layers of defense to present an attacker with progressively more critical challenges to overcome.

In general, attacks can be *targeted* or *indiscriminate* depending on conditions surrounding the impacted entity. In either situation, if a trusted component becomes compromised, an attacker may be able to gain access to other components and create cascading effects downstream. While the popular defense-in-depth techniques may work against indiscriminate attacks, these strategies alone are not sufficient against targeted attacks.

An indiscriminate attack is an attack that is not directed at a specific company, individual, or process. This may consist of a common virus distributed over email or drive-by downloads from malicious websites that infect random machines. The cyber incident involving Browns Ferry nuclear plant is indicative of such an event as excessive network traffic caused problems with recirculation pumps (U.S. Nuclear Regulatory Commission, 2007). The Browns Ferry Unit 3 suffered from a broadcast storm, which is representative of many unintentional ICS cyber incidents. Many nonnuclear facilities have also experienced similar broadcast storms that have impacted the operation of power plants, refineries, and energy management systems (Weiss, 2010). These indiscriminate attacks are generic and can impact many devices that cannot handle the flood of data. In the historical instances surrounding ICS environments, the attacks typically exploited Windows platforms. The effects on ICS operations were the indirect result of using systems that contained the vulnerability.

Targeted attacks are specific attacks designed to affect a particular person, network, process, or end device on a network. These are typically more complex than indiscriminate attacks. Developers of targeted attacks likely possess deep insider knowledge of the environment, such as architecture, software, and the interaction between components (Brunner et al., 2010). Such sophisticated attacks are becoming increasing popular and are difficult to combat due to the technical ingenuity and complexity. Intrusion detection or other defensive systems that rely solely on signatures may not recognize such attacks since there will be no signature for them. Stuxnet, discovered in 2010, is an example of a targeted attack containing advanced malware that was specifically designed to target Siemens Simatic-S7 product line used in ICS environments. The malware targeted field devices and related control components in a fashion never publicly seen before and demonstrates how a motivated adversary can cause significant havoc with steadfast preparation and execution.

## 2    ICS distributed applications

Sophisticated and targeted cyber intrusions against owners and operators of ICS across multiple critical infrastructure sectors have dramatically increased in the past two years (Industrial Control Systems Cyber Emergency Response Team Control Systems Security Program, 2012). In general, ICS is a term that can represent several different control systems such as a process control system (PSC), distributed control system (DCS), or supervisory control and data acquisition (SCADA) system (Macaulay and Singer, 2012). ICS gather information from a variety of endpoint devices about the current status of a production process and can be fully or partially automated. ICS can be relatively simple or incredibly complex depending on the application and underlying architecture that is implemented.

Figure 21 represents a notional model of example domains and actors associated with the ICS environment. This diagram demonstrates a smart grid implementation and shows the operational intricacies. The domains consist of customers, markets, service providers, operations, bulk generation, transmission, and distribution. Actors include devices, systems, or programs that make decisions and exchange information necessary for performing applications (Office of the National Coordinator for Smart Grid Interoperability, 2010). At the ICS level, each individual network can be separated physically or logically depending on the underlying architecture. The interconnection of asset owners, companies, consumers, and customers adds to the overall system complexity. Additionally, connections to the Internet provide convenience as well as introduce potential security risks.

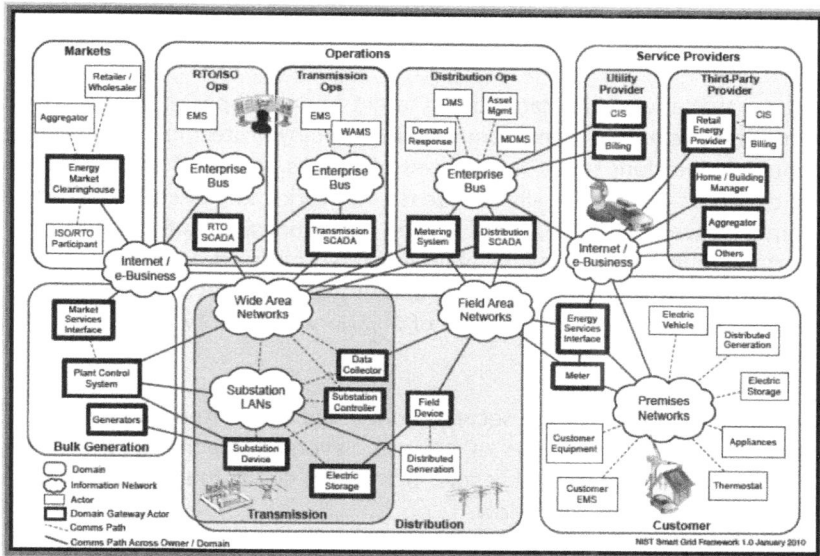

**Figure 21:** Conceptual model (Office of the National Coordinator for Smart Grid Interoperability, 2010)

Cyber threats to an ICS include myriad threat vectors, including non-typical network protocols, commands that cannot be blocked due to safety or production issues (e.g., alarm and event traffic), and otherwise valid communications used by an attacker in invalid ways (Macaulay and Singer, 2012). The numerous communication paths, various ingress and egress points, and diversity of control systems provide many opportunities for a motivated adversary to perform a cyber attack.

# 3   Current defense strategies

Government organizations and standards bodies recommend defense-in-depth as the primary strategy for achieving information assurance in computer networks and ICS communications (US-CERT, 2009), (Office of the National Coordinator for Smart Grid Interoperability, 2010),(National Security Agency, n.d.). Multiple layers of defense can be established to detect and mitigate many security issues. Several strategies are recommended for Internet facing control systems (Industrial Control Systems Cyber Emergency Response Team, 2011) but can also be applied to non Internet facing networks. Dividing control system functions into zones create clear boundaries to assist in effectively applying the appropriate level of defense.

Given that adversaries can attack a target from multiple points using either internal or external access, organizations deploy protection mechanisms at multiple locations to resist all classes of attacks. (National Security Agency, n.d.). Focus areas generally include the network and infrastructure perimeter, enclave boundaries, and trusted communication paths. Physical or virtual boundaries can be established based on functional responsibilities and may include an external zone, corporate zone, data zone, control zone, and safety zone and may consist of a variety of security mechanisms (US-CERT, 2009).

Figure 22 depicts typical security zones and associated security devices that provide several layers of defense. Several components can be integrated together to create a solid defense-in-depth foundation. The core elements are described below.

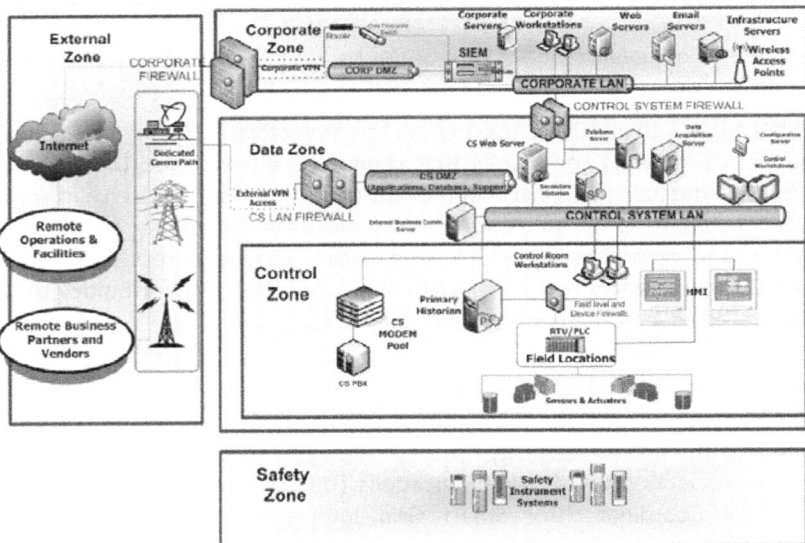

**Figure 22:** ICS zones and security mechanisms (US-CERT, 2009)

- Network segmentation is used to create demilitarized zones (DMZs). This can be accomplished with multiple routers and fire-

162

walls to provide granularity in defining access rights and privileges for separate functions.

- Firewalls are implemented at different networking layers to filter unwanted traffic. Many firewall options exist such as packet filter firewalls, proxy gateway firewalls, host based firewalls, or field-level firewalls that may be appropriate depending on the given control architecture.

- Passive intrusion detection systems (IDS) or active intrusion prevention systems (IPS), typically using signature-based checking, are used to monitor and sometimes take action on network activity that is unusual or unauthorized. Passive detection systems are generally used since availability is important in ICS applications. However, certain activity and abnormal traffic can trigger active responses depending on the location of the defensive system. Like a firewall, an IDS can be placed at ingress and egress points in the architecture or at the critical connectivity points such as security zones.

- Policies and procedures define guidelines for training all personnel, patching vulnerable components, analyzing event logs, responding to security incidents, and mitigating risk. A well-defined and properly executed plan is critical to the success of the defensive strategy. Security Incident Event Management (SIEM) technologies can collect, aggregate, and display log information for various events and provide insight for effective incident response, forensic activities, and for mitigation of risk.

Several security mechanisms are critical to defense-in-depth. Many defensive components are common in traditional information technology deployments; however, in ICS domains, it is important to adapt firewall rule sets, IDS attack signatures, and audit log software appropriately to protect data and communications. These defenses can improve security at several layers and assist in providing a secure network against indiscriminate attacks.

# 4   Case studies

Many components are necessary to successfully implement defense-in-depth strategies. Network architects and administrators implement multiple security zones, firewalls on the perimeters, intrusion detection systems, and other security mechanisms prevent attackers from penetrating

ICS networks. The degrees of protection can be limited by deployed tech-nologies and ICS configuration requirements. Implementations vary by industry and are sometimes constrained by limited resources. While de-fense-in-depth techniques have been prescribed, specific implementations may not conform exactly to the model nor may it contain every available defensive component. A network administrator or engineer for an ICS may interpret and implement defense-in-depth principles differently due to the uniqueness of an underlying SCADA system. The notional figure below was created to demonstrate a realistic SCADA configuration of an oil pipeline company (National Transportation Safety Board (NTSB) - NTSB/PAR-02/02; PB2002-916502, 1999) with defense-in-depth techniques applied.

While the depicted layers of defense can stop many indiscriminate attacks, it may only delay a motivated adversary. In the example above, with best practices applied, many vulnerabilities remain. An adversary may choose to exploit witting or unwitting insiders with USB drives, supply chain CD or DVDs, or exploit firmware upgrades. Dial-up modems, external terminal connections, and other unknown connections present additional weak-nesses and enable non-traditional access points. In addition, wireless de-vices and sensors may provide additional injection opportunities for an adversary. There are many avenues that a motivated adversary can explore and it is very difficult to safeguard against all attack vectors. Even with de-fense-in-depth security measures in place, ICS are still susceptible to so-phisticated cyber attacks or failures.

ICS have seen an increase in intentional and unintentional cyber attacks over the past ten years (Rebane, 2001). Several reported incidents are de-scribed below which highlight system damage from worms, virus, and other malicious cyber attacks. The attacks in this section are referred to as indiscriminate attacks which may have been prevented with proper de-fense-in-depth elements.

In 2003, the Sobig virus infected computers at the Amtrak dispatching headquarters, causing signaling systems to shut down and halt ten trains between Pennsylvania and South Carolina (Niland, 2003). The Slammer worm penetrated a computer at an Ohio nuclear plant in 2003, causing the safety monitoring system to be disabled for nearly five hours (Poulsen, 2003). At the Browns Ferry nuclear power plant in 2006, a "Data Storm" spike in traffic caused a programmable logic controller (PLC) to crash, resulting in the failure of recirculation pumps and forcing a manual reactor shutdown (United States Nuclear Regulatory Commission Office of Nuclear Reactor Regulation, April, 2007).

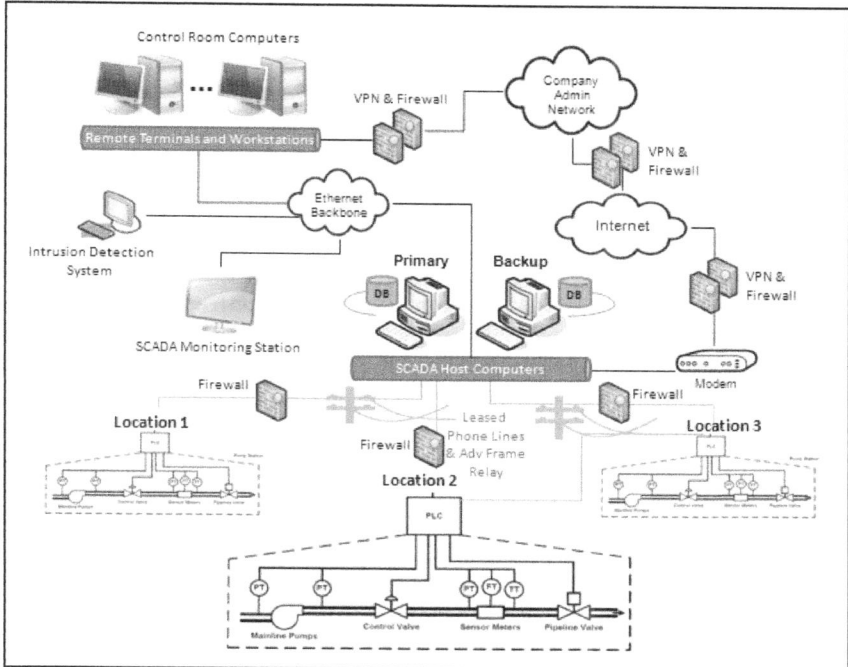

**Figure 23:** Notional SCADA network diagram

In August of 2012, Saudi Aramco, the world's biggest oil company, was attacked by the Shamoon virus which spread across the corporate network and erased 30,000 hard drives (Fineren and Bakr, 2012). According to reports, the virus did not directly impact the control systems or oil field data but instead affected the corporate network. This was only one of several attacks that have indirectly affected control systems and related networks. A few months earlier in April 2012, the National Iranian Oil Company, the second largest crude producer, was also affected by malicious software (Nasseri, 2012).

Many additional significant cyber incidents have occurred over the past several years (CSIS: Center for Strategic & International Studies, n.d.). Fortunately, the majority of historical events are the result of secondary effects and the damage has been minor. The absence of an overwhelming disaster, however, only perpetuates the false sense of security. Indeed, more sophisticated, targeted attacks could result in significant disruption or mass casualties.

# 5 Limitations of defense-in-depth strategies

Many layers of defense are described in this paper to potentially thwart cyber attacks. In the first set of case studies, the intrusions may have been detected, deterred, or possibly prevented if recommended security practices had been in place. While similar strategies may protect against indiscriminate attacks, they will likely not succeed in preventing sophisticated, targeted attacks. Indeed, cyber security is a weakest link issue, as nontraditional attack vectors are used in combination with sophisticated malware. This combination can allow adversaries to bypass network perimeters to gain access to areas that are assumed to be air-gapped. Traditionally, air-gapped networks, which were originally defined as having no external connections or direct access to the Internet, were thought to be secure. Note that many ICS were originally air-gapped, but are becoming more connected due to convenience.

A targeted attack can easily defeat traditional intrusion detection and related layered defensive technologies. Sophisticated, targeted malware generally presents unprecedented technical ingenuity and complexity and is difficult for traditional security devices to detect or thwart. Many existing solutions are reactive and require the presence of a known signature or predetermined behavior pattern for a threat to be detected. For example, an IDS can detect a wide range of attacks based on existing attack signatures, network traffic patterns, filenames, or file hashes. However, the signatures required to monitor for malicious traffic in many control networks are not adequate (US-CERT, 2009). Signature databases contain millions of signatures and most antivirus software solutions fail to detect between 40% and 90% of novel malware less than two weeks old (Macaulay and Singer, 2012).

The Stuxnet virus, discovered in 2010, is a prime example of sophisticated, targeted malware that bypassed traditional security defenses and used USB thumb drives to spread and bypass network perimeters. Additionally, in 2001, a disgruntled former employee launched a wireless attack on a sewage facility in Maroochy Shire, Queensland, which released millions of gallons of raw sewage into parks and rivers (Slay & Miller, 2008). The employee used authorized credentials and knowledge of the operating environment to achieve specific effects. Indeed, these two examples highlight scenarios where the defense-in-depth strategy is not sufficient.

Further examination of Stuxnet shows the malware was introduced into the target network, consisting of a Windows PC, using a USB drive and an unsuspecting human user. From the compromised machine, the malware propagated via the enterprise network through additional USB drives, infected PLC programming project files, network shares, and other methods utilizing several zero-day vulnerabilities in the Windows environment until it reached a control PC (Symantec: Nicolas Falliere, Liam O Murchu, and Eric Chien, 2011). The control PC is generally a Windows machine that is used to program PLCs. The malware traversed the network and installed on systems, avoiding detection by using valid (stolen) certificates. Stuxnet masked its presence on each PC by creating a root-kit and removing itself from USB devices after a set number of infections. Once the malware identified a control PC running WinCC or Step 7 PLC control software, alternate code was prepared, injected, and ultimately transferred to the specified PLC. The payload of Stuxnet was the compiled code that reprogrammed the end target PLC to manipulate the industrial processes. Disabling pumps, progressively activating turbines, and modifying speeds were a few of the Stuxnet operations. A targeted attack using nontraditional access is depicted in Figure 24.

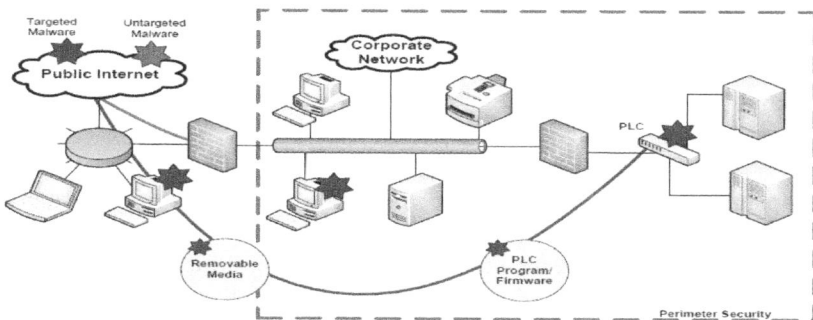

**Figure 24:** Targeted Stuxnet attack

Attackers that create targeted malware require deep insight and insider knowledge about the target environment settings to achieve desired goals.

This information can be gathered using various methods, including spear phishing to target an employee and compromise a legitimate account on the network. Additionally, a manager or remote operator may use virtual private network (VPN) access to perform maintenance or operational updates. Because these access points are considered trusted, they are not protected by the traditional defense-in-depth security mechanisms; compromise of any access point enables the attacker to become a trusted agent on the system.

Stuxnet demonstrates a new class and dimension of malware as it acts as a worm, virus, malware and exploit in a single package. Stuxnet uses a multi-staged attack vector to propagate to the targeted PLC. The worm is first introduced in the Windows environment. This is significant since the initial target is from a different operating system and environment than the end-target. It's difficult to notice infections from attacks such as Stuxnet on non-targeted systems since its presence is masked and does not impact the functionality of non-ICS operations.

Stuxnet highlights the nontraditional inputs (e.g., USB drive) that can be exploited by attackers using cyber methods. Unlike traditional cyber attacks, Stuxnet did not enter the network through the Internet via a compromised firewall or other ingress point. Non-traditional devices such as portable hard drives, personal laptops, music players, and cell phones can be extremely difficult to control and can allow a system to become infected with targeted malware bridging air-gapped networks. There are legitimate uses for the access points (e.g., applying system patches and updating software). As such, constraining the attack surface is nontrivial. In addition, new attack surfaces are introduced during system upgrades and architecture enhancements.

## 6 Alternative defense strategies

Implementing best practices or recommended security procedures, such as network segmentation and intrusion detection systems can often deter attacks, significantly reduce the time to detect an attack and reduce the impact of cyber attacks. However, as demonstrated, strategies consisting of defense-in-depth alone are not sufficient. Indeed, these techniques only attempt to the secure the network from the outside-in. To compliment this approach, the network must also be evaluated from the inside-out. This approach can help focus resources to more effectively combat targeted attacks.

New approaches to combating cyber attacks must also be proactive and evolve with time. Securing a network can begin with layered defenses to detect indiscriminate attacks. This can include reactive technologies which are efficient in detecting and characterizing known threats. However, for previously unseen cyber threats, additional strategies are needed to look for targeted malware. Existing recommendations can leave internal network components vulnerable to attack since defense-in-depth only protects the outer most perimeter and network layers. However, inside these boundaries lie trusted components that can generally communicate without limitation or supervision from defensive technologies. A new security paradigm is required. Individual components should not be blindly trusted because of their location inside a network. Currently, individual components lack validation. Processes and communications within the internal network, however, should remain untrusted until proven otherwise. With this approach, input and output validation at the component level is emphasized. Note that this notion is contrary to current security practices that do not evaluate every input and output connection, starting at the core. Building trust chains from inside-out allows evaluation and prioritization of assets in order to focus efforts and enable graceful degradation in the event of a cyber attack.

# 7   Conclusion and future work

This paper evaluates traditional security defense strategies from a perspective that challenges the current recommendations from standards organizations. Defense-in-depth is defined and applied in the context of ICS and network security. A notional ICS network, with security devices applied per standards organizations, is presented. Several examples demonstrate security challenges that ICS incur from cyber actors. The difference between indiscriminate and sophisticated, targeted attacks is described in detail. The necessity for additional evaluation methods, beyond the recommended defense-in-depth, becomes apparent when traditional strategies are not sufficient in cases such as Stuxnet. Alternative strategies are discussed that aim at protecting ICS in areas where defense-in-depth falls short. Finally, a new method to evaluate ICS cyber security is discussed as alternative strategies lay the ground work for a future evaluation model. Future work will introduce a new framework for analyzing exposures using input and output validation in an ICS environment containing malicious activity.

ICS networks and related components will continue to experience cyber attacks. Preventing destruction or severe effects across critical assets, which could have devastating consequences, is necessary. ICS networks need to be able to detect and withstand cyber attacks. Current standards organizations must evolve existing recommendations to expand defense-in-depth strategies. While experts agree that defense-in-depth is neces-sary, it has been demonstrated that it is not sufficient, especially when combating targeted, sophisticated cyber attacks.

# References

Brunner, M., Hofinger, H.K.C., Roblee, C., Schoo, P. and Todt, S. (2010) Infiltrating Critical Infrastructures with Next-Generation Attacks, December, [online], HYPERLINK "http://www.aisec.fraunhofer.de/content/dam/aisec/en/pdf/studien/AISEC_InfiltratingC riticalInfrastructures.pdf" http://www.aisec.fraunhofer.de/content/dam/aisec/en/pdf/studien/AISEC_InfiltratingCri ticalInfrastructures.pdf .

CSIS: Center for Strategic & International Studies Significant Cyber Events, [online], HYPERLINK "http://csis.org/files/publication/121113_Significant_Cyber_Incidents_Since_2006.pdf" http://csis.org/files/publication/121113_Significant_Cyber_Incidents_Since_2006.pdf [2012].

Fineren, D. and Bakr, A. (2012) Saudi Aramco repairing damage from computer attack, 26 August, [online], HYPERLINK "http://in.reuters.com/article/2012/08/26/saudi-aramco-hacking-idINL5E8JQ43P20120826" http://in.reuters.com/article/2012/08/26/saudi-aramco-hacking-idINL5E8JQ43P20120826 .

Industrial Control Systems Cyber Emergency Response Team (2011) ICS-ALERT-11-343-01—CONTROL SYSTEM INTERNET ACCESSIBILITY, 09 December, [online], HYPERLINK "http://www.us-cert.gov/control_systems/pdf/ICS-ALERT-11-343-01.pdf" http://www.us-cert.gov/control_systems/pdf/ICS-ALERT-11-343-01.pdf .

Industrial Control Systems Cyber Emergency Response Team Control Systems Security Program (2012) ICS-CERT Incident Response Summary Report: 2009-2011, July, [online], HYPERLINK "http://www.us-cert.gov/control_systems/pdf/ICS-CERT_Incident_Response_Summary_Report_09_11.pdf" http://www.us-cert.gov/control_systems/pdf/ICS-CERT_Incident_Response_Summary_Report_09_11.pdf .

Industrial Control Systems Cyber Emergency Response Team Control Systems Security Program (2012) ICS-TIP-12-146-01—TARGETED CYBER INTRUSION DETECTION AND MITIGATION STRATEGIES, 25 May, [online], HYPERLINK "http://www.us-cert.gov/control_systems/pdf/ICS-TIP-12-146-01.pdf" http://www.us-cert.gov/control_systems/pdf/ICS-TIP-12-146-01.pdf .

Macaulay, T. and Singer, B. (2012) Cyber Security for Industrial Control Systems: SCADA, DCS, PLC, HMI, and SIS, Boca Raton: CRC Press.

Nasseri, L. (2012) Iran Computer Worm Targets Oil Ministry, State Companies, 23 April, [online], HYPERLINK "http://www.bloomberg.com/news/2012-04-23/iran-detects-computer-worm-targeting-oil-ministry-mehr-says.html" http://www.bloomberg.com/news/2012-04-23/iran-detects-computer-worm-targeting-oil-ministry-mehr-says.html .

National Security Agency Defense in Depth: A practical strategy for achieving Information Assurance in today's highly networked environments, [online], HYPERLINK "http://www.nsa.gov/ia/_files/support/defenseindepth.pdf" http://www.nsa.gov/ia/_files/support/defenseindepth.pdf .

National Transportation Safety Board (NTSB) - NTSB/PAR-02/02; PB2002-916502 (1999) Pipeline Rupture and Subsequent Fire in Bellingham, Washington, 10 June, [online], HYPERLINK "http://www.ntsb.gov/doclib/reports/2002/PAR0202.pdf" http://www.ntsb.gov/doclib/reports/2002/PAR0202.pdf .

Niland, M. (2003) Computer virus brings down train signals, August, [online], HYPERLINK "http://www.informationweek.com/news/security/vulnerabilities/showArticle.jhtml?articleID=13100807" http://www.informationweek.com/news/security/vulnerabilities/showArticle.jhtml?articleID=13100807 .

Office of the National Coordinator for Smart Grid Interoperability (2010) 'NIST framework and roadmap for smart grid interoperability standards, release 1.0', U.S. Department of Commerce and National Institute of Standards and Technology, NIST Special Publication 1108, Available: HYPERLINK "http://www.nist.gov/public_affairs/releases/upload/smartgrid_interoperability_final.pdf" http://www.nist.gov/public_affairs/releases/upload/smartgrid_interoperability_final.pdf

Poulsen, K. (2003) Slammer worm crashed Ohio nuke plant network, August, [online], HYPERLINK "http://www.securityfocus.com/news/6767" http://www.securityfocus.com/news/6767 .

Rebane, J.C. (2001) The Stuxnet Computer Worm and Industrial Control System Security, New York: Nova Science Publishers, Inc.

Reed, T. (2004) At the Abyss - An Insiders History of the Cold War, New York: Ballantine Books.

Slay, J. and Miller, M. (2008) 'Lessons learned from Maroochy water breach', IFIP International Federation for Information Processing, vol. 253, pp. 73-82.

Symantec: Nicolas Falliere, Liam O Murchu, and Eric Chien (2011) W32.Stuxnet Dossier, February, [online], HYPERLINK "http://www.symantec.com/content/en/us/enterprise/media/security_response/whitepapers/w32_stuxnet_dossier.pdf" http://www.symantec.com/content/en/us/enterprise/media/security_response/whitepapers/w32_stuxnet_dossier.pdf .

U.S. DHS ICS-CERT (2012) Gas Pipeline Cyber Intrusion Campaign, April, [online], HYPERLINK "http://www.us-cert.gov/control_systems/pdf/ICS-CERT_Monthly_Monitor_Apr2012.pdf" http://www.us-cert.gov/control_systems/pdf/ICS-CERT_Monthly_Monitor_Apr2012.pdf .

U.S. Nuclear Regulatory Commission (2007) NRC Information Notice: 2007-15: Effects of Ethernet-Based, Non-Safety Related Controls on the Safe and Continued Operation of Nuclear Power Stations, April, [online], HYPERLINK "http://www.nrc.gov/reading-rm/doc-collections/gen-comm/info-notices/2007/in200715.pdf" http://www.nrc.gov/reading-rm/doc-collections/gen-comm/info-notices/2007/in200715.pdf [2012].

United States Nuclear Regulatory Commission Office of Nuclear Reactor Regulation (April, 2007) Effects of ethernet-based, non-safety related controls on the safe and continued operation of nuclear power stations, NRC Information Notice 2007-15.

US-CERT (2009) Recommended Practice: Improving Industrial Control Systems Cybersecurity with Defense-In-Depth Strategies, Department of Homeland Security's United States Computer Emergency Readiness Team (US-CERT).

Weiss, J. (2010) Protecting Industrial Control Systems from Electronic Threats, New York: Momentum Press.

# Replication and Diversity for Survivability in Cyberspace: A Game Theoretic Approach

**Charles Kamhoua[1], Kevin Kwiat[1], Mainak Chatterjee[2], Joon Park[3] and Patrick Hurley[1]**

[1]Air Force Research Laboratory, Information Directorate, Cyber Assurance Branch, Rome, New York, USA

[2]University of Central Florida, Electrical Engineering and Computer Science Dept, Orlando, Florida, USA

[3]Syracuse University, School of Information Studies (iSchool), Syracuse, New York, USA

charles.kamhoua @ rl.af.mil
kevin.kwiat @ rl.af.mil
mainak @ eecs.ucf.edu
jspark @ syr.edu
patrick.hurley @ rl.af.mil

*Originally Published in the Proceedings of ICCWS, 2013*

**Editorial Commentary**

The focus of this paper is the analysis of "malicious faults caused by an intelligent attacker," which might be considered an appropriate definition of an adversary in a cyberwarfare engagement. The intelligent attacker is assumed to have analyzed the system (eg, developed an intelligence data set that describes the system and appropriate means for attacking it effectively) and developed "sophisticated attacks that will cause the maximum damage." While one can quibble that maximum damage may not be the goal, as opposed to appropriate damage, the statement of assumptions lays the stage for the analysis by defining the parameters.

Applying a game theory approach to considering potential strategies from both the attacker and defender perspective, a key finding is that the relative skills of the adversaries are important to the outcome. However, when both are competent, then the design of the system becomes important. In particular, diversification (not having all your eggs in one basket) and replication (back ups for back ups) become critical features. As noted, "a less skillful defender that diversifies his replicas is always better off than the more skillful defender using similar replicas."

This is useful knowledge for both private and public entities. One of the realities that managers currently face is the lack of a skilled workforce. Highly talented individuals are rare and in high demand. Often managers are forced to fill positions with people who are not quite as skilled as they will eventually become. The analysis presented in this paper indicates that these weaknesses in human resources talents can be mitigated by system design. From the perspective of the military commander focused on developing attack and defense strategies, this analysis provides insights into how target selection might be considered and how defenders might be deployed.

**Abstract**: An effective defense-in-depth avoids a large percentage of threats and defeats those threats that turn into attacks. When an attack evades detection, it may disrupt the systems and networks, and then the need for survivability is more critical. In this context, mission assurance seeks to ensure that critical mission essential functions (MEFs) survive and fight through the attacks against the underlying cyber infrastructure. Survivability represents the quantified ability of a system, subsystem, equipment, process, or procedure to function continually during and after a disturbance. US Air Force systems carry varying survivability requirements depending on MEF's criticality and protection conditions. Almost invariably, however, replication of a subsystem, equipment, process, or procedure is necessary to meet a system's survivability requirements. Therefore, the degree of replication within a system can be paramount for MEF's survival. Moreover, diversity will prevent the same fault or attack from damaging all the replicas so that they can continue the mission. This research shows that the more dangerous vulnerabilities (that affect more replicas) in a system are sometimes less likely to be exploited. The attacker may be better off when exploiting small vulnerabilities because they will be less protected by the defender. In fact, diversity always gives extra challenges to attackers. This work uses the mathematical framework of game theory to show the significance of replica diversity for mission survival in cyberspace.

**Keywords:** cyber security, diversity, game theory, replication, survivability

# 1 Introduction

Today, most system and network operators in an organization (academic institute, industry lab, government facility) deploy fairly homogenous systems primarily because of ease of maintenance, monitoring, and upgrades. Homogeneity could provide advantages at the software systems, configuration files, security protection mechanisms, hardware or device level, network interfaces, etc. However, such homogenous environment also facilitates an attacker to concentrate their efforts on just a few types of systems. If the attackers are successful in finding any vulnerability, then they can exploit that to launch an attack that can potentially affect a large number of systems. Thus homogeneity acts as a catalyst that enhances the asymmetric advantages that attackers enjoy today. For example, in May 2012, the Flame virus was declared the most complex malware ever written by researchers at Kaspersky Labs after infecting approximately 1000 machines primarily located in Middle Eastern countries. Flame exploited a flaw in the Microsoft certificate licensing service to propagate and used several novel schemes to avoid detection and gather usage data illicitly. The success of the Flame virus is accelerated by the fact that most computers run identical software from Microsoft.

Approved for Public Release; Distribution Unlimited: 88ABW-2012-4886 dated September 10, 2012.

One of the ways to impede attackers is to make the expected payoff much lower than the cost of launching attacks. It is to be noted that, attackers would like to use the best possible and most efficient strategies to inflict the maximum damage. Thus, attackers can be discouraged by diversifying the technologies that the systems use. This is because a typical attack exploits a specific vulnerability and different systems are not likely to be affected. For example, if systems were different, the attackers will have to explore additional vulnerabilities as a vulnerability in one system might not be effective in other systems. This diversity would cause impediments for the attackers in two ways: i) by increasing their effort required to infect systems, and ii) by reducing the number of systems that could be infected because of the additional efforts required. In summary, the more diversity is introduced in a system the less will be the attacker's payoff from exploiting a system's vulnerability. In either case, the return on investment is reduced making it less profitable to attack.

Generally, although some survivability steps can be applied before an incident, some survivability models are effective after the security mechanisms have failed or after exploitable vulnerabilities have been discovered on a system. By definition, survivability is the capability of a system to fulfill its mission, in a timely manner, even in the presence of attack, failures, or accidents. To assure system survivability, replication and diversity become two strong components. Replication will allow the tolerance of the failure to a minimum number of replicas. For instance, a system using five replicas for the same mission will tolerate the failure of two replicas if using a simple majority vote. Diversity will prevent the same fault or attack from damaging all the replicas so that they can continue the mission.

The main contribution of this paper is to provide an analytical modeling of replicas diversity for critical mission survival using game theory. With the increased complexity of cyberspace, cyber survivability will increasingly rely on theoretical models. Analytical and theoretical approaches such as game theoretic modeling provide a general framework that can be applied to numerous problem specific scenarios. Game theory is the branch of applied mathematics that formalizes strategic interaction among intelligent rational agents. A game theoretic approach is appropriate because the attacks launched in critical systems are becoming more sophisticated and obviously originate from intelligent agents. Moreover, a game theoretic framework can use the Nash equilibrium profile to predict an intelligent attacker's behavior. This research shows that the more dangerous vulnerabilities (that affect more replicas) in a system are sometimes less likely to be exploited. The attacker may be better off exploiting small vulnerabilities because they will be less protected by the defender. To the best of our knowledge, there is no research that analyzes replica diversity in the framework of game theory.

The remainder of this paper is organized as follows. Section 2 is about the related works. Section 3 presents our game model. From the general framework of Section 3, Section 4 uses a typical scenario to illustrate our game model. Section 5 shows our numerical results that confirm the paramount importance of replicas diversity in a critical mission. Section 6 concludes the paper and expresses future research directions.

## 2    Related works

The interest of using game theory to address network security challenge has increased in recent years. This is because game theoretic modeling favors a comprehensive understanding of strategic cyber interaction. Several types of games have been used depending on the specific scenario.

Different scenario results in a distinct game model. Since the attacker's and defender's goals are purely conflicting, zero-sum games are used in (Nguyen 2009, Kamhoua 2012a). Most game theoretic models assume that all the players are rational. The research in (Sun 2008, Kamhoua 2011) relaxes the assumption of player's rationality and uses the mathematical framework of evolutionary game theory to model network security. In some scenarios, the security game is static (Jormakka 2005, Liu 2006), but in others, the game model is repeated, or more generally stochastic (Nguyen 2009, Shiva 2010, Kamhoua 2012b). A stochastic game is a generalization of a repeated game. In a repeated game, players play the same stage game in all periods, whereas in a stochastic game, the stage game can randomly change from one period to the next. Cyber security games also consider what information each player knows. When the rules of the game, and each player's strategy and payoffs are assumed to be common knowledge, the cyber game is of complete information as in (Jormakka 2005). Otherwise, we have a game of incomplete information that can be formulated as a Bayesian game as in (Liu 2006). The work in (Liu 2006, Agah 2004) modeled intrusion detection as a game. Information sharing in online social networks is modeled using a Markov decision process (Park 2012) and a zero-sum Markov game in (Kamhoua 2012a). The research in (Kamhoua 2012b) uses a repeated voting game among replicated nodes to extend the mission survival times in a critical mission. A key component of game theoretic modeling of cybersecurity is to find the Nash equilibrium of the cybersecurity game. At a Nash equilibrium profile, no player can increase his payoff by a unilateral deviation. Also, each player is playing his best response to other players' strategies. As a consequence, the network defender can use the Nash equilibrium profile to predict the attacker's behavior. A survey of game theory as applied to network security is provided in (Roy 2010, Alpcan 2010). A detailed presentation of game theory is found in (Myerson 1997). As we can see, game theory has provided a solid mathematical framework to model cyber security. Nevertheless, to the best of our knowledge, this is the first work that investigates replicas' diversity for cyber survivability in the framework of game theory.

# 3   Game model

Our game model focuses on malicious faults caused by an intelligent attacker. By intelligent, we mean that the attacker can analyze, understand the system and respond by launching sophisticated attacks that will cause the maximum damage given the defensive actions. Clearly, the attacker's goal is to impact the maximum number of replicas. In fact, the greater the number of compromised replicas, the more likely the mission will fail. On the other hand, the goal of the network defender is to minimize the number of compromised replicas. The conflicting nature of the objectives makes the scenario ideal to be modeled as a game. Moreover, a successful attack necessarily means a failure by the defender and a successful defense means a failed attack. Therefore, we model the conflict as a 2-payer zero-sum game.

Let us assume that there are $N$ diverse replicas of a node running a mission essential function. Let them be denoted as $R_i$ where $1 \leq i \leq N$. Diverse replicas mean that the replicas are not perfect copies of each other. Though we assume that the replicas execute the same function and should yield the same results, their protection mechanisms are different. That is, each node of those $N$ replicas is exposed to different vulnerabilities.

While we are dealing with a survivability model, let us also assume there are known vulnerabilities in the system. The vulnerabilities here include all the vulnerabilities in the replicas, where each replica may have its own set of vulnerabilities. Certainly, a critical system must be strengthened with a survivability model and a fight through capability to be able to continue its operation despite known vulnerabilities. Moreover, the network defender or system administrator must continuously scan their systems in search of new vulnerabilities before any attacker can exploit them. The defender must also find the potential attack strategies of an intelligent attacker as well as the best defense strategies against those attacks. Cautiously, the defender always acts as if the system is under attack by an intelligent attacker having knowledge of the system. For instance, 57th Information Aggressor Squadron executes cyberspace operations by emulating current and emerging threat capabilities and tactics and providing adversary operational and tactical influence operations and network operations (Online). In contrast, the attacker also scans the system and would like to exploit new vulnerabilities before the defender become aware of them. At anytime, the set of discovered vulnerabilities can be represented using a Venn diagram depicted in Figure 1.

Figure 1 shows 5 vulnerabilities (i.e., $V_1$, $V_2$, ...$V_5$). $V_1$ is a vulnerability only known to the attacker. The vulnerabilities $V_2$, $V_3$, and $V_4$ are common knowledge between the attacker and the defender. $V_5$ is a vulnerability only known to the defender. Finally, there could be other vulnerabilities that are unknown to both the attacker and the defender; however, these vulnerabilities will not appear anywhere in the game formulation or solution so they are omitted from the Venn diagram.

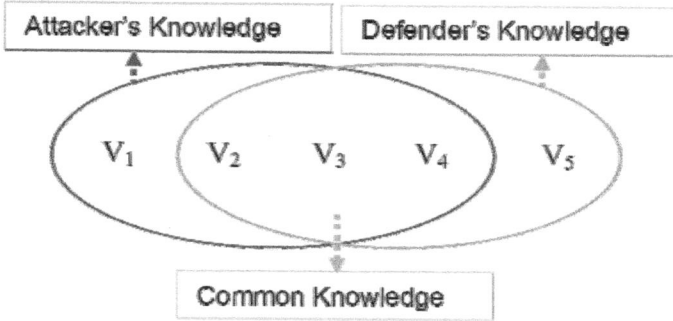

**Figure 1:** Venn diagram representation of discovered vulnerabilities

However, the defender does have a strategic advantage in the sense that the defender's scanning of their own systems is designed with the authority to by-pass any alarms that the attacker would have to try and avoid. Furthermore, the defender's scanning would also be designed to fully anticipate any defensive system agility (e.g., IP hopping) that are meant to confound an attacker. Therefore, we might reasonably assume that the defender has an edge in finding the vulnerabilities before the attacker. By then stating that we are letting the attacker have equal knowledge concedes an advantage to the attacker that he would not likely have otherwise - thus it might be considered a worst case scenario. Therefore, we assume that the subset of vulnerabilities affecting each of the replicas is common knowledge between the attacker and the defender. Thus, each player can design a vulnerability matrix that will help to optimize their attack and defense strategy accordingly.

Let the discovered vulnerabilities be denoted by $V_j (1 \leq j \leq K)$, where $K$ is the total number of the vulnerabilities in the system. Each of the replicas can be exposed to any number of vulnerabilities. In general, replica $R_i$ is exposed to $m$ vulnerabilities, where $0 \leq m \leq K$. To obtain the vulnerability matrix, we define a binary variable $X_{ij}$ $(1 \leq i \leq N, 1 \leq j \leq K)$ as follow:

$$X_{ij} = \begin{cases} 1 \text{ if replica } R_i \text{ can be affected by vulnerability } V_j \\ 0 \text{ if replica } R_i \text{ is safe from vulnerability } V_j \end{cases}$$

The vulnerability matrix can be represented as in Table 1.

**Table 1:** Vulnerability matrix

| | | Replicas | | | | | | |
|---|---|---|---|---|---|---|---|---|
| | | $R_1$ | $R_2$ | $R_3$ | ... | $R_i$ | ... | $R_N$ |
| | $V_1$ | $x_{11}$ | $x_{21}$ | $x_{31}$ | | $x_{i1}$ | | $x_{N1}$ |
| | $V_2$ | $x_{12}$ | $x_{22}$ | $x_{32}$ | | $x_{i2}$ | | $x_{N2}$ |
| | $V_3$ | $x_{13}$ | $x_{23}$ | $x_{33}$ | | $x_{i3}$ | | $x_{N3}$ |
| Vulnerabilities | ... | | | | | | | |
| | $V_j$ | $x_{1j}$ | $x_{2j}$ | $x_{3j}$ | | $x_{ij}$ | ... | $x_{Nj}$ |
| | ... | | | | | ... | | ... |
| | $V_K$ | $x_{1K}$ | $x_{2K}$ | $x_{3K}$ | | $x_{iK}$ | ... | $x_{NK}$ |

We consider that the attacker can only exploit one of the vulnerabilities at a time. Similarly, the defender, defending all the replicas, can choose to defend any of the vulnerabilities; however, it can defend only against one of the vulnerabilities at a time. We also consider that the attack can still be successful with probability $p$ $(0 \leq p \leq 1)$ although the defender defends against the vulnerability exploited by the attacker. We consider the value of $p$ to be common knowledge between the attacker and the defender.

Let the strategies of the attacker be $E_j$ $(1 \leq j \leq K)$ which correspond to exploiting vulnerabilities $V_j$ $(1 \leq j \leq K)$ respectively. Similarly, the defender strategies are $P_k$ $(1 \leq k \leq K)$ which correspond to protecting against vulnerabilities $V_k$ $(1 \leq k \leq K)$ respectively. In fact, $P_j$ is the only suitable defense strategy against the attack $E_j$ because $P_j$ protects the replicas against the vulnerability $V_j$ being exploited by the attacker. We consider $E_j$ and $P_j$ at the abstract level, including primitive operations. Although exploiting the vulnerability $V_j$ is abstracted by a single strategy $E_j$, many of the strategies may consist of a multi-stage process involving step such as scanning, collecting information, and launching the attack. Similarly, the defender strategy $P_k$ may consist of multiple actions such as system monitoring, reconfiguration, and patching.

The attacker's payoff is the number of compromised replicas while the defender's payoff is the opposite since the game is zero-sum. When the attacker plays $E_j$ ($1 \leq j \leq K$) while the defender plays $P_k$ ($1 \leq k \leq K$), the attacker payoff is:

$$U_A(E_j, P_k) = \begin{cases} \sum_{i=1}^{N} X_{ij} \; if \; k \neq j \\ p \sum_{i=1}^{N} X_{ij} \; if \; k = j \end{cases} \tag{1}$$

In the first case, we have $k \neq j$. The attack $E_j$ is successful because the defender chooses a strategy other than $P_j$. Therefore, the attacker may compromise all the replicas that are subject to vulnerability $V_j$. In the second case, when $k = j$, the defender protects vulnerability $V_j$ being exploited by the attacker. Nevertheless, there is still a probability $p$ of a successful attack. Thus, the attacker's payoff is probabilistic. There are two distinct interpretations of the probability $p$ that yields the same payoff as in (1). First, it can be that all the replicas that share a vulnerability fail together or survive together when that vulnerability is exploited by the attacker. Then, $p$ will be the probability that all the replicas that share a vulnerability fail given that the attacker exploits that vulnerability while the defender protects against it. In the second case, the replicas that share a vulnerability may fail independently. Thus, $p$ may be interpreted as the probability that a replica having a vulnerability fail given that the attacker exploits that vulnerability while the defender protects against it. In either case, the optimum defense strategy will depend on the specific normal form game that in turn depends on the number of replicas, the number of vulnerabilities, and the corresponding vulnerability matrix.

Moreover, the defender can have an actual appraisal of the loss only after the attacker exploits a vulnerability. In turn, the attacker would not know the potential losses the defender will incur for the different attacks it can launch. Without knowing the defender's defense strategy and payoff, the attacker will not have a definite strategy that maximizes the damage. Such a game with incomplete information can be modeled as a Bayesian game by considering that the distribution over the payoff from exploiting a vulnerability is common knowledge among the two players. Such consideration is not the primary focus of this paper. In this paper, we propose our game theoretic approach for mission survivability using replication and diversity based on the following scenario with complete information in the game.

# 4    Model illustration

An illustrative example (see Table 2) shows 9 replicas ($N = 9$) and 5 vulnerabilities ($K = 5$) in the entire set of replicas. Note that, replica 6 is exposed to all 5 vulnerabilities, whereas replica 3 is exposed to none. We highlight that the same replica can be affected by different vulnerabilities and a given vulnerability can affect several replicas. Also, from an attacker's perspective, an exploitation of vulnerability 1, 2, 3, 4, or 5 will affect 2, 3, 4, 4, 6 replicas respectively (the attacker payoff). Those are the numbers $\sum_{i=1}^{9} X_{ij}$ we mentioned in (1). They are obtained by summing the "1" in each row of Table 2, i.e., $\sum_{i=1}^{9} X_{i1} = 2, \sum_{i=1}^{9} X_{i2} = 3, \sum_{i=1}^{9} X_{i3} = 4, \sum_{i=1}^{9} X_{i4} = 4, \sum_{i=1}^{9} X_{i5} = 6$. From the general game model described above, the vulnerability model described in Table 2 can be matched into the Normal form game of Table 3 when we consider $p = 0$.

When the attacker plays $E_1$ while the defender plays $P_1$, the attacker gets a payoff of zero because the defender has protected the replicas against the vulnerability $V_1$. Since the game is zero-sum, the defender also gets a payoff of zero. However, when the attacker plays $E_1$ while the defender plays a different strategy than $P_1$ (say, $P_2$, $P_3$, $P_4$, or $P_5$), the defender has failed to protect against the vulnerability $V_1$. The two replicas $R_1$ and $R_6$ are compromised (see table 2). The attacker gets a payoff of 2 while the defender gets -2. The same rationale holds for the other four attack strategies.

We can see that no strategy is dominated. By definition, at a Nash equilibrium profile, no player can increase his payoff by a unilateral deviation. Moreover, each player plays a best response to the behavior of other players. We can see that there is no pure strategy Nash equilibrium in the game of Table 3. To check that there is no pure strategy Nash equilibrium, if, for instance, the attacker plays $E_5$ when the defender plays $P_5$, both players get a payoff of zero. The attacker's best response will be to change his strategy to $E_4$ and increase its payoff to 4. After that, the defender's best response should be to change his strategy to $P_4$ and so on. No pure strategy profile will be stable. One of the players will have incentive to deviate.

**Table 2:** Vulnerability Matrix (9 replicas with 5 vulnerabilities)

| | | Replicas | | | | | | | | |
|---|---|---|---|---|---|---|---|---|---|---|
| | | $R_1$ | $R_2$ | $R_3$ | $R_4$ | $R_5$ | $R_6$ | $R_7$ | $R_8$ | $R_9$ |
| Vulnerabilities | $V_1$ | 1 | 0 | 0 | 0 | 0 | 1 | 0 | 0 | 0 |
| | $V_2$ | 0 | 1 | 0 | 0 | 0 | 1 | 0 | 1 | 0 |
| | $V_3$ | 1 | 0 | 0 | 1 | 0 | 1 | 0 | 0 | 1 |
| | $V_4$ | 0 | 1 | 0 | 0 | 1 | 1 | 0 | 1 | 0 |
| | $V_5$ | 1 | 1 | 0 | 1 | 0 | 1 | 1 | 0 | 1 |

**Table 3:** Normal form game (attacker's payoff, defender's payoff)

| | | Defender's Strategies | | | | |
|---|---|---|---|---|---|---|
| | | $P_1$ | $P_2$ | $P_3$ | $P_4$ | $P_5$ |
| Attacker's Strategies | $E_1$ | 0,0 | 2,-2 | 2,-2 | 2,-2 | 2,-2 |
| | $E_2$ | 3,-3 | 0,0 | 3,-3 | 3,-3 | 3,-3 |
| | $E_3$ | 4,-4 | 4,-4 | 0,0 | 4,-4 | 4,-4 |
| | $E_4$ | 4,-4 | 4,-4 | 4,-4 | 0,0 | 4,-4 |
| | $E_5$ | 6,-6 | 6,-6 | 6,-6 | 6,-6 | 0,0 |

To obtain the mixed strategy Nash equilibrium profile, the defender randomizes to make the attacker indifferent. Also, the attacker randomizes to make the defender indifferent. Then the attacker and the defender play the best response to each other. The mixed strategy Nash equilibrium profile is: ($0E_1$, $0E_2$, $0.375E_3$, $0.375E_4$, $0.25E_5$; $0P_1$, $0P_2$, $0.25P_3$, $0.25P_4$, $0.5P_5$). The attacker's payoff is 3 and the defender's payoff is -3. Let us make two important observations about this Nash equilibrium profile:

- The vulnerabilities V1 and V2 are neither exploited by the attacker nor protected by the defender. This is because they yield a lower value (in term of the number of vulnerable replicas) relative to the other three vulnerabilities.
- The vulnerabilities that are present in more replicas are protected by the defender with a higher probability. This constraints the attacker to exploit those vulnerabilities less often, e.g., the attacker plays E5 25% of the time and plays E4 and E3 37.5% of the time although E5 has a higher value.

We will now consider the case when the attack can still be successful with probability *p* although the defender defends against the vulnerability exploited by the attacker. In that case, the game in Table 3 is translated to a more general game in Table 4.

**Table 4:** Normal form game (attacker's payoff, defender's payoff)

| | | Defender's Strategies | | | | |
|---|---|---|---|---|---|---|
| | | $P_1$ | $P_2$ | $P_3$ | $P_4$ | $P_5$ |
| | $E_1$ | 2p,-2p | 2,-2 | 2,-2 | 2,-2 | 2,-2 |
| | $E_2$ | 3,-3 | 3p,-3p | 3,-3 | 3,-3 | 3,-3 |
| Attacker's | $E_3$ | 4,-4 | 4,-4 | 4p,-4p | 4,-4 | 4,-4 |
| Strategies | $E_4$ | 4,-4 | 4,-4 | 4,-4 | 4p,-4p | 4,-4 |
| | $E_5$ | 6,-6 | 6,-6 | 6,-6 | 6,-6 | 6p,-6p |

The Nash equilibrium profile will depend on the specific value of $p$. In addition, as the probability $p$ increases, the attacker's strategies $E_1$, $E_2$, $E_3$, and $E_4$ become strictly dominated by $E_5$. The same holds for the corresponding defense strategies. For instance, $E_5$ strictly dominates $E_1$ if $\frac{1}{3} < p \leq 1$. That is because the minimum payoff the attacker gets by playing $E_5$ (6p) is greater than the maximum payoff (2) the attacker can get by playing $E_1$. Similarly, $E_5$ strictly dominates $E_1$ and $E_2$ if $\frac{1}{2} < p \leq 1$ and $E_5$ strictly dominates $E_1$, $E_2$, $E_3$, and $E_4$, if $\frac{2}{3} < p \leq 1$. The pure strategy profile ($E_5$, $P_5$) is a strict Nash equilibrium for $\frac{2}{3} < p \leq 1$.

When similar replicas are used, the vulnerability matrix of Table 2 is changed. All the "0" are replaced by "1". That is because each of the vulnerabilities automatically affects all the 9 replicas. As a consequence, the resulting game in Normal form is represented in Table 5. The mixed strategy Nash equilibrium profile is: ($0.2E_1$, $0.2E_2$, $0.2E_3$, $0.2E_4$, $0.2E_5$; $0.2P_1$, $0.2P_2$, $0.2P_3$, $0.2P_4$, $0.2P_5$). The attacker payoff increase with probability $p$ as shown in Figure 2. We will see that this game is always favorable to the attacker.

**Table 5:** Normal form game (attacker's payoff, defender's payoff)

| | | Defender's Strategies | | | | |
|---|---|---|---|---|---|---|
| | | $P_1$ | $P_2$ | $P_3$ | $P_4$ | $P_5$ |
| | $E_1$ | 9p,- 9p | 9,-9 | 9,-9 | 9,-9 | 9,-9 |
| | $E_2$ | 9,-9 | 9p,- 9p | 9,-9 | 9,-9 | 9,-9 |
| Attacker's | $E_3$ | 9,-9 | 9,-9 | 9p,- 9p | 9,-9 | 9,-9 |
| Strategies | $E_4$ | 9,-9 | 9,-9 | 9,-9 | 9p,- 9p | 9,-9 |
| | $E_5$ | 9,-9 | 9,-9 | 9,-9 | 9,-9 | 9p,- 9p |

# 5  Numerical results

This section provides a more detailed analysis of our model illustration of the last section. Of particular importance will be the probability $p$. In fact, the probability $p$ measures the defense capability compared to the attacker. When an experienced and skillful network defender is faced by a weak attacker, the attacker has no chance to successfully exploit a vulnerability that is protected by the defender and thus $p = 0$. On the contrary, when an expert attacker oppose an unskilled defender, that attacker can always go around the protection mechanism implemented by the defender and then $p = 1$. We should have $0 < p < 1$ when both the attacker and defender are competent.

Figure 2 shows the changes in attacker's payoff with probability $p$ in two scenarios: without replica diversity and with replica diversity. The defender's payoff is the opposite since we have a zero-sum game. As expected, the attacker's payoff increases with probability $p$ in both scenarios. A more skillful attacker will get a higher payoff. With diverse replicas, the attacker payoff slowly and linearly increases with a slope of 1.5 until the probability $p$ reaches a value of 2/3. Then the attacker payoff starts a faster linear increase with the slope of 6. This is due to a change from a mixed strategy Nash equilibrium to a pure strategy Nash equilibrium as shown in Figure 3. On the other hand, with similar replicas, the attacker payoff linearly increases with probability $p$ with the slope of 1.8. We can see that diversity always gives extra challenges to attackers. With diverse replicas, the attacker get on average less than half of the payoff they should get if similar replicas were used. Moreover, even though $p = 1$ and diverse replicas are used, the attacker is still worse off compared to the case $p = 0$ and similar replicas are used. This indicates that a less skillful defender that diversifies his replicas is always better off than the more skillful defender using similar replicas.

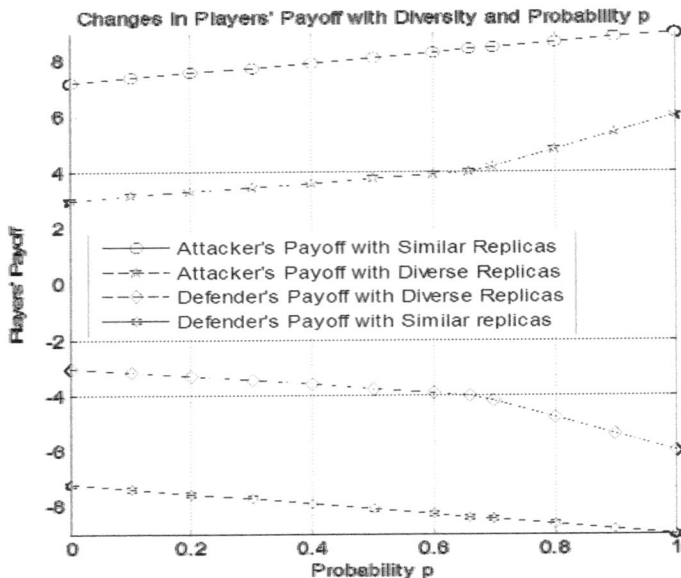

**Figure 2:** Reduction of attacker's payoff with replicas' diversity

Figure 3 shows how the players adjust their strategy with $p$, using diverse replicas as proposed. The game has two fragments depending on $p$. In the first part, $0 \le p \le \frac{2}{3}$, both players adopt a mixed strategy. The attacker's strategy ($0E_1$, $0E_2$, $0.375E_3$, $0.375E_4$, $0.25E_5$) remains unchanged. However, the defender modifies his strategy with $p$. As $p$ increases, playing $E_5$ becomes substantially more profitable to the attacker. Thus, to counteract, the defender increases his probability to play $P_5$. As a result, the attacker has no incentive to change his strategy. In the second segment, $\frac{2}{3} < p \le 1$, both players adopt a pure strategy. This is because $E_5$ is the dominant strategy for the attacker while $P_5$ is the dominant strategy for the defender. Recall that the attacker's strategies $E_1$ and $E_2$ are never used. The same is true for the defender's strategies $P_1$ and $P_2$. Those strategies are not represented in Figure 3.

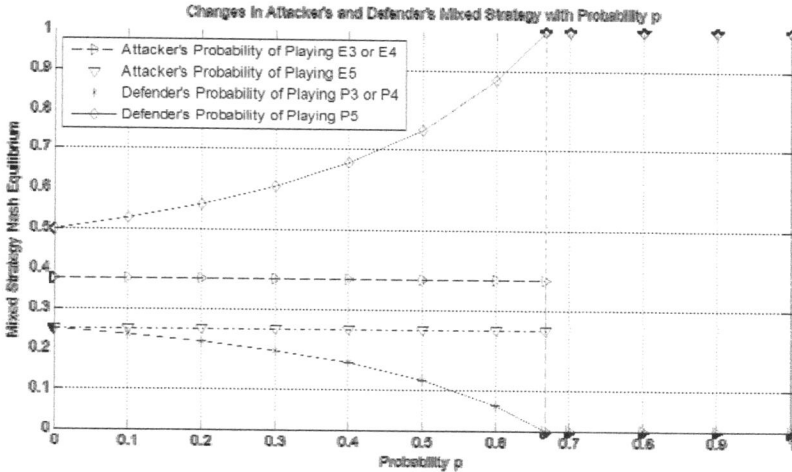

**Figure 3:** Changes in the Nash equilibrium strategy profile with probability *p* (with replicas' diversity).

Therefore, replicas' diversity can offer a tremendous advantage to a cyber defender while diminishing the attacker's payoff and incentive. In fact, population diversity leads to population survivability because avoiding monoculture prevents any single infection from disabling the entire population. Diversity should be applied at all stage of the design process, in hardware as well as software. The less similarity between the replicas, the less likely is, that any vulnerability found in one replica will be found in others. Thus, the attacker's payoff is substantially reduced as shown in Figure 2, while the defender's payoff is considerably increased.

# 6   Conclusion

This work has used a game theoretic model to demonstrate the importance of diversity in cyber survivability. As opposed to common belief, we have shown that the more dangerous vulnerabilities in a system are sometimes less likely to be exploited. The attacker may be better off when exploiting small vulnerabilities because they will be less protected. Our results show that the defender is always better off when using diverse replicas. That is because any vulnerability will affect all the replicas when the replicas are perfectly similar to each other. In the future, we will consider incomplete information game in which the attacker skill level and thus the probability *p* is not common knowledge but private information. We will also look into the case that the attacker can simultaneously exploit multiple vulnerabilities while the defender can also simultaneously protect against several vulnerabilities.

## Acknowledgements

This research was performed while Dr. Joon Park held a National Research Council (NRC) Research Associateship Award at the Air Force Research Laboratory (AFRL). This research was supported by the Air Force Office of Scientific Research (AFOSR).

## References

Agah, A. Das, S. K. Basu, K. Asadi, M. (2004) Intrusion Detection in Sensor Networks: A Non-Cooperative Game Approach, nca, pp.343-346, Network Computing and Applications, Third IEEE International Symposium on (NCA'04), 2004.

Alpcan, T. and Basar T. (2010) Network Security: A Decision and Game-Theoretic Approach Cambridge University Press; 1 edition (November 30, 2010)

Jormakka, J. and Molsa, J. V. E. (2005) Modelling information warfare as a game, Journal of information warfare; vol.4(2), 2005.

Kamhoua, C. Kwiat, K. Park, J. (2012a) A Game Theoretic Approach for Modeling Optimal Data Sharing on Online Social Networks, in proceedings of the 9th IEEE International Conference on Electrical Engineering, Computing Science and Automatic Control (IEEE CCE 2012), Mexico City, Mexico, September 2012.

Kamhoua, C. Kwiat, K. Park, J. (2012b) Surviving in Cyberspace: A Game Theoretic Approach, in the Journal of Communications, Special Issue on Future Directions in Computing and Networking, Academy Publisher, Vol. 7, NO 6, June 2012.

Kamhoua, C. Pissinou, N. Makki, K. (2011) Game Theoretic Modeling and Evolution of Trust in Autonomous Multi Hop Networks: Application to Network Security and Privacy, in proceedings of the IEEE international conference on communications (IEEE ICC 2011). Kyoto, Japan, June 2011.

Liu, Y. Comaniciu, C. Man, H. (2006) A Bayesian game approach for intrusion detection in wireless ad hoc networks, ACM International Conference Proceeding Series; vol. 199, 2006.

Myerson R. Game theory: analysis of conflict Harvard University Press, 1997.

Nguyen, K. C. Alpcan, T. Basar, T. (2009) Stochastic games for security in networks with interdependent nodes, in proceedings of Intl. Conf. on Game Theory for Networks (GameNets), 2009.

Park, J. Kim, S. Kamhoua, C. Kwiat, K. (2012) Optimal State Management of Data Sharing in Online Social Network (OSN) Services in the 11th IEEE International Conference on Trust, Security and Privacy in Computing and Communications (IEEE TrustCom-2012), Liverpool, United Kingdom, June 2012.

Roy, S. Ellis, C. Shiva, S. Dasgupta, D. Shandilya, V. Qishi, W. (2010) A Survey of Game Theory as Applied to Network Security, 43rd Hawaii International Conference on System Sciences (HICSS). Honolulu, HI, USA. March 2010.

Shiva, S.  Roy, S.  Bedi, H.  Dasgupta, D.  Wu, Q. (2010) A Stochastic Game with Imperfect Information for Cyber Security, 5th International Conference on i-Warfare & Security (ICIW), 2010.

Sun, W.  Kong, X.  He, D.  You, X. (2008) Information security problem research based on game theory, International Symposium on Publication Electronic Commerce and Security, 2008.(Online) http://www.nellis.af.mil/library/factsheets/factsheet.asp?id=4098

# Exercising State Sovereignty in Cyberspace: An International Cyber-Order Under Construction?

**Andrew Liaropoulos**

University of Piraeus, Department of International and European Studies, Piraeus, Greece

andrewliaropoulos@gmail.com

*Originally Published in the Proceedings of ICCWS, 2013*

---

**Editorial Commentary**

What is the appropriate level of control that a state may or should exercise over cyberspace? Where must that control end? Is it legitimate for a state to create a walled-off area of cyberspace to both protect itself and its citizens, where "protection" is operationally defined by the ruling party? As noted by Liaropoulos, activities in cyberspace have "challenged the traditional political, social and economic structures of the international society." These challenges have not been met apathetically; to the contrary, we have witnessed events such as Egypt turning off the internet during the unrest of 2011, China creating the "Great Firewall of China" to restrict types of information available to ordinary users, and Iran creating a internal version of the internet with built in surveillance capabilities. But additionally we have seen the growth of attacks on internet connected devices, for which governments have some responsibility in protecting their citizens and national interests. One question among many is if it is "possible for states to exercise their authority and control in a borderless world" and, if so, should the structural challenges be analyzed from the perspective of a Westphalian state or from some other construct.

Liaropoulos presents a cogent discussion of what constitutes "sovereignty" and the challenges associated with expressing control of associated elements in the domain of cyberspace. He argues, citing a broad range of sources and authorities, that the expression of sovereignty in cyberspace is a needed and appropriate course of action for states, and that it is a necessary condition for the development of an international cyber order. Acknowledging the limitations of the paper size to delve into such a deep topic, he provides an impressive set of references for readers to pursue in their understanding and appreciation of this topic. This paper, combined with the following paper, contribute to a growing body of research into the evolution of the state and international control structures in the context of the challenges presented by cyberspace. These papers should be considered from the perspective of the Clausewitzian Centers of Gravity concept and the development of virtual non-state actors presented previously.

**Abstract:** Cyberspace is erroneously characterized as a domain that transcends physical space and thereby is immune to state sovereignty and resistant to international regulation. The purpose of this paper is to signify that cyberspace, in common with the other four domains (land, sea, air and outer space) and despite its unique characteristics, is just a reflection of the current international system, and thereby is largely affected by the rules that characterize it. The issue of state sovereignty in cyberspace is critical to any discussion about future regulation of cyberspace. Although cyberspace is borderless and is characterized by anonymity and ubiquity, recent state practices provide sufficient evidence that cyberspace, or at least some components of it, are not immune from sovereignty. The increasing use of Internet filtering techniques by both authoritarian regimes and democracies is just the latest example of attempting to control information flows. Cyberspace is non-territorial, but in sharp contrast to the land, sea, air and outer space, cyberspace is not a part of nature, it is human-made and therefore can be unmade and regulated. States have continuously emphasized their right to exercise control over the cyber-infrastructure located in their respective territory, to exercise their jurisdiction over cyber-activities on their territory, and to protect their cyber-infrastructure against any trans-border interference by other states or by individuals. As a result, states are filtering and monitoring cyber-bytes. Over the past years, there is a growing number of states that is publishing national cyber-policies and establishing cyber-centers that aim to protect the national cyber-infrastructure and control their citizens' access to information. The issue of state sovereignty in cyberspace raises critical questions about the need to regulate the cyber domain and gradually reach an international cyber-order.

**Keywords:** cyberspace, sovereignty, state sovereignty, international law, international cyber-order

# 1 Introduction

Over the past three decades, cyberspace has expanded and affected many aspects of human life. States, organizations and individuals have extensively exploited the opportunities that cyberspace offers. The cyber domain has challenged the traditional political, social and economic structures of the international society. It has radically increased the speed, volume and range of communications, and thereby, largely altered the way states are governed, the way companies deliver services and public goods, the way individuals interact and build social networks in Internet and the way citizens participate in civil society (Betz and Stevens, 2011: 9-11). Along with these developments, the emergence of cyberspace has also raised major challenges to individual and collective security. Critical national infrastructure is vulnerable to cyber-attacks, world economy is threatened by cyber-crime and cyber-espionage and individuals are terrorized by hackers (Carr, 2011). In the cyber domain, cyber-attacks cross national borders, they are hard to trace and affect both civilian and military networks. Militaries, terrorist groups and even individuals, now have the capability to launch cyber-attacks, not only against military networks, but also against critical infrastructures that depend on computer networks (Liaropoulos, 2011b: 541). News reports are replete of cases, where private and public communications were disrupted, banking systems were manipulated and even military communication systems were destroyed.

A number of questions is inevitable raised. How will states adapt to cyberspace? How does the condition of anarchy affect international politics in cyberspace? Is it possible for states to exercise their authority and control in a borderless world? In order to deal with these questions we need first to define the security challenges that the Westphalian state faces in cyberspace. In a latter phase we will examine a key concept in international politics, that of sovereignty and apply it in cyberspace. By conceptualizing sovereignty, we will be able to address a number of critical issues regarding the establishment of common principles and norms in cyberspace. Paraphrasing Hedley Bull's concept of international order, we could argue that exercising state sovereignty in cyberspace, is a necessary step for establishing an international cyber-order. According to Bull, states act in such a way as to preserve international order, because this order is in their own interest. (Bull, 1977). The question we need to ask is, whether states will act in the same way in cyberspace, in order to preserve an international cyber-order.

## 2   Security in cyberspace

A few recent examples of cyber-conflicts vividly illustrate the challenges that the Westphalian state system faces in cyberspace. In April 2007, the

Estonian government's decision to move a Soviet-era war memorial, the Bronze Soldier, triggered a cyber-conflict, in the form of a three-week wave of distributed denial-of-service (DOS) attacks that crippled the country's information technology infrastructure (Blank, 2008: 227-247). The cyber-attacks temporarily disrupted the Estonian communications networks, by targeting the government, newspapers, mobile phones, emergency response systems and banks. The target included the Estonian presidency, its parliament and many government ministries. Although the cyber-attacks cannot be attributed to a specific actor, it is widely believed in Estonia that Moscow was behind these attacks. Russia claimed that the attacks came from cyber-patriots and not on the order of the Russian government (Crosston, 2011: 104-5). Regardless of the true identity of the attacker, the important issue is that the inability to trace the origin of the attack (the attribution problem), hinders any attempt of retaliation (Tsarougias, 2012).

Likewise, during the conflict that broke out on August 2008, between Russia and Georgia, over South Ossetia, cyber-attacks were launched against Georgian governmental websites, media, and communication services (Korns and Kastenberg, 2009). As with the Estonian case, there is no proof of who was behind these attacks. Georgia accused Russia, claiming that the route traffic pointed to the Russian Business Network (RBN). The Georgian case clearly shows that cyber-attacks that take place in a borderless world, where the traditional law of armed conflict cannot be applied, might be a very handy strategy when states choose to exercise coercive diplomacy. The barriers to entry to cyberspace are lowering due to the proliferation of low-cost information and communication technology (ICT) and therefore, the cyber option seems to be a very attractive and less costly one, compared to the use of traditional military means.

Cyber-attacks can take many forms and the examples of Ghost Net and the Google hacking, are indicative of the above. Both incidents have been related to China and raise many questions regarding the way the victims could respond. Ghost Net was a massive cyber-espionage operation that was discovered by the Information Warfare Monitor in March 2009. The operation used malware and attacked non-governmental organizations and embassies working on Tibetan issues, in 103 countries (Information Warfare Monitor, 2010). In January 2010, Google announced that a computer attack originating from China had penetrated its corporate infrastructure and stolen information from its computers, most likely source code. The attacks also targeted Gmail accounts of human-rights activists and infiltrated the networks of 33 companies (Thomas, 2010: 101-33 and Morozov, 2011: 1-33). The borderless and complex nature of cyberspace might explain why Beijing regards Google as an element of US power (Klimburg, 2011: 52) and social networks as a threat to national security.

The latest and most definite cyber-attack is the Stuxnet worm. Stuxnet is malicious software (malware) that was designed specifically to strike the Iranian nuclear facility at Natanz. It spread via Microsoft Windows and targeted Siemens industrial software. The value of the Stuxnet lays not so much on its technical characteristics, but on the political and strategic context, within which it operated (Farwell and Rohozinski, 2011: 23-40). The scenario of launching an air strike to stop or slow down Iran's nuclear program has troubled security experts for years. The outcome of such an operation would be doubtful and the risks for the regional and international security, potentially disastrous. A preventive air strike on Iranian nuclear facilities would most probably start a conflict in the Middle East and would be unlikely to prevent the eventual acquisition of nuclear weapons by Iran. So did Stuxnet offer a better and risk-averse alternative to a conventional attack? Even better, what if it was launched by a criminal organization or by a group of patriot-hackers? What if nations outsource cyber-attacks to third parties, to cyber-mercenaries, thereby bypassing the attribution issue?

The above incidents demonstrate that malicious actors, state and non-state, have the ability to compromise and control millions of computers that belong to governments, private enterprises and ordinary citizens. These developments have challenged social scientists to redefine key concepts like politics (Karatzogianni, 2009, Chadwick and Howard, 2009 and Morozov, 2011), power (Dunn Cavelty et.al, 2007, Betz and Stevens, 2011 and Nye, 2011), ethics (Dipert, 2010 and Liaropoulos, 2011a), international law (Tikk et.al, 2010, Hughes, 2010 and Schmitt, 2013) and security (Dunn Cavelty et.al, 2007, Kramer et.al, 2009 and Ryan, 2011). There is a growing body of literature that covers in depth many cyber-related issues, but anyone attempting to untangle the complexities of cyberspace, cannot afford to ignore the concept of sovereignty. After all, state sovereignty largely defines the current international order. The United Nations are based on the principle of sovereign equality of all its members and preserving state sovereignty is a top priority for both international organizations and individual states (Franzese, 2009: 7). The reasons for concentrating on the concept of sovereignty are two. First, to explore how the state, being a territorial entity, can exercise sovereignty, thereby authority and control, in a non-territorial and borderless domain like cyberspace. Second, by framing the debate on sovereignty in cyberspace, we will develop a useful framework to address other cyber-related issues. As a preliminary to this discussion, however, some exegesis of the key terms cyberspace and sovereignty is required. This may seem as a semantic exercise, but semantics are important; how words are understood defines expectations and expectations are important in shaping policy.

## 3   Cyberspace and sovereignty

The relevant literature offers various definitions of cyberspace, depending on the conceptual understanding of the author. A definition that is widely accepted among the cyber-experts is that of Daniel Kuehl. He defines cyberspace as *a global domain within the information environment whose distinctive and unique character is framed by the use of electronics and the electromagnetic spectrum to create, store, modify, exchange, and exploit information via interdependent and interconnected networks using information-communication technologies* (Kramer, 2009: 28).

Cyberspace refers to the fusion of all communication networks, databases and information sources into a global virtual system. Cyberspace is composed of three layers. The first one is the physical layer that consists of electrical energy, integrated circuits, communications infrastructure, fiber optics, transmitters and receivers. The second layer is the software, meaning the computer programs that process information. The last and least concrete layer is that of data (Tabansky 2011: 77-8). Cyberspace is non-territorial, but in sharp contrast to the land, sea, air and outer space, cyberspace is not a part of nature, it is human-made and therefore can be unmade and regulated (Herrera, 2007). The modern system of communications seems boundless, but it is not. Cyberspace is bounded by the existing physical structures. Much of what actually constitutes cyberspace is located in the sovereign territory of states (Betz and Stevens, 2011: 35). In common with the Westphalian era, states will always try to control the information flow. Cyber-bytes cannot escape this practice (Demchak and Dombrowski, 2011: 41). Recent developments demonstrate that states are trying to overcome the border paradox and delimitate borders by asserting sovereignty over cyberspace (Von Heinegg, 2012).

Sovereignty is regarded as a fundamental concept in the current international order. Sovereignty signifies authority within a distinct territorial entity, but also asserts membership of the international system. Defining what constitutes sovereignty in international politics can be a puzzling task. A useful typology of sovereignty for the purposes of our analysis is provided by Stephen Krasner. He identifies four ways in which sovereignty can be understood: domestic sovereignty, interdependence sovereignty, international legal sovereignty and Westphalian sovereignty (Krasner, 1999: 3-25).

Domestic sovereignty refers to the way public authority is organized within a state and to the level of effective control these authorities can exercise. Political authorities either organized in a parliamentary or presidential system, in a monarchical or republican way, or in an authoritarian or democratic way, are responsible for regulating and controlling developments within their own territory. Interdependence sovereignty relates to the ability of public authorities to control trans-border movements, the flows of people, materials and ideas across borders. If a state fails to regulate what passes its borders, it will also fail to control what happens within them. Therefore, loss of interdependence sovereignty can affect domestic sovereignty, in terms of inefficient control. Advocates of globalization argue that there is a number of activities, like environmental pollution, currency crises and terrorism, where state's control is declining. International legal sovereignty refers to the mutual recognition of states in the international system. Finally, Westphalian sovereignty highlights the right that states have to determine their political life and makes reference to the exclusion of external actors from influencing or determining domestic authority structures (Krasner, 1999: 11-25).

## 4  Exercising sovereignty in cyberspace

Krasner's typology of sovereignty will assist us to debunk the myth that cyberspace is immune from state sovereignty. This myth is based on a widely-held belief that cyberspace *is not a physical place* and therefore defies the rules that apply to land, sea, air and outer space. Actions in the cyber domain seem to take place *outside* the state in a *virtual* manner, but their implications affect the *real* world, *inside* states. Getting back to the description of cyberspace and the physical layer, it is obvious that cyberspace requires a physical infrastructure in order to operate. This infrastructure is terrestrially based and therefore not immune from state sovereignty (Von Heinegg, 2012: 9). Even more, cyberspace cannot operate in a chaotic manner, but needs regulation and oversight. Companies that operate in cyberspace need the laws of state to operate their business (Wu, 1997). Finally, states need to be present in cyberspace and exercise control for reasons of national security. National critical infrastructures, like banking and finance, oil, gas and electricity, water and transportation, all depend upon computer networks to operate and therefore cannot escape the control of the state (Franzese, 2009: 13-4).

Regarding domestic sovereignty, cyberspace has affected domestic authority and control, in both liberal democracies and authoritarian regimes. There is a growing number of states that attempts to control their citizens' access to information, on the basis that certain types of content constitute threat to the domestic order or national security (Deibert, 2009). According to a report by OpenNet Initiative, the flow of information in cyberspace in many Muslim countries emulates the flow of information in the *real* space (Noman 2011: 2). In the West, the threat of terrorism, serves in a similar way. Western governments, mainly the US and EU members, have increased their filtering surveillance techniques and limited anonymity in cyberspace. The unrestricted flow of information in cyberspace has definitely challenged the interdependence sovereignty. Terrorist use of the Internet as a means of propaganda is a classic case where the state is unable to control what passes its borders. Governments have attempted to restore control by removing videos with terrorist content from the Web (Betz and Stevens, 2011: 69-70). Cyberspace poses no challenge to international legal sovereignty. The claim that cyberspace, due to its unique nature should acquire international legal status is not popular among the states (Franzese, 2009: 11). The most essential challenge that cyberspace poses, is to Westphalian sovereignty. As stated above in the cases of the cyber-conflicts in Estonia and Georgia, as well as in the case of Stuxnet, cyber-attacks in another's country information infrastructure, consists a violation of the Westphalian sovereignty.

States have to solve a number of critical issues, both of technical and political nature, in order to successfully establish sovereignty and thereby order in cyberspace. The lack of attribution is a major obstacle in exercising sovereignty. Unless states gain the ability to identify actors and trace back cyber-attacks, any claim to exercise power in cyberspace will be fragile. Creating an international investigative body, modeled after the International Atomic Energy Agency (IAEA), to review and investigate cyber-attacks, might not answer the attribution problem, but definitely points to the right direction (Austin and Gady, 2012: 12). Reaching a consensus about regulating cyberspace is another major issue. The role of great cyber-powers like USA, Russia and China is critical. Washington, Moscow and Beijing are trying to implement their policies in multilateral and international fora, where cyber issues are debated. According to US officials, the United States faces a real danger of cyber-attacks from both state and non-state actors. Such attacks could be as destructive as the terrorist attack on 9/11 and could virtually paralyze the state. US officials stress the need to develop offensive capabilities to defend the nation and its allies. China and Russia do not share the US position that existing international laws should apply to cyberspace. China and Russia have argued that new rules and laws need to be created. In September 2011, the two countries submitted to the UN General Assembly a proposal for a code of conduct in cyberspace. The proposed code calls for states to respect domestic laws and sovereignty and to settle disputes within the framework of the United Nations. Cyberspace is another example where great power politics are exercised. China views its cyberwarfare capabilities as a powerful asymmetric tool to deter the US. For Russia, the ability of states to have control over the information space is intrinsic. Moscow has been actively proposing international cyber security legislation that constrains the free flow of information (Giles, 2012: 2). Many states in the West do not share the same views with Russia, since they view cyberspace as a mean to spread democracy and freedom.

## 5   Conclusion

To conclude, cyberspace is not immune to state sovereignty, but at the same time states have still a long way to go until they establish an effective mechanism of authority and control. Cyberspace is rather a reflection of the current international system in a new domain. Therefore, international politics in cyberspace will be shaped by state rivalry and geopolitical concerns, as well as common interests and existing norms. Cyberspace is a domain where national interests clash, but also where states cooperate. Although it is premature to refer to an international cyber-order, it is fair to say that such a process seems to be underway. Echoing Hedley Bull's concept of international order, we need to examine closely the role of the following 'institutions' in cyberspace: the balance of power, international law, diplomacy, war and the role of great powers. Bull's work on international order could serve as a useful guide for international relations scholars to investigate the behavior of states in cyberspace. Obviously, a short paper like this can only scratch the surface, and I urge the reader to delve into the reference list for further information.

## Acknowledgements

The author would like to thank his colleagues, Professor P. Ifestos, for his insightful discussions regarding the concept of sovereignty in international relations, Associate Professor P. Liacouras, for clarifying the legal aspects of territorial sovereignty and finally Dr. I. Konstantopoulos for his general comments and research support.

## References

Austin, G. and Gady, F-S. (2012) Cyber Détente between the United States and China: Shaping the Agenda, East-West Institute, New York.

Betz, D.J. and Stevens, T. (2011) Cyberspace and the State: Toward a Strategy for Cyber-Power, Routledge, International Institute for Strategic Studies, Oxon.

Blank, S. (2008) "Web War I: Is Europe's First Information War a New Kind of War?", Comparative Strategy, Vol 27, No.3, pp.227-47.

Bull, H. (1977) The Anarchical Society, Macmillan, London.

Carr, J. (2011) Inside Cyber Warfare, O'Reillly, Sebastopol.

Chadwick, A. and Howard, P. eds (2009) Routledge Handbook of Internet Politics, Routledge, London and New York.

Crosston, M. (2011), "World gone Cyber MAD. How Mutually Assured Debilitation is the best hope for cyber deterrence", Strategic Studies Quarterly, Vol 5, No.1, pp.100-16.

Deibert, R. (2009) The Geopolitics of Internet Control: Censorship, sovereignty and cyberspace' in Chadwick, A. and Howard, P. eds, Routledge Handbook of Internet Politics, Routledge, London and New York.

Demchak, C. and Dombrowski, P. (2011), "Rise of a Cybered Westphalian Age", Strategic Studies Quarterly, Vol 5, No.1, pp.32-61.

Dipert, R.P. (2010) "The Ethics of Cyberwarfare", Journal of Military Ethics, Vol 9, No.4, pp.384-410.

Dunn Cavelty, M. et.al (2007) Power and Security in the Information Age: Investigating the role of the state in cyberspace, Ashgate, Burlington.

Farwell, J. and Rohozinski, R. (2011) "Stuxnet and the future of Cyber War", Survival, Vol 53, No.1, pp.23-40.

Franzese, P.W. (2009) "Sovereignty in Cyberspace: Can it exist?", Air Force Law Review, Vol 64, pp.1-42.

Giles, K. (2012) Russian Cyber Security: Concepts and Current Activity, Chatham House, London.

Herrera, G.L (2007) Cyberspace and Sovereignty: Thoughts of Physical Space and Digital Space in Dunn Cavelty, M. et.al Power and Security in the Information Age: Investigating the role of the state in cyberspace, Ashgate, Burlington.

Hughes, R. (2010) "A Treaty for Cyberspace", International Affairs, Vol 86, No.2, pp.523-41.

Information Warfare Monitor, (2010) Shadows in the Cloud: Investigating Cyber Espionage 2.0, JR03-2010, Shadowserver Foundation, web version http://shadows-in-the-cloud.net, last day accessed, 20.10.2012.

Karatzogianni, A. ed. (2009) Cyber Conflict and Global Politics, Routledge, London and New York.

Klimburg, A. (2011) "Mobilizing Cyber Power", Survival, Vol 53, No.1, pp.41-60.

Korns, S.and Kastenberg, J. (2009) "Georgia's Cyber Left Hook", Parameters, Vol 38, No.4, pp.60-76.

Kramer, F.D., et.al (2009) Cyberpower and National Security, Potomac Books, Inc, Washington D.C.

Krasner, S.D. (1999) Sovereignty: Organized Hypocrisy, Princeton University Press, New Jersey.

Liaropoulos, A.N. (2011a) War and Ethics in Cyberspace: Cyber-conflict and Just War Theory, in Ryan, J. ed, Leading Issues in Information Warfare & Security Research, vol.1, Academic Publishing International Ltd, Reading.

Liaropoulos, A.N. (2011b) Power and Security in Cyberspace: Implications for the Westphalian state system, in Panorama of Global Security Environment, Centre for European and North American Affairs, Bratislava.

Morozov, E. (2011) The Net Delusion. The Dark Side of Internet Freedom, Public Affairs, New York.

Noman, H. (2011) In the name of God: Faith-based Internet Censorship in majority Muslim Countries, OpenNet Initiative.

Nye, J.S. (2011) The Future of Power, Public Affairs, New York.

Ryan, J. ed. (2011) Leading Issues in Information Warfare & Security Research, vol.1, Academic Publishing International Ltd, Reading.

Schmitt, M.N. ed. (2013) Tallinn Manual on the International Law applicable to Cyber Warfare, Cambridge University Press, Cambridge.

Tabansky, L. (2011) "Basic Concepts in Cyber Warfare", Military and Strategic Affairs, Vol 3, No.1, pp.75-92.

Thomas, T. (2010) "Google Confronts China's Three Warfares", Parameters, Vol 40, No.2, pp.101-113.

Tikk, E., et.al (2010) International Cyber Incidents: Legal Considerations, NATO CCD COE Publications, Tallinn.

Tsarougias, N. (2012) "Cyber attacks, self-defense and the problem of attribution", Journal of Conflict & Security Law, Vol 17, No.2, pp.229-244.

Von Heinegg, W.H. (2012) Legal Implications of Territorial Sovereignty in Cyberspace, in Czosseck, C. et.al, 2012 4th International Conference on Cyber Conflict, NATO CCD COE Publications, Tallinn.

Wu, T.S. (1997) "Cyberspace Sovereignty? The Internet and the International System", Harvard Journal of Law & Technology, Vol 10, No.3, pp.647-66.

# Establishing Cyberspace Sovereignty

**Kris Barcomb, Dennis Krill, Robert Mills and Michael Saville**
Air Force Institute of Technology, Wright-Patterson AFB, USA
Kris.Barcomb@us.af.mil
Dennis.Krill@us.af.mil
Robert.Mills@afit.edu
Michael.Saville@afit.edu

*Originally Published in the Proceedings of ICIW, 2012*

**Editorial Commentary**

In this paper, the authors start with definitions of sovereignty and then use historical examples to draw analogies on how to proceed in creating a useful definition of state sovereignty in cyberspace. Taking exception to the notion that cyberspace should be appropriately treated as global commons, they lay out an analysis framework based on a five layer internet protocol stack in order to differentiate where control lies and where sovereignty might appropriately be established. The context of the analysis is the experience of the United States, with references to control and use of exoatmospheric space and the development of international norms for such control.

The analysis is thought provoking, particularly when combined with the previous paper. It is useful and important to keep the differences between space and cyberspace in perspective. Several crucial differences include accessibility, knowledge required to participate, infrastructure required to participate, interactivity of elements, and the turn-over rate of required knowledge. An additional crucial difference is in the human resources component.

For exoatmospheric space, access is quite limited by both technology and cost, as well as availability of launch platforms. The knowledge required to participate is very high and very specialized, as is the infrastructure. Most space components are not interactive: they are designed for specific purposes and do not by default interact with other components. This is particularly true of those assets referred to by the authors as "national technical means". The turn-over rate of required knowledge is quite low: once the knowledge has been obtained, it changes fairly slowly. Finally, the people who play in the space arena are relatively rare: the inclination to access the required knowledge and apply it to the space domain attracts only a small percentage of highly educated individuals.

Contrasting that to cyberspace, access is almost unlimited by any of the considerations. Cyberspace is both highly accessible and being made more so in order to both optimize the benefits of cyberspace and to reduce disadvantages associated with lack of access. The knowledge required to participate is freely available from many sources, although a variety of tuition based training and education options are available. The infrastructure required to participate ranges from trivial to massive, but even those starting out in cyberspace have a reasonably easy task in developing their segment of the infrastructure. With the development of cloud-based services, it becomes even easier. By default, most components of cyberspace are interactive at least on some level, thus creating exponential connectivity. But the knowledge turn-over rate is quite high, requiring people to continually keep up with the technology.

These considerations notwithstanding, the point is made that "international norms governing appropriate conduct in cyberspace are immature. As nations become more cyberspace-dependent, they are struggling to clearly define their claims within it and to determine appropriate responses when those claims are jeopardized." This is, of course, true and serves as a fitting conclusion to the thoughts developed through the presentations of all the papers in this volume.

**Abstract:** International norms governing appropriate conduct in cyberspace are immature, leaving politicians, diplomats, and military authorities to grapple with the challenges of defending against and executing hostilities in cyberspace. Cyberspace is unlike the traditional physical domains where actions occur at specific geographic places and times. Rules governing conduct in the traditional domains emerged over centuries and share a common understanding of sovereignty that helps establish and justify the use of force. In cyberspace, sovereignty is a more abstract notion because the geographic boundaries are often difficult to define as data and applications increasingly reside in a virtual, global "cloud." This paper proposes a construct for establishing sovereignty in cyberspace by studying similarities between space and cyberspace. The characteristics of the space domain challenged traditional notions of sovereignty based on geography. As nations deployed space-based capabilities, the concept of sovereignty needed to mature to deal with the physical realities of space. Sovereignty is defined, and general requirements for claiming sovereignty are presented. The evolution of sovereignty in space is then discussed, followed by a construct for how sovereignty could be defined in cyberspace. The paper concludes with a brief discussion on how military doctrine offers useful insights into how nations may choose to assert sovereignty within these domains.

**Keywords:** cyberspace, space, sovereignty, critical infrastructure

# 1    Introduction

Cyberspace exists within the realm of electronic data where activity happens at "network speed" through a vast array of interwoven networks, computers, and repositories spanning the globe. International norms governing appropriate conduct in this new domain are still developing, leaving politicians, diplomats, lawyers, and military authorities to grapple with the challenges of defending against and executing hostilities in cyberspace. Cyberspace is unlike the traditional physical domains where actions occur at specific geographic places and times. Rules governing conduct in these traditional domains emerged over centuries through diplomacy and conflict. They also share a common understanding of sovereignty that helps establish and justify the use of force (*jus ad bellum* and *jus in bello*). In cyberspace, sovereignty is a more abstract notion because geographic boundaries in air, land and sea are difficult to define as data and applications increasingly reside in a global, virtual "cloud."

Like cyberspace, the space domain is also relatively new, and its characteristics challenged traditional notions of sovereignty based on geography. Technological advancements outpaced the development of a legal framework for establishing internationally accepted practices in the domain, and the international community's understanding of sovereignty needed to mature to deal with the physical realities of space. Studying the emergence of space as a domain in its own right will help national leaders establish a concept of sovereignty in cyberspace. Once nations generally agree on the aspects of cyberspace where sovereignty might apply, they can then develop and employ means to protect those claims.

# 2    Sovereignty

Sovereignty is a complex concept in political science. The Stanford Encyclopedia of Philosophy (2010) defines sovereignty as the "supreme authority within a territory." Generally, a nation has sovereignty when it meets two conditions. First, it must have "formal" or "technical" sovereignty in the sense of formal recognition of sovereignty by other governments. This is known as *de jure* sovereignty.

Second, it must have both practical control and jurisdiction over a territory. This is known as *de facto* sovereignty. (Colangelo, 2009, p. 626) To claim *de facto* sovereignty, a nation must be able to control the territory it claims and protect it from outside influence. The point at which a nation can claim *de facto* sovereignty is also a useful demarcation for delineating the difference between an "environment" and a "domain". For example, space did not become a domain until nations began to assert their presence within it; prior to that point, space was simply an environment.

Sovereignty's historical relationship to geographic territory complicates applying sovereignty to both space and cyberspace. The international community generally acknowledges geographic boundaries in the air, land, and maritime domains, but boundaries do not always apply directly to space and cyberspace. Fortunately, laws and customs governing both *de jure* and *de facto* sovereignty in space have successfully been developed over the last 50 years. Understanding the historical development of sovereignty in space is useful as nations attempt to define sovereignty within cyberspace.

## 2.1   The evolution of sovereignty in space
In light of the unique challenges of establishing military norms in cyberspace, the United States Air Force has turned toward the space domain to draw parallels. We can see this in the structural similarity between space and cyberspace doctrine discussed later in this article as well as in the fact that United States Air Force cyberspace forces are now organized, trained and equipped under Air Force Space Command. Like cyberspace, space is a relatively new domain that has only been accessible for a little more than 50 years.

As the prospect of man-made satellites transitioned from science fiction to reality, the international community struggled to determine whether or not geographic sovereignty should be extended into space. Long-accepted notions of sovereignty dictated that a nation had a right of self-defense against any action below, on, or above the geographic areas it claimed. In 1957, the Soviet Union launched Sputnik, which orbited the globe without regard for the territories over which it passed. After the launch, the Soviets reversed their previously held position that the sovereignty of a State extended to unlimited altitude and instead advocated that no state could claim sovereignty in space. (Reinhardt, 2005) This opened the door to U.S. space advocates who, prior to the launch of Sputnik, were concerned that a U.S. satellite launch could be considered an act of aggression. Donald Quarles, then Deputy Secretary of Defense stated, "the Russians have done us a good turn, unintentionally, in establishing the concept of freedom of international space." (Terrill, 1999, p. 29) Furthermore, no countries objected to the Sputnik's overflight of their territory. These events set a precedent for customary space law allowing for the free flight of satellites in space. (Terrill, 1999, p. 30)

In May of 1960, the Soviet Union shot down Francis Gary Powers' U-2 aircraft which was flying within the recognized boundaries of the Soviet Union. (Department of State, 1960) The Soviets thus exercised their *de facto* sovereignty by defending their airspace. Around that same time, the U.S. was close to launching a satellite capable of collecting intelligence similar to that provided by the U-2. The Corona imagery reconnaissance satellite, cloaked under the "Discoverer" program, provided the U.S. with a new means of assessing the strength of the Soviet nuclear program. (Ruffner, 1995, p. xiv) President Eisenhower ended the contentious U-2 overflights of the Soviet Union in favor of gathering similar data from space. The international precedent for satellite overflight established by Sputnik helped safeguard the Corona program. The first successful Corona launch occurred in August, less than four months after Powers was shot down. (Ruffner, 1995, p. xi)

In 1967, 10 years after the launch of Sputnik, international diplomatic efforts culminated in a basic framework for international space law called the Outer Space Treaty. Among other things, the treaty barred participants from placing nuclear weapons in space. (United Nations, 1967, Article IV) It also stated, "outer space, including the Moon and other celestial bodies, is not subject to national appropriation by claim of sovereignty, by means of use or occupation or by any other means." (United Nations, 1967, Article II) However, the state launching an object into space retained jurisdiction and control over that object. (United Nations, 1967, Article VII) The Outer Space Treaty effectively established space as a *global commons*, similar to the high seas, where no country can make territorial claims, and any nation with appropriate technological capability can use its resources.

Beginning with the Strategic Arms Limitation Talks in 1969 and continuing beyond the end of the Cold War with the New Strategic Arms Reduction Treaty in 2010, the United States and Soviet Union negotiated agreements and treaties to maintain the balance of nuclear power between the two nations. They established that both parties would use "national technical means of verification" (i.e., reconnaissance satellites) and that each party would not interfere with the other's means. These statements codified the critical relationship between national technical means and national security. In light of the dependency between space assets and treaty verification, and the growing reliance on other space-based capabilities, the most recent U.S. National Space Policy claims the U.S. has an "inherent right of self-defense" of space assets. (United States of America, 2010, p. 3) The document further clarifies that the U.S. will *deter* others from interference and attack, *defend* against hostile action and, if deterrence fails, *defeat* efforts to attack U.S. and allied space systems. The National Space Policy serves as a statement of the *de facto* sovereignty of the U.S. over its space assets.

The International Telecommunications Union also plays a role in space sovereignty. That organization is responsible to the United Nations (UN) for allocating geostationary orbital slots to nations and for managing satellite communication frequencies. (International Telecommunication Union, 2011) These functions play an important role in determining *de jure* sovereignty over space assets. Intentional intrusions into another nation's assigned orbits or interference with its satellite frequency allocations could be considered a hostile action on the international stage.

## 2.2   Cyberspace sovereignty

Those engaged in defining international law as it pertains to cyberspace can learn from the historical development of space law and policy. Decades passed before the modern, generally-accepted notion of sovereignty emerged in the space domain. Likewise, the U.S. must also decide which cyberspace assets are so important that it is willing to *deter*, *defend*, or if necessary *defeat* efforts to attack them. Each of these identified assets must be clearly traceable to national security objectives, just as national technical means were explicitly linked to nuclear treaty verification.

The following sections outline potential methods for evaluating sovereignty in cyberspace. This is a critical step in laying the foundation for establishing control within the domain. Violations in any of these areas could provide a basis for taking action. Under normal circumstances, an aggressor who is a U.S. citizen would be subject to national law, with law enforcement agencies being responsible for enforcement and prosecution. Responses to aggressive actions from outside the nation would be dealt with using various instruments of national power, as deemed appropriate by national leadership.

## 2.2.1    Current state of cyberspace sovereignty

Within the United States, many organizations are engaged in identifying "critical infrastructure," which include cyberspace elements. The primary organization tasked with this responsibility is the Department of Homeland Security (DHS), but coordination when deciding what constitutes critical infrastructure spans Congress, the State Department, Department of Defense (DoD), law enforcement, and the intelligence community. The Patriot Act of 2001 defined critical infrastructure as "systems and assets, whether physical or virtual, so vital to the United States that the incapacity or destruction of such systems and assets would have a debilitating impact on security, national economic security, national public health or safety, or any combination of those matters." (United States of America, 2001, Sec. 1016 (e))

In 2009, DHS authored the National Infrastructure Protection Plan (NIPP), which identified the 18 sectors of critical infrastructure and key resources (CIKR) shown in Table 1. (Department of Homeland Security, 2009, p. 3) This list has grown from only 13 sectors originally identified in 2002. (Department of Homeland Security, 2002, p. 30) Interestingly, the NIPP does not explicitly identify space systems as critical infrastructure, although it does reference communications satellites under the telecommunications category and describes space-based position, navigation and timing services as "components of multiple CIKR sectors." DHS states that cyber elements span all of these sectors. When describing the relationship between U.S. critical infrastructure and cyberspace, The *National Strategy to Secure Cyberspace* even goes so far as to declare in that "Cyberspace is their nervous system—the control system of our country." (Department of Homeland Security, 2003, p. 1)

The *National Strategy to Secure Cyberspace* lays out three strategic objectives for securing cyberspace: (1) Prevent cyber attacks against U.S. critical infrastructures; (2) reduce national vulnerabilities to cyber attack; and (3) minimize the damage and recovery time. (Department of Homeland Security, 2003, pp. 13-15) These three functions are analogous to the National Space Policy's *deter*, *defend*, and *defeat*, although the tone is much more focused on *deterrence* and *defense*, than on *defeat*. In fact, the word "defeat" is found only once in the *National Strategy to Secure Cyberspace* and refers to defeating a certain class of attack through a defensive versus offensive action. (Department of Homeland Security, 2003, p. 31)

**Table 1:** 18 Critical infrastructure and key resource sectors

| 18 Critical Infrastructure and Key Resource Sectors | | |
|---|---|---|
| Agriculture and Food | Banking and Finance | Chemical |
| Commercial Facilities | Communications | Critical Manufacturing |
| Dams | Defense Industrial Base | Emergency Services |
| Energy | Government Facilities | Healthcare and Public Health |
| Information Technology | National Monuments and Icons | Nuclear Reactors, Materials and Waste |
| Postal and Shipping | Transportation Systems | Water |

To date, the U.S. has not faced an attack in cyberspace sufficiently damaging to elicit a military response. In fact, an action of this magnitude has not occurred even internationally, although many hostile cyberspace actions, such as those conducted against Georgia and Estonia, have sparked intense debate over what responses are acceptable.' (Tikk, 2008) (Evron, 2008) Given that the cyberspace domain exists to facilitate the flow of information, most "cyber attacks" either destroy, disrupt, or intercept that flow and typically fall under the categories of crime or espionage. By customary international law, neither of those activities is generally considered an acceptable justification for going to war. Loss of life or physical property of sufficient magnitude to meet the criteria for jus ad bellum has not occurred as a direct consequence of an attack generated in cyberspace.

Unless significant progress can be made under peaceful circumstances, the issue will likely go unresolved until a sufficiently significant event forces the international community to deal with its ramifications under emergency conditions.

### 2.2.2 *Recommendations for establishing sovereignty in cyber-space*

The United States should define its critical infrastructure more precisely. The 18 current areas established by DHS cover an extremely wide variety of subjects. The diversity and breadth of those subjects make their prioritization extremely difficult. Eventually, if not already, it will be hard to find an example of what is *not* considered critical, and the U.S. will be no better off for having gone through the process. Just as space-based, national technical means were identified as critical to national security, critical infrastructure components must be identified according to their relationship to national security objectives. This is a foundational step for asserting sovereign claims in cyberspace. The next step is to make those claims with respect to the inner workings of this domain. Cyberspace is composed of many technical layers and understanding how each contributes to the overall whole is critical for setting sound policy.

One way to approach cyberspace sovereignty is to consider it holistically according to all of the layers shown in Figure 1. The depiction, commonly known as the Internet Protocol (IP) stack, illustrates the different layers of functionality required to support operations in cyberspace. Each layer has unique responsibilities for facilitating the flow of electronic information and most have international governing bodies overseeing their management. Having at least a basic understanding of the purpose and the management structure for all aspects of the Internet Protocol Stack will help policy makers make better decisions concerning sovereignty in cyberspace.

The *physical layer* consists of the actual hardware, such as routers, network links, and switches that provide the foundation of cyberspace. A physical attack on that infrastructure could be considered a "use of force" according to customary understandings of warfare, such as those found in Articles 2(4) and 51 of the UN Charter. Such an act would allow nations to act in "self-defense" to protect their sovereign territory. (United Nations, 1945)

The physical layer presents difficulties for those who have attempted to label cyberspace as a "global commons" similar to space and international waters. (Department of Defense, 2005, p. 1) (Atlantic Council, 2010, p. 1). This interpretation stems from the perception that cyberspace is free, open and global. Unlike cyberspace, though, space and the high seas are natural domains that existed prior to their discovery and use and humanity played no part in their creation. The physical layer of cyberspace presents a challenge to any notion of cyberspace as a global commons because every piece of infrastructure exists in some specific geographic location and is owned, operated and maintained by some entity, whether government, military or private sector. Treating cyberspace as a global commons fails to recognize that the underlying physical resources remain subject to private property rights (Kanuck, 2010, p.1579) and policy makers must account for this when defining cyberspace sovereignty.

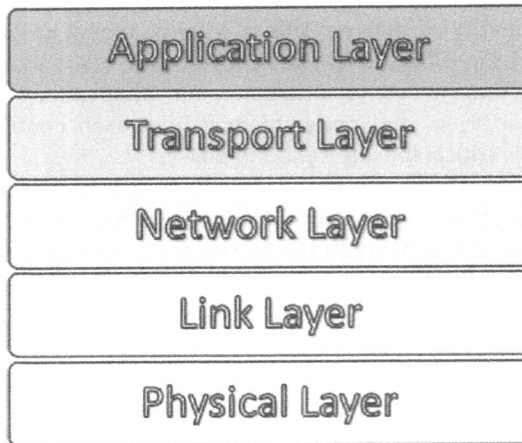

**Figure 1:** Internet Protocol Stack (Kurose & Ross, 2009, p. 51)

The *link layer* provides a bridge between the physical hardware and the network. Every hardware device connected to the Internet has a unique Media Access Control (MAC) address. The Institute of Electrical and Electronics Engineers (IEEE) manages the distribution of MAC addresses to hardware manufacturers by assigning them a 24-bit Organizationally Unique Identifier (OUI). Each hardware interface produced by that manufacturer will contain the OUI along with an additional 24-bit address that serves to identify the individual device uniquely. (Institute of Electrical and Electronics Engineers, 2011) These device identifiers provide a means of distinguishing one component from another on a local area network and could be used to delineate spheres of control in cyberspace akin to sovereign territory.

The *network layer* is the first layer that represents cyberspace subdivisions completely independently of the physical world. It serves to logically group and separate the realm of cyberspace. This layer is responsible for routing information from one node to another through all of the intermediary nodes along the way. Typically, it manages this according to the Internet Protocol (IP) address of the sender and receiver of the information. The Internet Assigned Numbers Authority is the international body responsible for the global coordination and assignment of IP addresses. (Internet Assigned Numbers Authority, 2011)

Both the assigned MAC and IP addresses of the link and network layers of the protocol stack could provide a basis for establishing internationally-recognized (*de jure*) sovereignty. Since international governing bodies manage these addresses, the global community might consider intentional actions taken to manipulate or infringe upon them as hostile. Anyone attempting to illegally impersonate an assigned IP address by falsifying his own network information or denying legitimate services intended for the address would be committing a criminal act. Any damage or loss associated with either of these activities could provide a basis for seeking restitution either on the national stage through law enforcement or on the international stage by exercising various instruments of national power, depending on the nature and effects of the attack.

The *transport layer* provides a means to logically link end systems together. For example, the Transmission Control Protocol establishes a logical connection between two processes for data transfer. This connection only exists as long as the two machines require it. During that period, though, the connection could be thought of as being owned by those two machines and no one else should be able to interfere with or duplicate it. The transport layer also allows systems to define ports that tie data connections to programs at the application layer. These ports act like doorways that allow information systems to access data or services on host machines.

No internationally-recognized agency allocates ports or connections to physical systems or organizations. Therefore, it would be difficult to claim any form of *de jure* sovereignty at this layer. Yet, these connections while transient in nature are essentially the property of the two connected systems for the duration of the connection. Any intentional attempt to hijack or circumvent those connections could be considered a hostile action.

Finally, the *application layer* provides a series of protocols by which systems exchange semantic information. Popular examples include Hypertext Transfer Protocol, Domain Name System (DNS), and Simple Mail Transfer Protocol (SMTP). DNS and SMTP are the most relevant to sovereignty. DNS automatically binds organizational names in a human-readable form to IP addresses. DNS makes using the web more efficient by freeing users from having to remember numeric IP addresses. For example, it is easier to remember "www.google.com" than 72.14.204.104, although one could use either to get to the same web page. The Internet Corporation for Assigned Names and Numbers (ICANN) is the internationally-recognized organization that manages the association of domain names to IP addresses. In executing this role, ICANN's efforts could provide a basis for establishing *de jure* sovereignty at the application layer. Intentionally corrupting the automatic translation from domain names to IP addresses performed by DNS servers would violate the victim's recognized identity. DNS also manages the name assignments associated with e-mail servers operating over SMTP, which is the protocol responsible for handling e-mail. An organization's e-mail address is a form of identification. Intentionally tampering with or impersonating an e-mail address by spoofing SMTP would also violate the identity of the victim.

In conjunction with identifying the sovereign aspects of cyberspace, nations asserting sovereignty must also develop and employ capabilities to patrol and protect those sovereign assets against the hostile actions from others. The first step is to organize, train, and equip cyberspace forces and then employ them to establish and maintain superiority in the domain. *Superiority* is the degree of dominance of one force over another which permits the conduct of operations by the former at a given time and place without prohibitive interference by the opposing force. (Department of Defense, 2010, p. 30) *Control* is the mechanism by which the U.S. achieves its stated objective of domain superiority. (United States Air Force, 2010, p. ii) (Department of Defense, 2009, p. II-5) The following sections provide an overview of joint doctrine covering space and cyberspace control. These topics are important for understanding how the U.S. asserts and exercises a form of *de facto* sovereignty in the space and cyberspace domains from a military perspective.

# 3  Space and cyberspace control

The U.S. establishes space superiority by though space control by "surveilling space and terrestrial areas of interest that could impact space activities; protecting the ability to use space; preventing adversaries from exploiting US, multinational, or neutral space services and capabilities; and negating the ability of adversaries to exploit space services and capabilities." Space control consists of three functions: offensive space control (OSC), defensive space control (DSC), and space situational awareness (SSA). (Department of Defense, 2009, p. II-5)

OSC is the flexible set of responses, including the denial, deception, disruption, or destruction, to negate enemy space capabilities. Joint doctrine clarifies that the "enemy" can include either state or non-state actors. (Department of Defense, 2009, p. II-6)

DSC includes both active and passive operations that maintain the ability to employ space capabilities and protect friendly space capabilities from attack, interference, or unintentional hazards. DSC has three components: *prevention, negation, and protection. Prevention* is not limited to military power alone. It entails the use of diplomatic, informational, and economic instruments of national power to thwart aggression before a situation escalates to a point where military force is necessary. *Negation* employs active or offensive measures to subvert an adversary's space capabilities. Finally, *protection* is a combination of active and passive defensive measures that keep U.S. and friendly space systems safe from hostile action and from space environmental factors.

Lastly, SSA provides the foundation for accomplishing all other space control tasks. It underpins OSC and DSC by characterizing the space capabilities operating in the space domain. Contributors to SSA include components of Intelligence Surveillance and Reconnaissance (ISR), systems designed to monitor the space environment, and threat warning systems.

Current U.S. military doctrine for cyberspace activity is similar in structure to U.S. space doctrine. It also consists of an offensive, defensive and intelligence gathering triad. The U.S. establishes cyberspace superiority through Computer Network Operations (CNO). The three mission areas of CNO are computer network attack (CNA), computer network defense (CND), and computer network exploitation (CNE). Joint doctrine defines computer network operations (CNO) as an information operations core capability. (Department of Defense, 2006, p. II-5)

CNA is comprised of "actions taken through the use of computer networks to disrupt, deny, degrade, or destroy information resident in computers and computer networks, or the computers and networks themselves." CND involves actions taken using computer networks "to protect, monitor, analyze, detect, and respond to unauthorized activity within DOD information systems and computer networks." CND actions protect DOD systems from both external and internal threats, and are a necessary function in all military operations. CNE is the set of network-based operations and intelligence collection capabilities conducted to gather data from target or adversary automated information systems or networks. (Department of Defense, 2006, p. II-5)

Having the ability to both patrol and protect assets within space and cyberspace is a critical component of *de facto* sovereignty over those assets. SSA and CNE capabilities provide a means to patrol the space and cyberspace domains, respectively. Protection has both offensive and defensive facets. The offensive capabilities in both domains serve to deter adversaries from taking hostile actions against critical assets. Defensive operations help protect assets when attacks occur. It is not enough to simply have strong perimeter defenses—*de facto* sovereignty requires the ability to actively seek out and identify undesirable activities within sovereign cyberspace assets, and then take appropriate action to nullify or mitigate those activities.

## 4    Conclusions

International norms governing appropriate conduct in cyberspace are immature. As nations become more cyberspace-dependent, they are struggling to clearly define their claims within it and to determine appropriate responses when those claims are jeopardized. The United States should continue to refine the aspects of cyberspace that it considers sovereign. The 18 critical infrastructure sectors defined by DHS provide a glimpse into what the U.S. may be willing to defend by the use of military force if necessary. The sovereign aspects of cyberspace should not be limited to only the physical infrastructure that supports the flow of electronic information, but should also include key aspects of all the layers of the Internet Protocol Stack. The U.S. should clearly link its sovereign claims in cyberspace to national security objectives to both support their prioritization and help define appropriate responses in case hostile actions are taken against them.

Assertions of sovereignty are unsustainable unless a nation has a sufficient ability to patrol and protect its claims. The United States should also continue to invest in cyberspace capabilities that allow it to maintain superiority within cyberspace and protect its sovereign claims within the domain. These steps will help ensure it is prepared to face the combination of technological, legal, and military challenges it faces as the world's reliance on information technologies continues to expand at an exponential rate.

This article evaluated the requirements to patrol and protect national sovereign claims in cyberspace largely from a U.S. military perspective. Subsequent analysis is still needed to distinguish the appropriate roles for military and law enforcement agencies within the framework of national and international law.

*The views expressed in this article are those of the authors and do not reflect the official policy or position of the United States Air Force, Department of Defense, or the U.S. Government.*

# References

Atlantic Council (2010). "ACT Workshop Report: NATO in the Global Commons". [Online]
Available at: http://www.act.nato.int/images/stories/events/2010/gc/report01_wash.pdf
Colangelo, A., (2009). De facto Sovereignty: Boumediene and Beyond. In: George Washington Law Review 77, no. 3. [Online] Available at:
http://docs.law.gwu.edu/stdg/gwlr/issues/pdf/Colangelo-77-3.pdf
Department of State, (1960). State Department press release #249 concerning U-2 incident. [Online] Available at:
http://eisenhower.archives.gov/Research/Digital_Documents/U2Incident/5-6-60_No249.pdf
Department of Defense. (2005). Strategy for Homeland Defense and Civil Support. [Online] Available at: http://www.defense.gov/news/Jun2005/d20050630homeland.pdf
Department of Defense. (2006). Joint Publication 3-13, Information Operations. [Online] Available at: http://www.dtic.mil/doctrine/new_pubs/jp3_13.pdf
Department of Defense. (2009). Joint Publication 3-14, Space Operations. [Online] Available at: http://www.dtic.mil/doctrine/new_pubs/jp3_14.pdf

Department of Defense. (2010). Joint Publication 1-02, Department of Defense Dictionary of Military and Associated Terms. [Online] Available at: http://www.dtic.mil/doctrine/new_pubs/jp1_02.pdf. Generalized from "maritime superiority" and "air superiority" definitions.

Department of Homeland Security. (2002). National Strategy for Homeland Security. [Online] Available at: http://www.dhs.gov/xlibrary/assets/nat_strat_hls.pdf

Department of Homeland Security. (2003). National Strategy to Secure Cyberspace. [Online] Available at: Department of Homeland Security. (2009). National Infrastructure Protection Plan. [Online] Available at: www.dhs.gov/xlibrary/assets/NIPP_Plan.pdf

Evron, G., (2008). Battling Botnets and Online Mobs: Estonia's Defense Efforts during the Internet War. Winter/Spring 2008. pp. 121-126. In: Georgetown Journal of International Affairs, [Online] Available at: http://dx.fi/media/blogs/dx/0000699.pdf

Insitute of Electrical and Electronics Engineers, (2011). Registration Authority General Information. [Online] Available at: http://standards.ieee.org/develop/regauth/general.html

International Telecommunication Union, (2011). Radiocommunication Sector. [Online] Available at: http://www.itu.int/ITU-R/index.asp

Internet Assigned Numbers Authority. (2010). [Online] Available at: http://www.iana.org

Kanuck, S., (2010). Sovereign Discourse on Cyber Conflicts Under International Law. Texas law Review, Vol. 88, Issue, 7, 1 June 2010, 1579, [Online] Available at: http://www.texaslrev.com/sites/default/files/issues/vol88/pdf/Kanuck.pdf

Kurose, J. & Ross, K., (2009). Computer Networking: A Top-Down Approach, 5th ed., Addison Wesley.

Reinhardt, D., (2005). The Vertical Limit of State Sovereignty. McGill University [Online] Available at: http://www.dtic.mil/cgi-bin/GetTRDoc?Location=U2&doc=GetTRDoc.pdf&AD=ADA436627.

Ruffner , K., (1995). Corona: America's First Satellite Program. Center for the Study of Intelligence. Central Intelligence Agency. Washington D.C. [Online] Available at: https://www.cia.gov/library/publications/additional-publications/corona-between-the-sun-and-the-earth/corona.pdf

Stanford Encyclopedia of Philosophy, (2010). Sovereignty. [Online] Available at: http://plato.stanford.edu/entries/sovereignty/

Terrill, D., (1999). The Air Force Role in Developing International Outer Space Law. Maxwell AFB, AL: Air University Press.

Tikk, E. et al., (2008). Cyber Attacks Against Georgia: Legal Lessons Identified. Cooperative Cyber Defense Centre of Excellence. [Online] Available at: http://www.carlisle.army.mil/DIME/documents/Georgia%201%200.pdf

United Nations. (1945). Charter of the United Nations. [Online] Available at: http://www.un.org/en/documents/charter

United Nations, (1967), Outer Space Treaty. [Online] Available at: http://www.oosa.unvienna.org/oosa/en/SpaceLaw/gares/html/gares_21_2222.html

United States Air Force. (2010). Air Force Doctrine Document 3-12, Cyberspace Operations. [Online] Available at: http://www.e-publishing.af.mil/shared/media/epubs/afdd3-12.pdf

United States of America, (2001). U.S. Patriot Act, [Online] Available at: http://frwebgate.access.gpo.gov/cgi-bin/getdoc.cgi?dbname=107_cong_public_laws&docid=f:publ056.107.pdf

United States of America. (2010). National Space Policy of the United States of America. [Online] Available at: http://www.whitehouse.gov/sites/default/files/national_space_policy_6-28-10.pdf

# Syllabus to Accompany Leading Issues in Cyber Warfare Volume 2

This syllabus is designed for a high level discussion type of course. Please note all links were working at time of publication.

## Class 1: Administration and Context of Course
Readings:  none

Discussion questions to set the stage for the course:
- What is warfare?
- What is offensive warfare, and how does that differ from defensive warfare?
- What are nations or states?
- What are legitimate constraints on warfare?
- Can all technologies be used for war?
- What is the role of the international community in setting and enforcing limits to war?

## Section 1:  Considering The Future of Cyberwarfare

## Class 2:  "Cyber Can Kill and Destroy Too: Blurring Borders Between Conventional and Cyber Warfare" by Marina Krotofil

Supplemental Readings:
- Lee, Dave and Nick Kwek.  "North Korean hackers 'could kill', warns key defector," BBC News, 29 May 2015. http://www.bbc.com/news/technology-32925495
- Lu, Quan Hai T.  "Cyber Attacks: The New WMD Challenge to the Interagency," InterAgency Journal Vol. 6, Issue 2, Special Edition, Spring 2015.  pg 48 - 57.  Available online at

http://thesimonscenter.org/wp-content/uploads/2015/05/IAJ-6-2-Spring-2015-48-57.pdf

Discussion questions:
- When would an attack with lethal consequences be an act of war, versus criminal behavior?
- What would be appropriate reactions for a sovereign nation?
- What would be appropriate reactions for an organization?
- How should the international community approach these types of challenges?

### Class 3: "Cyberspace from the Hybrid Threat Perspective" by Hakan Gunneriusson and Rain Ottis

Supplemental Readings:
- Van Puyvelde, Damien. "Hybrid War — Does it Even Exist?" NATO Review Magazine, 2015. http://www.nato.int/docu/review/2015/Also-in-2015/hybrid-modern-future-warfare-russia-ukraine/EN/
- Korman, Michael and Matthew Rojansky. "A Closer Look at Russia's Hybrid War", Kennan Cable No. 7, April 2015. http://www.wilsoncenter.org/sites/default/files/7-KENNAN%20CABLE-ROJANSKY%20KOFMAN.pdf
- Schadlow, Nadia. "The Problem with Hybrid Warfare," War on the Rocks, April 2015. http://warontherocks.com/2015/04/the-problem-with-hybrid-warfare/

Discussion questions:
- How can states defend themselves legitimately against attacks that may be protected speech?
- When does competition in cyberspace rise to the level of national security consideration?

## Class 4: "Comparing Models of Offensive Cyber Operations" by Tim Grant, Ivan Burke, and Renier van Heerden

Supplemental Readings:
- O'Dwyer, Gerard. "Denmark To Develop Offensive Cyber Capability," Defense News, Jan 8, 2015. http://www.defensenews.com/story/defense/policy-budget/cyber/2015/01/08/denmark-cyber-hackers-china-terma/21448705/
- Gellman, Barton and Ellen Nakashima. "U.S. spy agencies mounted 231 offensive cyber-operations in 2011, documents show", Washington Post, August 30, 2013. https://www.washingtonpost.com/world/national-security/us-spy-agencies-mounted-231-offensive-cyber-operations-in-2011-documents-show/2013/08/30/d090a6ae-119e-11e3-b4cb-fd7ce041d814_story.html
- Need, Maren. "Offensive Cyber Capabilities at the Operational Level: The Way Ahead", CSIS, September 2013. http://csis.org/files/publication/130916_Leed_OffensiveCyberCapabilities_Web.pdf
- Gadd, Franz-Stefan. "Does China Really Know How to Wage Cyber War?" The Diplomat, Feb 20, 2015. http://thediplomat.com/2015/02/does-china-really-know-how-to-wage-cyber-war/

Discussion questions:
- What are important distinctions between espionage and warfare?
- Is it ever possible for corporate espionage rise to the level of warfare?
- Under what conditions?
- How could intelligence activities be designed to detect the development of offensive capabilities in an adversary state?
- Is it possible to do that without engaging in cyberwarfare as well? How?

**Class 5: "Duqu's Dilemma: The Ambiguity Assertion and the Futility of Sanitized Cyber War" by Matthew Crosston**

Supplemental Readings:
- Knake, Robert K. "Untangling Attribution: Moving to
- Accountability in Cyberspace," Council on Foreign Relations, July 15, 2010.
- Clark, David D. and Susan Landau. "Untangling Attribution", Proceedings of a Workshop on Deterring CyberAttacks: Informing Strategies and Developing Options for U.S. Policy http://www.nap.edu/catalog/12997.html, also available online at http://cs.brown.edu/courses/csci1950-p/sources/lec12/ClarkandLandau.pdf
- Finklea, Kristin. "Attribution in Cyberspace: Challenges for U.S. Law Enforcement", CRS Insights, April 17, 2015. https://www.fas.org/sgp/crs/misc/IN10259.pdf

Discussion questions:
- If attribution cannot be absolutely determined, how can attacks be countered?
- If attribution cannot be absolutely determined, what level of attribution would be acceptable for legitimate defense purposes?
- What are the tensions between mandated true attribution and socially useful aspects of hiding true identity?

**Class 6: "Unrestricted Warfare Versus Western Traditional Warfare: A Comparative Study" by Gregory Commin and Eric Filiol**

Supplemental Readings:
- Guiora, Amos N. "Determining a Legitimate Target: The Dilemma of the Decision-Maker", TEXAS INTERNATIONAL LAW JOURNAL, Volume 47, Issue 2. http://www.tilj.org/content/journal/47/num2/Guiora315.pdf

- BBC. "In an ethical war, whom can you fight?", Ethics Guide. http://www.bbc.co.uk/ethics/war/just/whom_1.shtml
- ICRC. "Practice Relating to Rule 8. Definition of Military Objectives", Customary IHL. https://www.icrc.org/customary-ihl/eng/docs/v2_rul_rule8

Discussion questions:
- How should nations with different approaches to warfare interact with each other when conflict arises?
- How should the international community react or proactively act, if at all?

## Class 7: Seminar discussion of classes 1 through 5

Discussion questions:
- How does all the material from the previous class discussions combine logically?
- What are the most important aspects that need to be considered by citizens, leaders, managers, and technologists?
- What are the most pressing areas of concern facing humanity?
- What recommendations would each student make?

## Section 2: Structural Considerations for Cyberwarfare

## Class 8: "Hofstede's Cultural Markers in Computer Network Attack Behaviors" by Char Sample and Andre' Ara Karamanian

Supplemental Readings:
- Pfeifle, Sam. "PRIVACY IN POPULAR CULTURE: Privacy Is 'More Complicated Than We Realized'", The Privacy Advisor, Aug 23, 2013. https://privacyassociation.org/news/a/privacy-in-popular-culture-privacy-is-more-complicated-than-we-realized
- Monash University. "Cultural Linguistics: A new multidisciplinary field of research", Profile of Sharifian.

http://profiles.arts.monash.edu.au/farzad-sharifian/cultural-linguistics/
- Earley, P. Christopher and Elaine Mosakowski. "Cultural Intelligence", Harvard Business Review, October 2004. https://hbr.org/2004/10/cultural-intelligence

Discussion questions:
- Could different cultures accept or reject different actions associated with cyberwar? In what ways, and how would the behavior emerge or be displayed?
- Could aggressors use cultural aspects as the designing features of attacks?
- How should nations or groups consider this problem, if at all?

**Class 9: "Virtual Non-State Actors as Clausewitzian Centers of Gravity: An Examination for Sensemaking, Elaboration, and Discussion" by Larisa Breton**

Supplemental Readings:
- Strange, Joe and Richard Iron. "Understanding Centers of Gravity and Critical Vulnerabilities." http://www.au.af.mil/au/awc/awcgate/usmc/cog2.pdf
- Ullman, Harlan. "Hybrid War: Old Wine in a New Bottle?" Atlantic Council, March 9, 2015. http://www.atlanticcouncil.org/publications/articles/hybrid-war-old-wine-in-a-new-bottle

Discussion questions:
- Could actions by virtual non-state-actors ever rise to the level of warfare?
- If so, how should state-actors be able to respond legitimately?
- If not, how should affected organizations or nations respond legitimately?

**Class 10: "On the Military Geography of Cyberspace" by Tim Grant**

Supplemental Readings:
- O'Brien, John. "Coup d'ceil: Military Geography and the Operational Level of War." School of Advanced Military Studies, US Army Command and General Staff College. 1991. http://www.dtic.mil/dtic/tr/fulltext/u2/a243343.pdf
- Morgan, Timothy Prickett. "A Rare Peek Into The Massive Scale of AWS," Enterprise Tech, Nov 14, 2014. http://www.enterprisetech.com/2014/11/14/rare-peek-massive-scale-aws/

Discussion questions:
- Given the level of interconnectedness, the Internet-of-Things, and attribution challenges, what are the most important questions associated with trying to develop a military geography concept for cyberwarfare?
- What effect would rapid reconfiguration of systems and networks have on such a concept?
- What level of virtualization of services might render such a concept meaningless from a practical perspective?
- Is there a useful alternative way to conceptualize the ideas in an operational sense?

**Class 11: "Intelligence Preparation of the Cyber Environment (IPCE): Finding the High Ground in Cyberspace" by Antoine Lemay, Scott Knight and José Fernandez**

Supplemental Readings:
- UNODC. "Criminal Intelligence Manual for Analysts" http://www.unodc.org/documents/organized-crime/Law-Enforcement/Criminal_Intelligence_for_Analysts.pdf
- Dugdale-Pointon, T. (22 August 2007), The Role of Intelligence in War, http://www.historyofwar.org/articles/concepts_intelligence_in_war.html

Discussion questions:
* Can intelligence preparation activities be distinguished from offensive actions in cyberspace?
* Should guidelines or international norms be developed to serve as acceptable behavior standards?
* Can this type of activity legitimately be done in advance of aggression or defense?
* What defenses are appropriate for nations?

## Class 12: "Strategies for Combating Sophisticated Attacks" by Chad Arnold, Jonathan Butts, and Krishnaprasad Thirunarayan

Supplemental Readings:
* Abrams, Marshall and Joe Weiss. "Malicious Control System Cyber Security Attack Case Study–Maroochy Water Services, Australia". http://csrc.nist.gov/groups/SMA/fisma/ics/documents/Maroochy-Water-Services-Case-Study_report.pdf
* Smith, Gerry. "Stuxnet: U.S. Can Launch Cyberattacks But Not Defend Against Them, Experts Say," Huffington Post, June 1, 2012. http://www.huffingtonpost.com/2012/06/01/stuxnet-us-cyberattack_n_1562983.html
* Better, Kim and Andy Greenberg. "Why The OPM Breach Is Such a Security and Privacy Debacle," Wired. June 11, 2015. http://www.wired.com/2015/06/opm-breach-security-privacy-debacle/

Discussion questions:
* In a highly interconnected world, where each node is potentially a weak link that subverts all other security measures, is defense even a viable option?
* What should be done to develop the capacity for combatting sophisticated attacks?
* Who should be responsible?

- Should the administrators of systems with poor security controls be held criminally liable for negligence?
- What other approaches might be considered?

**Class 13: "Replication and Diversity for Survivability in Cyberspace: A Game Theoretic Approach" by Charles Kamhoua, Kevin Kwiat, Mainak Chatterjee, Joon Park, and Patrick Hurley**

Supplemental Readings:
- none

Discussion questions:
- Consider the questions from Class 12 again, after having read this paper.

**Class 14: "Exercising State Sovereignty in Cyberspace: An International Cyber-Order Under Construction" by Andrew Liaropoulos**

Supplemental Readings:
- US News Debate Club. "Should There Be an International Treaty on Cyberwarfare?" http://www.usnews.com/debate-club/should-there-be-an-international-treaty-on-cyberwarfare
- Arimatsu, Louise. "A Treaty for Governing Cyber-Weapons: Potential Benefits and Practical Limitations," 2012 4th International Conference on Cyber Conflict. https://ccdcoe.org/cycon/2012/proceedings/d3r1s6_arimatsu.pdf
- Plummer, Brad. "How easy is it to shut off a country's Internet?" Washington Post. December 1, 2012. http://www.washingtonpost.com/blogs/wonkblog/wp/2012/12/01/how-easy-is-it-to-shut-off-a-countrys-internet/
- McKinnon, Rebecca. "Ghettoization of the Chinese Internet?", RConversation, October 31, 2007.

http://rconversation.blogs.com/rconversation/2007/10/ghettoization-o.html

Discussion questions:
- Is access to the internet a fundamental human right?
- Is it legitimate for states to limit access to the internet?
- If so, to what level?
- When does limiting access violate human rights, if ever?
- How should countries, both dictatorial and democratic, approach this issue from a policy and technology perspective, particularly given all the discussions developed to this point in previous classes?

### Class 15: "Establishing Cyberspace Sovereignity" by Kris Barcomb, Dennis Krill, Robert Mills and Michael Saville

Supplemental Readings:
- Fukuyama, Francis. "Review of 'Beyond Westphalia: State Sovereignty and International Intervention'", Foreign Affairs, September 1995, https://www.foreignaffairs.com/reviews/capsule-review/1995-09-01/beyond-westphalia-state-sovereignty-and-international-intervention
- "The Problem of Humanitarian Intervention", http://www.globalization101.org/the-problem-of-humanitarian-intervention/

Discussion questions:
- Summarize the important issues and problems from the semester
- Develop a set of recommendations for research, policy, and technology

Lightning Source UK Ltd.
Milton Keynes UK
UKOW06f0755241015

261298UK00002B/65/P